M000159080

# WELCOME TO
# OUR REAL MATRIX

## ONE WITH NO ESCAPE

# TOM ARANT

Copyright © 2021 by Thomas Arant

Illustration credit:
Gardner, Sawyer. "The Allegory of the Cave," 2021
Arant, Tom. "The Matrix Model," 2021

All rights reserved. No part of this publication may be reproduced, distributed or transmitted in any form or by any means, including photocopying, recording or other electronic or mechanical methods, without the prior written permission of the author, except in the case of brief quotations embodied in reviews and certain other non-commercial uses permitted by copyright law.

Printed in the United States of America
ISBN: 978-1-953910-71-4 (hardcover)
ISBN: 978-1-953910-72-1 (paperback)
ISBN: 978-1-953910-73-8 (ebook)

**Canoe Tree
Press**

4697 Main Street
Manchester Center, VT 05255

Canoe Tree Press is a division of DartFrog Books.

*To the giants whose shoulders I stand on.*
*May what I have built enable others to climb even higher.*

Once you finish the book, if you don't want to take the blue pill and acknowledge there is no red pill, you can choose to become a Purplepill and join the discussion at www.purplepillssociety.org

# TABLE OF CONTENTS

## List of Figures

## List of Tables

# 1 PROLOGUE

*The difficulty lies, not in the new ideas, but in escaping the old ones, which ramify, for those brought up as most of us have been, into every corner of our minds.*
John Maynard Keynes

## 1.1 ORIGINS

A few years ago, I was working my way through some popular books on genetics and other topics – *Genome: The Autobiography of a Species in 23 Chapters*,[1] *Your Inner Fish: A Journey into the 3.5-Billion-Year History of the Human Body*,[2] *The Beak of the Finch: A Story of Evolution in Our Time*,[3] *Gödel, Escher, Bach: An Eternal Golden Braid*,[4] *On the Origin of Species*,[5] and *I Am a Strange Loop*.[6] Two of these books won the Pulitzer Prize, and a third one would have if it had been published after 1917.

Somewhere in there, I re-watched the movie, *The Matrix*.

During the movie, I had an epiphany. If the latest demonstrable scientific evidence of biology, evolution, and genetics is correct, I concluded that each of us (and all living things) must then be made of and live in our own analogous, interlinked matrix (set of matrices). These individual and linked matrices are what constitute what I will now call the Real Matrix, which has been constructed over time by the chemicals making up our genome and cells, and is ubiquitous with no escape hatch. The Real Matrix determines our perception of reality and our motivations within it.

I decided to dig into all the interrelated topics to develop, validate, and enhance my position, using generally accepted science as the foundation. This book is the result.

To distinguish from related theories I have stumbled across, I am *not* proposing that we live in a *simulated universe*, nor do I believe there is a *supreme/superior consciousness* that created it. I believe, but cannot prove nor disprove, that those theories are just wishful thinking.

There is a *Reality* out there (i.e., the universe) that somehow came into existence. But the Real Matrix does (and must necessarily) stand between us and that Reality. I have no plans, nor need, to tackle where the universe came from, what it is (well, a little), or how it operates.

## 1.2 What is Our Real Matrix?

So, what is this Real Matrix I am proposing?

The Real Matrix is both the biological processes for all organisms and the biomass resulting from those processes. It includes each living organism's (including each human's) individual, unique, and interrelated perception of, and response to, Reality, which resides internally in the organism. This perception and response give the false appearance of being Reality when it is only the interpretation of the signals received by each organism's sensory receptors. Furthermore, the Real Matrix emerged and continues to emerge in a *non-directional way* through the processes of abiogenesis (emergence of life) and evolution.

## 1.3 The Book Outline

After some important disclaimers and challenges, I provide an overview of the movie *The Matrix* and introduce some basic terms that I will later use to compare to our analogous Real Matrix.

Then, about a half of the book is taken up with an introduction to abiogenesis (the initial emergence of life) that includes a necessary education on chemistry, biochemistry, and biology, plus a detailed discussion of sensory and response systems. Abiogenesis led to the emergence of biological organisms that then continued (and still continue) to change through evolutionary mechanics.

I then discuss the major implications of all these theories and experiments in the context of human perception and behavior within the Real Matrix. At this point, I go back and compare the Real Matrix to the movie's Matrix to help you understand the similarities and differences.

I spend the rest of the book on life considerations given this new-found knowledge – how to live life, why to live life, and how we can further explore and share our interpretations of this knowledge.

## 1.4 Use of a Glossary

The science can get heavy at times, and since I assume no prior scientific knowledge, I define every term I use. Where it does not impede the flow, I have placed the definitions of these terms in a glossary you will find at the end. I identify those terms by using the small-caps font. I have organized the glossary to follow the structure of these science sections, so please refer to it if you need some help. The definition will only appear once, in either the body or the glossary.

## 1.5 How to Read This Book

I have written this book to be a comprehensive one-stop-shopping guide to help you along a journey of understanding. How I suggest that you read it will depend on your interests, your education, and your time. Let me offer a few options:

1. **Complete mastery** – I try to leave no stone unturned in building my case and supporting my conclusions. This has resulted

in a book that provides a thorough primer on necessary topics in biochemistry, biology, abiogenesis, and evolution, in both the main text and glossary. In addition, I address many of the implications that are also quite complex. If you do not want to trust me while gaining the highest level of understanding, then you will have to read the book in its entirety a few times. This will take a few weeks.

2. **Gain an understanding** – if you are willing to partially trust me and are fine with my throwing around some terms that you may not understand, you can skip the chapter on the emergence of life and its accompanying glossary. That will take out about half the content, but you will still get the point. This will reduce your commitment to about a week.

3. **Skip to the end** – if you are a buff of *The Matrix* and do not really care about all the science and reasoning behind my conclusions, then you can also toss the chapter on evolution and lose another fifth of the content. It becomes just an enjoyable read. This will take a weekend to get through.

# 2 Author's Note

*This is an era of specialists, each of whom sees his own problem and is unaware of or intolerant of the larger frame into which it fits.*
Rachel Carson

I am not a specialist nor a scientist. I want everything in this book to be:

- Understandable to other non-scientists.
- Correct, if incomplete, providing enough to support my conclusions.
- Give you (both scientists and non-scientists) implications to think about and new pathways to follow.

## 2.1 The Required Science

*Even if the open windows of science at first make us shiver after the cozy indoor warmth of traditional humanizing myths, in the end the fresh air brings vigor, and the great spaces have a splendor of their own.*
Bertrand Russell

Once I had my epiphany about the Real Matrix, as a non-scientist, I had to study and try to understand the relevant chemistry, biochemistry, genetics, evolution, and even philosophical topics, then simplify them. This has been tough, adding over a year to the writing of this book, but I think I have accomplished it well enough.

I hope to teach you enough to support my conclusion but also to entertain you. Anything more is just unnecessary complexity. I will not spend any time on the history behind this, such as the famous scientists, the early discoveries, or the evolution of relevant theories – that would just be using interesting stories to increase the page count. I am going to skip over this history to get to the point.

I also will not be doing a comprehensive review of anatomy. Where something happens is not nearly as interesting as what and how it happens, except when you are studying for your MCATs or in the operating room.

This book is founded on materialism and physicalism – that everything (in theory) can be shown to be based on physical processes. You can do a web search and spend a few hours reading up on these concepts. This book also assumes that basic genetics and evolutionary theory (and all related science disciplines) in their current level of maturity are correct, with no fundamental errors. I will make no effort to re-litigate their validity.

Evolution is a scientific fact.[7] If you have trouble with the science (and deny the relevance of science itself), then come back when you do not. If you are ignorant or curious about the science, accept it, or just want to get beat up, then strap in and enjoy where knowledge can take you. If you steadfastly believe in a god/designer and not in evolution, then you are fully baked, and I do not want to confuse you with the facts. Please donate this book to a public library, unread. Sorry, no refunds.

Finally, the book assumes that you have seen the movie *The Matrix* (see Chapter 3). If you are not familiar with it, go watch the first movie (the sequels are not necessary viewing). When you have, I think you will enjoy the analogy with our "real" one – the Real Matrix.

## 2.2 MY DEPENDENCY ON OTHERS

*I had fallen victim to the fallacy of the 'growing edge;' the belief that only the very frontier of scientific advance counted; that*

*everything that had been left behind by that advance was faded and dead.*
Isaac Asimov

Being a non-scientist (B.A. in Economics and an MBA) means that I am 100% dependent on science found in textbooks, journals, articles, and websites. I have none of my own research, interviews, or class notes. Most of the time it took me to write this book was spent on self-education in these scientific fields. Every time I write something scientific but do not leave a citation, it is a generally-accepted subject that is taught in high-school science classes (I do admit that they were required at my high school). Where I do include citations (found in Chapter 14, Notes) is when I come across a better explanation or additional information – typically recent scientific journal articles. Also, I have intentionally avoided reading or rereading anything that might directly parallel my premise – I wanted to develop this independently without borrowing what may be similar themes from others. Regardless, I am not aware of any other work that directly parallels mine.

## 2.3 THE NON-FALSIFIABLE/NON-SCIENCE

*Cherish those who seek the truth but beware of those who find it.*
Voltaire

As scientists understand, a theory in the empirical sciences can never be proven, but it can be falsified, meaning that it can (and should) be scrutinized with decisive experiments.

Although I did promise to stick to the science, in some places, I will venture into what may be "non-falsifiable," i.e., what is outside the ability of the scientific method to theoretically prove false. I have found it sometimes necessary and will point out when this occurs.

But I promise not to venture into metaphysics and pure philosophy, including epistemology (the study of the nature of knowledge, justification, and the rationality of belief), ontology (the study of the nature of being, becoming, existence, or reality), identity, causality, cosmology, mind and matter, or determinism and free will, mostly because post *On the Origin of Species and the Real Matrix*, it is mostly nonsensical stuff.

## 2.4 Scientific Arguments I Plan to Avoid

*Definitions are temporary verbalizations of concepts, and concepts – particularly difficult concepts – are usually revised repeatedly as our knowledge and understanding grows.*
Ernst Mayr

I am going to do my best to avoid scientific language/terminology debates that are mostly an attempt to place transitional or unknown things on a discrete spectrum or to just label those entities for discussion convenience. Although important to many researchers, to me, they are mostly pointless word games that do not move us closer to real understanding. I liken it to arguing over the number of angels on a pinhead. Menger's dictum is, "Definitions are dogmas; only the conclusions drawn from them can afford us any new insight."[8] Countless PhDs earn their keep by anally debating some of the following.

### 2.4.1 The Inanimate Versus the Animate

There are thousands of articles on the difference between animate and inanimate, how life started from the inanimate and somehow transformed/transitioned into animate, and where the exact tipping point was. Like the joke about economists, if you put five people in a room (a physicist, a biochemist, a geneticist, a philosopher, and a priest) and ask them to define life, you will come up with six opinions. Interestingly, 95% of the articles discussing the transition from inanimate to animate never actually define inanimate – they assume everyone knows what it is – and focus on inconclusively defining animate. There is even a paper, "Vocabulary of Definitions of Life Suggests a Definition,"[9] that analyzed the vocabulary of 123 tabulated definitions of life to determine the common set for a concise and inclusive definition.

I do not have to be successful here because it does not matter to my objectives. We can agree that life did start with the inanimate and somehow became animate. Since we were not there, the precise transition (which also requires, but is lacking, a precise definition) will remain eternally open to debate. At least one paper, "Looking for the Last Universal Common Ancestor (LUCA),"[10] tries to demonstrate that, even theoretically, there cannot be a demarcation line between animate and inanimate. I will be spending a lot of space on the latest research on the process that resulted in life (abiogenesis) within the Real Matrix without worrying about that demarcation line.

With that said, the most commonly agreed-upon characteristics of a living entity from my reading are:

1. It must have a maintained selective boundary between itself and its environment.
2. It must have a capacity for autocatalysis, leading to metabolic homeostasis, disequilibrium with the environment, and growth.
3. It must be able to respond to stimuli.
4. It must pass a variation of itself to its descendants.

## 2.4.2 SENTIENCE/INTELLIGENCE/CONSCIOUSNESS/THE SELF/FREE WILL

Same thing here – thousands of articles and many books. We live in a world of sentient, intelligent, and conscious beings operating under free will, and yet there is no agreement as to what constitutes sentience, intelligence, consciousness, quantum mind, intuition, the self, or free will (try reading some of the literature). If anyone can rigorously, and without dispute, offer a single definition of any of these concepts from a neurological, psychological, biochemical, and metaphysical perspective, and if that definition is universally understood and supported, then we can have a meaningful discussion on the nature of these concepts in the context of the Real Matrix. Until then, the exercise is futile. I also believe that Gödel's Incompleteness Theorems (explored in Section 2.6: Potential Threats) are the primary, permanent block to this understanding.

I think we can all agree (except perhaps Deepak Chopra) that, whatever our favorite definitions of these concepts, a molecule does not have any of these things, living things have varying degrees of them, and they are all the result of abiogenesis and evolution.

### 2.4.3 ORIGIN OF LIFE (OoL) RESEARCH

On the surface, Origin of Life (OoL) research seems to be a big part of what I am doing here. So, why am I explicitly excluding it?

My problem is that it is based on a question that is unimportant, sophomoric, and full of vocabulary problems – "What is the origin of life?" Does this question even make sense? One now must spend time defining "origin" and "life." I think looking for the "origin" is looking for something through a false worldview that does not exist. A good example of this misguided approach is "A Strategy for Origins of Life Research,"[11] where the challenge is so great that 37 people had to get together to ineffectively (both their opinion and mine) try to come up with an approach – science by committee. It reminds me of an old Milton Berle joke where he described a committee as something where minutes are kept and hours are wasted.

What comes with this is an ancillary statement: "Understanding the origin of life (OoL) is one of the major unsolved scientific problems of the century."[12] Back to definitions. How can one prove or disprove this statement? Let us say that everyone agrees that there are 20 things necessary for life to "originate." If we can only show 18 of them without any doubt, then by this approach, we have failed in our inquiry. The referenced paper (with another 25 authors) wraps itself in circular definitions and spends a large part of its page-count trying to figure out how all the disciplines could play nicely together. From the same paper, "The main reason the OoL research field is still divided on so many issues is that it seems virtually impossible to find definite answers for all of our questions."

When I step back, I see this line of inquiry to be a residual response to creationism. Just like the supernatural roots of Newton's occult studies and Einstein's rejection of quantum indeterminism ("God does not play dice"), the OoL participants seem to set up their arguments solely to beat down that historical, religious, cultural opponent. The unintended consequence is that, since there is no final answer to the question they framed, creationists use this and drop their creator into the empty answer box! (Do not look for any citations from creationism websites. I refuse to feed that beast.)

### 2.4.4 NAMING/SEQUENCING TRANSITIONAL ENTITIES

Later, we will discuss the required mechanics of evolution, but what happened before there was life? An important scientific question is, "How did life first start?" In other words, "What were the precursors to DNA?" We will explore the pre-evolution/pre-life mechanics (abiogenesis) but will not get wrapped up in what to call everything and what came first, second, and third. This would just get in the way of the important points of the discussion. In the end, it does not matter to my argument.

### 2.4.5 RESULTS OF SYNTHETIC BIOLOGY (MOSTLY)

The literature overflows with labs trying to test/recreate conditions supporting the emergence of life.[13] Most of them are extremely technical and beyond my means, but I have found a small sample to be illuminating, and I will reference them wherever helpful. Much of it is misused because some feel that if we cannot create life in a lab, then neither could the natural world, which is where the creator again is conveniently dropped in.

## 2.5 THE UBIQUITOUS PRESENCE OF TELEOLOGY

*Nature does not act by purposes.*
Erwin Schrödinger

When I started writing this book, the term "teleology" was an unknown concept to me. As I dug deeper, I discovered its trap throughout the literature without yet knowing the name for it and even tried to come up with my own. Then, I discovered the term.

Teleology is a big word with major implications for this discussion. For my purposes, I am going to use a succinct definition, which is *the explanation of a phenomenon by intent.* There are broader definitions that include natural source, purpose, utility, or design, but those are just ways for us humans to make *intent* seem cooler. To get to the root understanding of the Real Matrix, I have had to ferret out teleological explanations found in many sources.

Some uses of teleology are explicitly rejected by science, e.g., "God is the Creator." Others use what I will call "stealth terms" to sneak teleology in the back door. Whenever you see someone taking that approach, please look at their credentials (if you can find them). You will no doubt find words like *religious studies, philosophy, philosophy of science,* or nothing meaningful at all.

For example, David L. Abel of the Department of ProtoBioCybernetics/ProtoBioSemiotics writes an incredible 56-page article, "The First Gene, Chapter 9 - Examining specific life-origin models for plausibility,"[14] citing 461 sources that purport to review the science-based theories of abiogenesis. By using a selective reading of the literature while highlighting any gray areas, he forces the conclusion he was after, which is that the "reality of Prescriptive Information's control of life is undeniable." *Prescriptive*

*Information* is his stealth term for a designer, which is some intelligent force (being or god?) directing things.

One of my biggest disappointments in this area is with one of my favorite philosophers, Karl Popper. Concerning evolution and teleology, I think he was stuck in his upbringing, fame, and the period in which he lived. He proposed the *spearhead model of evolution*, in which living organisms themselves have goals and act according to these goals, each guided by a central control.[1] I completely reject this and any other teleology I come across.

Another example is in an otherwise excellent paper that I will draw from later, "The nature and mathematical basis for material stability in the chemical and biological worlds."[15] The authors state, "There is an entire area of biology, functional biology, which continually asks "what is its function, how does it work" type questions, as the purposeful (teleonomic) character of living systems is empirically irrefutable." Sorry, no. Function does not equal purpose. Both are labels we humans place on entity processes, not what these entities place on themselves. The authors put biology on the slippery slope from *function* down to *purpose* down to *intent* down to *design intent* right out the door to the *supernatural*.

I will not list the thousands of articles, books, and especially textbooks that I have come across in my research that ubiquitously, subconsciously, and lazily use teleological terms in their explanations of biological (and even chemical) *stuff*, but here is a good example from a research paper titled, "Defining Life or Bringing Biology to Life."[16] Teleology is embedded in their entire argument, but they never explicitly stated that these "entities" exhibited conscious intent. Examples from the paper (that irritated the hell out of me) include:

- "Life builds"
- "Components are responsible"
- "Organisms act to ensure"
- "Organisms develop"
- "Life is able to maintain"

- "Nature would not overcome"
- "Strategies of evolution"
- "Organisms tinker"
- "Organisms make use of"
- "Organism acts to maintain and reproduce itself"
- "The organization of organisms implies that the components and processes of the organized entity are not only responsible for producing each other and the whole but get subjugated under the power of that entity to carry out global, highly coordinated, actions: i.e., to behave like an agent."
- "Life maintains itself because it keeps evolving"
- "Organisms maintain themselves"

I would not want the job to remove all the false and misleading teleology from the text. Such literature even slips into anthropomorphism, whereby non-thinking entities are given human characteristics.

While they are too late to change, I also disagree with the common misuse of the evolutionary terms "adaptation" and "competition" without accompanying definitions because they imply intent and purpose.

The best (or worst) example phrase that you will find *everywhere* is that "life evolves." This implies (stealthily) that there is some direction or intent. Sorry, but life does not evolve – evolution (or better yet, descent with modification) takes place.

Another is "natural selection." Nature does not select – variant entities survive or do not, and replicate or do not. Darwin liked this term because he spent a lot of time studying "artificial selection," whereby breeders could make dramatic changes in animals and plants over time through their breeding choices. Darwin's original definition of natural selection was, "This preservation of favourable individual differences and variations, and the destruction of those which are injurious." Shortly after the publication of *On the Origin of Species*, Darwin noted to Charles Lyell that he preferred the term "natural preservation," and I agree with him – less teleology. But by then, it was too late – that ship had sailed.

However, there still exist purely scientific arguments in favor of the use of teleology that promote its framing and communication strengths but not its underlying validity. One famous proponent is Ernst Mayr in Chapter 3 of *Toward a New Philosophy of Biology: Observations of an Evolutionist.*[17] In it, Mayr defends the use of teleology in biological studies, but only because it makes explanations easier to write, easier to understand, and easier to extend. He, in a sense, flips teleology on its head. Instead of sincerely *believing* intent is the real explanation of a natural phenomenon (teleology), he uses the wording of intent *without* believing in it to simplify his explanations. He uses it to mask complexities in the same way that chemists use a hierarchy of approximations and simplifications to mask the fundamental physics point of view of molecules and their reactions – not focusing on "time-dependent multi-particle quantum systems in order to attain models of more practical educational value."[18]

I will attempt to keep casual teleological vocabulary out of my writing. One way I will do this will be to use the terms "emerge" or "emergent," which are more passive without intent than the active ones that imply teleology. Let me know if I unintentionally slip up, likely due to it being so ingrained in all scientific literature or because I was raised Catholic.

## 2.6 POTENTIAL THREATS

*Problems worthy of attack / prove their worth by hitting back.*
Piet Hein

Getting to some of the non-falsifiable early, I do believe that there are "things" that could act against me in attaining a complete understanding of the Real Matrix, and there is no way I can use the scientific method to prove or disprove my belief.

## 2.6.1 THE DEMON, THE AGENT

*If you would be a real seeker after truth, it is necessary that at least once in your life you doubt, as far as possible, all things.*
René Descartes

In 1641, René Descartes wrote *Meditations on First Philosophy*. The book is made up of six parts. In "Meditation One," he first discards all his beliefs in things that are not absolutely certain. He then imagines "some malicious demon of the utmost power and cunning has employed all his energies in order to deceive me." This evil demon is imagined to present a complete illusion of an external world, so much so that Descartes says, "I shall think that the sky, the air, the Earth, colors, shapes, sounds and all external things are merely the delusions of dreams which he has devised to ensnare my judgment."

In "Meditation Two," he discusses the evil demon again, saying, "But what shall I now say that I am, when I am supposing that there is some supremely powerful and, if it is permissible to say so, malicious deceiver, who is deliberately trying to trick me in every way he can?"

It makes sense to me that there would have emerged, within the Real Matrix, ways to keep us from understanding it, because by understanding it, we may develop the means to thwart it (I do not at the moment understand what attempting to thwart it would entail or accomplish). This is the equivalent of Descartes' "demon," and, if you recall from the movie, the Matrix's "agent." A stronger position would be that the total Real Matrix is a non-sentient evil demon. This evil demon may act in several ways:

1. Make it difficult to, or keep me from, completing this book.
2. Keep me from completely/accurately describing the Real Matrix.
3. Keep readers from understanding, accepting, and effectively acting on my conclusions.

## 2.6.2 THE INCOMPLETENESS THEOREMS

In 1931, Kurt Gödel established two different, but related, theorems, usually called the First and Second Incompleteness Theorems. His work was stimulated by his reading of "Principia Mathematica" by Bertrand Russell and Alfred North Whitehead, which was an attempt to analyze the roots of mathematics (whole numbers) to "prove" its validity using logic. The incompleteness theorems blew a hole in "Principia Mathematica" that even a later edition could not overcome.

Please take your time and study the theorems closely. Because of their impact on all of mathematics, Gödel's theorems are the most important mathematical results of the 20th century. The two theorems can be summarized as follows:[19]

- **First** – any consistent, formal system within which a certain amount of elementary arithmetic can be carried out is incomplete, i.e., *there are statements of the language of the system that can neither be proved nor disproved in that system.*
- **Second** – for any consistent system within which a certain amount of elementary arithmetic can be carried out, *the consistency of the system cannot be proved in that system itself.*

Many mathematicians have tried to overturn these theorems, yet they still stand strong today.

I am going to extend (without proof) the Incompleteness Theorems to *any system* (not dependent on whole-number arithmetic) and include the Real Matrix in this set of systems. Given that one cannot escape from reality (the Real Matrix I am describing), one is indeed trapped within the system. It is like being trapped within arithmetic (like Milo in *The Phantom Tollbooth*). If this extension is valid, then I must conclude that:

- I may be correct in my understanding of the Real Matrix but be unable to prove it.

- I cannot prove the consistency of the Real Matrix since all I can use is my existence within the Real Matrix to try to prove it.

One could argue that the never-ending struggles that various scientific disciplines have with the definition of "Life" and many other concepts (that I am intentionally dodging) have the Incompleteness Theorems at their failure's root cause.

I have no choice now but to ignore this theorem set and pretend that I can fight my way out of this limitation. I provide an evaluation of my efforts at the end of the book.

## 2.6.3 MY PROTECTION

The primary source of these threats is inside my mind, which emerged within, and is part of, the Real Matrix. The next source would be anyone I have to collaborate with to complete this book. I plan to stand firm. Since I am recognizing early the sources of these threats, I hope that I am building enough mental protections against their influence.

The fact that you are holding this book in your hands is evidence that I was at least partially successful in countering these threats (or, of course, that they never existed).

Two years into writing this book, another possible source of protection came to mind – there is a chance that the Real Matrix does not block this type of inquiry, like the possibility that the sentient machines in *The Matrix* permitted the Resistance. Otherwise, how could it have come into existence if everyone had been connected and under their control? Interesting.

# 3 The Matrix Movie

*None are more hopelessly enslaved than those who falsely believe they are free.*
Johann Wolfgang Von Goethe

*That you are a slave, Neo. Like everyone else, you were born into bondage. Into a prison that you cannot taste or see or touch. A prison for your mind.*
Morpheus from *The Matrix*

## 3.1 Terminology

*The Matrix* is a beautiful movie, and it goes far (but not far enough) along the path I am taking here. Please take my earlier advice and watch it again. If you want to be a real groupie, you can find the movie script at dailyscript.com.[20] It was my epiphany concerning humanity's (and all life's) existence. To aid in my storytelling, let me lay out the terms and present a model of the world of *The Matrix*. I will later compare these terms and use the model as an analogy to the Real Matrix that all life exists within and is made up of.

I am going to give a synopsis of the movie that is sufficient to explain some key terms. I will need those terms later. This terminology was primarily abstracted from *The Matrix Wiki*.[21]

- In **reality**, there was a war between **humans** and a race of sentient **machines**. In their last effort for survival, the humans blotted out the sun, hoping to deny the machines their energy source. In response, the machines enslaved and grew humans in **power plants** to use their bodies as batteries.

- To subdue and deceive the humans, the machines built a virtual-reality program called the **Matrix** that simulated reality and then connected the humans to it. The Matrix program was continually rewritten by the machines to fix problems. In the movie, there were two unstable and six stable versions of the Matrix.
- The **Source** was the central computing core for the machine mainframe.
- The **Architect** was a program of the machine world as well as the creator of the Matrix. As the chief administrator of the system, he was possibly a collective manifestation, or at the very least, a virtual representation of the entire machine mainframe.
- The humans in the power plants were physically connected to the Matrix by inserting a data probe into a **headjack** located at the base of their skulls. The humans not only provided heat and electrical power – their brains became part of a massive biocomputing cluster that generated and maintained much of the Matrix itself.
- The connected humans were called (by free humans) the **Bluepills**. They were not aware that the reality they were experiencing was a virtual reality of the Matrix. Their experience was imagined in their minds through their **avatars** that represented their persona inside the Matrix. A better term would be the "Nopills," since 99.99% of them were never offered a pill.
- **Agents** were programs within the Matrix whose primary function was to eliminate anyone or anything that could potentially reveal the truth of the Matrix to its inhabitants or cause harm to its system.
- The **Resistance** consisted of free humans on Earth not connected to the Matrix (either at some point disconnected or never connected) who were fighting against the machines to regain control of the planet. They lived in the human city of Zion underground for warmth, power, and protection.
- The **Nebuchadnezzar** was a hovercraft that was part of the real

world and upon which all real-world activities take place in the first *Matrix* movie.

- The avatar of a connected human could choose to take a **red pill** that disconnected them from the Matrix and allowed humans outside the Matrix (in the Resistance) to find their physical bodies in the power plant and retrieve them. This was a virtual pill given by an operative (who materialized inside the Matrix as an avatar) to a human's avatar still living out a life within the Matrix. The pill was a tracing program that disrupted the carrier signal of the pod-human's mind, making it possible for a hovercraft operator to locate the pod that held the human, and then send commands that forced it to go offline and awaken its inhabitant.

- The contacted avatar could instead have chosen to take a **blue pill** after being informed of the existence of the Matrix to wipe their memory of that knowledge and return them to their ignorant life within the Matrix.

- **Redpills** were humans whose bodies and minds had been freed from the power plant by Zion hovercraft teams. Upon returning to the Matrix, a redpill's awareness of the virtual reality allowed them to bend the Matrix's rules and exceed normal physical limitations.

- A **telephone line** served as the connection point that the redpills in the Matrix could connect with and use to return to reality.

- **Neo** was a human whose destiny was to release humans from the prison of the Matrix and domination by the sentient machines. Before he emerged as "The One," he suspected the existence of the Matrix but did not understand its full extent until shown by **Morpheus** and after taking the red pill.

- At the end of the movie, Neo could "see" the Matrix's underlying program, visualized as executing **binary code**.

## 3.2 The Matrix Model

Using the terms defined above, I have drawn my own picture that represents the universe of *The Matrix* movie. Study it, and make sure you understand it before proceeding.

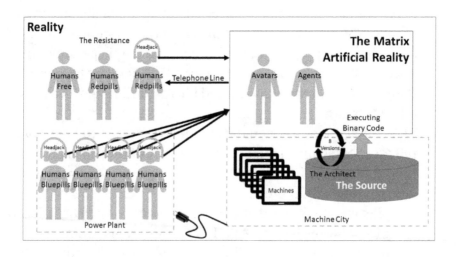

*Figure 1 – The Matrix Model*

## 3.3 Simulacra and Simulation

I do not want to waste any more than this space to say that although *Simulacra and Simulation* by Jean Baudrillard[22] was required reading for the main actors of *The Matrix*, it does not contribute to this discussion or my objectives. Baudrillard reportedly said that the movie "stemmed mostly from misunderstandings" of his work.[23] Go ahead and read it if you want to waste some time and end up in confusion. Let me know if you agree or disagree with me about its utility afterward.

## 3.4 PLATO'S ALLEGORY OF THE CAVE

*Figure 2 – Plato's Allegory of the Cave*

Since *The Matrix* is a modern adaptation of the 2,400-year-old "Allegory of the Cave" found in Plato's *The Republic*, I thought it would be helpful to give an overview of the source material.

**Imprisonment in the Cave**

Imagine a cave where people have been imprisoned since childhood. These prisoners are chained so that their legs and necks are fixed, forcing them to look at the wall in front of them, unable to look around at the cave, each other, or themselves. There is a fire behind the prisoners, and between the fire and the prisoners is a raised walkway with a low wall. People walk behind this low wall, carrying objects or puppets "of men and other living things" that cast shadows, while the bodies and their shadows are hidden. The prisoners cannot see any of what is happening behind them – they are only able to see the shadows cast upon the cave wall in front of them. The shadows are the only reality for the prisoners because they have never seen anything else.

**Departure from the Cave**

Suppose now that one prisoner is somehow freed. This prisoner looks around and sees the fire. The light hurts his eyes and makes it difficult for him to see the objects casting the shadows. If he were told that what he is seeing is real instead of the other version of reality he sees on the wall, he would not believe it. In his pain, the freed prisoner would turn away and run back to what he is accustomed to.

Now suppose that someone forces him up the rough ascent and never stops until he drags him out into the light of the sun. The prisoner would be angry and in pain, and this would only worsen when the radiant light of the sun overwhelms his eyes and blinds him.

Slowly, his eyes adjust to sunlight. First, he can only see shadows. Gradually, he can see the reflections of people and things in water, and later, he can see the people and things themselves. Eventually, he can look at the stars and moon at night until finally, he can look upon the sun itself.

## Return to the Cave

The freed prisoner now thinks that the world outside the cave is superior to the world he experienced in the cave and attempts to share this with the prisoners remaining in the cave.

The returning prisoner, whose eyes have become adapted to the sunlight, would be blind upon reentering the cave, tripping over everything and causing a ruckus, just as he was when he was first exposed to the sun. The prisoners would conclude from the returning man's blindness that the journey out of the cave had harmed him and that they should not undertake a similar journey. The prisoners would then kill the returning prisoner.

Please do not hurt me!

# 4 THE EMERGENCE OF LIFE

I now enter the heavy-lifting section of the book. The challenge is that this is where we stop talking about movies and start talking about real science.

This section is going to take you from the prebiotic (i.e., before biological organisms) to the biotic (i.e., biological organisms). The challenge for you is that it is now necessary to teach you some science before you can begin to understand it. After introducing abiogenesis, I will take you through the required chemistry, biochemistry, and biology. With those terms, I will then explain the mechanics of abiogenesis.

Keep in mind while reading through this section that this process – and the matter and energy utilized that have resulted in and continue to enable biological organisms – is the Real Matrix. To understand one is to begin to understand the other.

While none of this section directly applies to my epiphany about the existence of our Real Matrix, it does clearly demonstrate that it emerged in a non-directional way from the inanimate.

## 4.1 INTRODUCTION TO ABIOGENESIS

*Abiogenesis* is the process by which life arises from non-living matter, also called the *chemical phase*, while evolution is the *biological phase*.

### 4.1.1 THE EMERGENCE OF LIFE

I said back in Section 2.4.3 that I would not be covering the origin of life in this book. Instead, my focus is on the *emergence* of life. *Origin* implies a single significant point, while *emergence* does not.

Many articles about abiogenesis are stupid and simplistic or overly philosophical and obtuse. They are usually written to conjecture on the possible ways that life could have originated (some list three, others list six, and others list seven or more). They can also be written with the intent to disprove or at least disclaim the theoretical likelihood of abiogenesis. Such articles point out that it is silly to imagine you can get a human from a rock, and they also disparage experiments that weakly claim to prove this, or muddle their analysis with all the different possible ways that abiogenesis might have happened. All the while, these articles focus on the improbability and irreducible complexity of abiogenesis, seemingly with the objective of throwing up their hands and claiming that creationism or some other mysterious force of nature is the only way.

Even "scientific" articles can run into trouble. They just use bigger words and more complex experiments and theories, then trip over teleology. Scientists are human, and many just cannot help themselves in falling back on this explanation. For example, "Nature's most fundamental drive, *dictated by logic itself*, is toward greater stability."[24] Teleology is just black magic sneaking in the back door. It is sometimes represented as a breakthrough when it is just lazy thinking trying to appear as brilliance. I think it is one of the threats I discussed in Section 2.6 making its presence known.

The remaining scientific articles make clear that nothing is settled. I am not suggesting that this research is not important. It is. It simply does not help us much here. One of the challenges for the non-scientist is that the content of these articles is extremely complex, particularly because the theory and terms have not coalesced. Thank me now for not spending excessive space on the many hypotheses I have discovered that are being actively explored, including:

- RNA world
- Protein enzyme (metabolism) world
- Pre-enzyme, pre-compartment autocatalytic world
- Virus world

- Nucleopeptide theory
- Lipid world (compartmentalization)
- Lipid-RNA world
- Polycyclic aromatic hydrocarbons (PAHs) world
- Iron-sulfur world
- Zinc world
- Green rust world
- Introns-early vs. introns-late
- SimSoup
- Between the sheets of muscovite mica
- Hypercycles
- Chemotons
- Coevolution
- Compositional

My objective here is to discuss the required mechanics, not the timing or naming, focusing on the emergence of biology. I will spend some time on the first four listed – RNA, protein/metabolism, auto-catalytic, and virus world – but more to get you thinking than to argue for one over another. To paraphrase from a paper I draw from later,[25] *structure is more relevant than sequence.*

## 4.1.2 THE CULMINATION OF ABIOGENESIS

Before we discuss the mechanics, it is important to understand where abiogenesis ends and biology (now driven by evolution) begins. Notice that I am directing you to this transitional topic instead of the fruitless one of defining when life began.

One position says that abiogenesis ended at the Last Universal Common Ancestor (LUCA, aka LCA or cenancestor). It is at this single point that all future organisms began to evolve. Based on a recent systematic and global study of the evolution of domain structure and organization in proteins, organismal timelines showed Archaea was the most ancestral superkingdom, followed by Viruses, then

Eukarya and Bacteria.[26] This study and others[27,28] present evidence that viruses may have predated Archaea and even LUCA. This proposed virus world existed before any cellular organisms, and RNA and DNA viruses originated at this time, contributing features to the first cellular organisms (see the end of Section 4.8.7).

The simplest consensus of what LUCA would have looked like is:[29]

- **Genetic code** – a core of ribosomal proteins, tRNA, and translation factors (for initiation and elongation).
- **Membrane** – signal recognition particles, a system for protein secretion, and the complex ATP process working with a transmembrane gradient.

In the paper I referenced way back in Section 2.4.1 about the demarcation between inanimate and animate,[30] the authors also argued that the quest for LUCA is unattainable because the driving forces and paths of evolution cannot be separated from each other, making it a non-computable task. It is an interesting argument, but I take issue with their approach because they build up a strawman definition of LUCA only to knock it down in their argument. They state that LUCA is the first "animate" entity and the first living being and that it represented a huge departure from its immediate ancestor. Then, they base their entire argument on that definition. I call bullshit. LUCA is *not* defined by its ancestors, nor by its unique characteristics. It is defined by the success of its *descendants*. In and of itself, LUCA is not special.

There is an earlier place to look for that fundamental (and *special*) transition. The *Darwinian Threshold* is the term used to define when protocells reach the tipping point from primarily horizontal to vertical gene transfer (i.e., heredity), upon which evolutionary mechanics operate. These protocells are referred to as *Initial Darwinian Ancestors* (IDAs). This is where I will draw my fuzzy line between the operation of abiogenesis and evolution mechanics. There is no avoiding it, but the terms are circular since I am saying that evolution began to operate when there were entities that began to operate under evolution. The helpful thing is that we now have a hook on which to hang our descriptors of this transitional protocell/organism.

IDAs would be able to:

- Self-organize.
- Store information and replicate that information.
- Translate the information into the components that can produce their functional structures.
- Obtain metabolic components and energy.
- Transform the components and energy into biochemical networks.[31]

To summarize, abiogenesis did not end with the rise of LUCA but with the rise of IDAs. Notice that "LUCA" is singular, while "IDAs" is plural. The implication is that many IDAs were operating under evolution, but there was just one LUCA from which all biological organisms subsequently descended. We were not there, so we will never know for sure.

## 4.1.3 RESOURCE AND TIME CONSTRAINED

*Time is what keeps everything from happening at once.*
Ray Cummings (commonly misattributed to Albert Einstein)

I could never compete with these smart and educated people who developed thermodynamic laws and incompleteness theorems. Despite that, I would like to propose something that I have not come across before that will frame this section – *spatial/temporal theorems (laws?)*.

1. All matter and energy occur spatially and temporally.
2. Only one instance of matter or energy can exist at a unique location and time.

3. Every action occurs in a location.
4. Every action takes time.

Obviously, these statements are built into reality and the Real Matrix, so they are built into this entire discussion and, at times, will be addressed explicitly.

## 4.2 THE CHEMISTRY

Now that I have introduced you to abiogenesis, I will start with some fundamental chemistry terms that we will need later when detailing abiogenetic mechanics at a very technical level.

**Chemical force** – an attractive force between two or more atoms. This attractive force can be intramolecular or intermolecular.

- **Intramolecular force** – exists *within* molecules to hold *atoms* together, i.e., a molecular bond. *Supramolecules* are molecules that share electrons through the intramolecular force. *Covalent bonds* occur between two non-metals, *metallic bonds* between two metals, and *ionic bonds* between metal and non-metal. Breaking up these types of bonds requires a lot of energy. For example, a peptide bond that holds together the amino acids in polymers is an amide-type covalent chemical bond.
- **Intermolecular force** (Noncovalent Interactions) – exists *between* molecules to hold them together in a three-dimensional shape. *Supermolecules* are molecules that are more loosely linked using these *noncovalent* interactions that do not involve a sharing of electrons. Although noncovalent interactions are weak, they can produce highly stable and specific associations when there are hundreds or thousands

of them. Multiple noncovalent interactions can stabilize the three-dimensional shape of supermolecules and can control the interactions between molecules. Also, as a key to many of our mechanics, noncovalent interactions are *readily reversible*. The three principal types of noncovalent interactions are electrostatic, hydrophobic, and hydrogen. What holds together DNA's double helix is a noncovalent hydrogen interaction – its secondary structure.

**Chemical reactions** are processes in which one or more substances, the *reactants*, or *substrates (biochemistry)*, convert to one or more different substances when combined with a *catalyst*. A chemical reaction causes the rearrangement of the constituent atoms of the reactants that results in different substances called *products*. A catalyst is a molecule that speeds up the rate at which a chemical reaction occurs without being used up in that reaction.

**Autocatalytic reactions** produce at least one reactant. In other words, if energy is continually provided, then the reaction can create more similar reactions. A set of chemical reactions is "collectively autocatalytic" if some of those reactions produce catalysts for enough of the other reactions to create an entire set of chemical reactions that is self-sustaining, given an input of energy and food molecules.

**Metabolism** is a vast autocatalytic set within a biological cell, in that all its molecular constituents are produced by reactions involving the same set of molecules. Metabolism is the set of all enzyme-catalyzed reactions that take place within each cell of a living organism and provide energy for biological processes.

## 4.3 The Biochemistry

*The king of Siam once asked his wise men for a proverb that would be appropriate for any occasion. They suggested 'This, too, shall pass'.*
*Well, in biochemistry an equally appropriate saying for all occasions is 'Things are more complicated than they seem.'*
Michael J. Behe

Biochemistry is the chemistry of living systems. Even though we are going to start the discussion of the emergence of life with abiogenesis (before biology), I must introduce some fundamental biochemistry terms because the abiogenetic process had to somehow result in the biochemistry of life. Thus, I need these terms to discuss how they may have emerged. A comprehensive understanding of this and later sections is not required – just a familiarity – and the GLOSSARY is available to dig deeper. Do not worry if some of it flies over your head – it did for me for quite a while. If you are scientifically minded, go read the citations.

### 4.3.1 Enabling Properties of Water

The existence of life on Earth depends on the capacity of water to dissolve polar molecules that are fuels, building blocks, catalysts, and information carriers. Concentrations of these polar molecules can coexist in water, where they diffuse and interact with one another and the water molecules. Several properties of biomolecules derive from their interactions with water molecules in the surrounding environment, including the following:[32]

- **Water is a polar molecule**. The water molecule is bent and carries an asymmetric distribution of electronic charge. The electronically negative oxygen atom draws the electrons in the covalent bond to the hydrogen atoms away from the hydrogen nuclei, which leaves the region around the hydrogen nuclei with a partial positive charge. The water molecule is thus an electronically polar structure.

- **Water is highly cohesive**. Water molecules interact with one another through hydrogen bonds. The cohesive nature of water affects the interactions between molecules in aqueous solutions.

## 4.3.2 Monomers and Polymers

A monomer is a molecule that can react with other monomer molecules to form a larger polymer chain or three-dimensional network in a process called polymerization.

A polymer is a large molecule, or supermolecule, composed of many repeated monomers held together by intramolecular and intermolecular bonds.

## 4.3.3 Biological Supermolecules (Biomolecules)

We will spend a lot of space discussing the emergence of biomolecules during abiogenesis, so it is important to understand them here.

Biomolecules are compounds primarily composed of carbon. The four main classes of biomolecules that make up most of the bodies of living things are NUCLEIC ACIDS, PROTEINS, CARBOHYDRATES (the polymers), and LIPIDS (the non-polymers). Each biomolecule type has multiple structures and functions. The monomer units of biomolecules are polar (having heads and tails). When they polymerize in a head-to-tail fashion, the resulting polymers also have heads and tails.

Biomolecules are held together internally by covalent bonds. The three-dimensional structures of these biomolecules are primarily maintained by noncovalent interactions. The weak interactions keep the biomolecule's shape stable but also allow it to open for copying and use. Noncovalent interactions are found in enzyme catalysis, protein structures, DNA strands, RNA structures, and lipid bilayer membranes.

### 4.3.4 BIOMOLECULAR STRUCTURES

Biomolecules exhibit different levels of structures that enable many biological processes. These structures are:[33]

- **Primary** – the initial polymer structure (determined by the sequence of monomers) held together by covalent bonds. The primary structure determines the polymer's secondary and tertiary structures by dictating the folding of the chain.
- **Secondary** – the twisting and folding of the polymer (helixes and sheets) by mostly hydrogen (noncovalent) bonds.
- **Tertiary** – the structure at which these chains become functional; formed due to various covalent and non-covalent attractive forces. At this level, the biomolecule has a three-dimensional shape and presents functional groups on its outer surface, allowing it to interact with other molecules and giving it its unique function. The structure of this folding is due to the amino-acid-side chain interactions on the polypeptide chain.
- **Quaternary** – the cluster of two or more biomolecular chains forming a larger protein structure. Insulin and silk are two examples.

### 4.3.5 BIOLOGICAL PATHWAYS

I mention pathways throughout, so try to follow – it is a bit complex. A biological pathway is a series of actions among molecules in a cell that leads to a certain product or change in the cell. The molecules that make up biological pathways interact with signals, as well as with each other. When multiple biological pathways interact with each other, they form a biological network. This is an incredibly complex topic that I must grossly simplify (mostly due to my lack of education). The KEY BIOLOGICAL PATHWAYS include metabolic, genetic information processing, environmental information processing, cellular processes, organismal systems, human diseases, and drug development.

If you have the time and interest, you can find comprehensive online pathway databases containing related content, modeling techniques, and analysis tools.[34,35,36]

### 4.3.5.1 METABOLIC PATHWAYS

Metabolism is the set of all enzyme-catalyzed reactions that take place within each cell of a living organism and provide energy for biological processes. The product of a pathway may be used immediately, initiate another metabolic pathway, or be stored for later use. The three main results of metabolism are the conversion of food to energy to run cellular processes, the conversion of food/fuel to building blocks for proteins, lipids, nucleic acids, and some carbohydrates, along with the elimination of wastes.

The key metabolic pathways are CATABOLIC, ANABOLIC, and OXIDATION-REDUCTION REACTIONS.

### 4.3.5.2 GENE-REGULATION PATHWAYS

A genetic regulatory network is a collection of molecular regulators that govern the gene expression levels of DNA, RNA, protein, and complexes of these. Each mRNA molecule makes a specific protein (or set of proteins). Proteins can be structural or enzymes, or they can activate other genes.

### 4.3.5.3 SIGNAL-TRANSDUCTION PATHWAYS

Signal transduction is the process by which a chemical or physical signal is transmitted through a cell as a series of molecular events that ultimately results in a cellular response. Proteins responsible for detecting stimuli are called *receptors* (see Section 4.4.11: Cell Signaling). The changes elicited by signal sensing in a receptor give rise to a biochemical cascade, which is a chain of biochemical events known as a signaling pathway.

When signaling pathways interact with one another, they form networks, which allow cellular responses to be coordinated. These events control cell growth, proliferation, metabolism, cell communication, and many other processes.


## 4.4 THE BIOLOGY

> *We are biology. We are reminded of this at the beginning and the end, at birth and at death. In between, we do what we can to forget.*
> Mary Roach

### 4.4.1 THE BIG IDEAS

Before we get down in the weeds, I thought it would be instructive to list the "Big Ideas" of biology as defined during a National Science Foundation-sponsored workshop.[37]

1. Living organisms are *causal mechanisms* whose functions are to be understood by applications of the laws of physics and chemistry.
2. *The cell* is the basic unit of life.
3. Life requires *information flow* within and between cells and between the environment and the organism.
4. Living organisms must obtain matter and energy from the external world.
5. This matter and energy must be *transformed* and *transferred* in varied ways to build the organism and to perform work.
6. *Homeostasis* (aka *stability*, more generally) maintains the

internal environment in a more or less constant state that is compatible with life.

7. Understanding the behavior of the organism requires understanding the relationship between *structure and function* (at each and every level of organization).

8. *Evolution* provides a scientific explanation for the history of life on Earth and the mechanisms by which changes to life have occurred.

9. All life exists with an *ecosystem* composed of physicochemical and biological worlds.

## 4.4.2 BIOLOGICAL PROCESSES

The BIOLOGICAL PROCESSES include homeostasis, metabolism, growth, adaptation, response to stimuli, reproduction, and interaction between organisms.

## 4.4.3 BIOMOLECULAR AGGREGATES

We now need to build from the ground up our understanding of biological entities and their contents. The emergence of biological entities during abiogenesis was critical to the emergence of life. Biomolecular components and aggregates, in order, include the AMPHIPHILE, MICELLE, BIOLOGICAL MICELLE, VESICLE, LIPID, LIPID BILAYER, LIPO-SOME, PROTOCELL, CELL, ORGANISM, and the HOLOBIONT.

## 4.4.4 CELL TYPES

There is a lot of debate on the first emergence of prokaryote versus eukaryote organisms, and even whether the concept of prokaryote organisms is a valid distinction, but let me introduce them for now. A PROKARYOTE is a cell that lacks a membrane-bound nucleus, mitochondria, or any other membrane-bound organelle, while a EUKARYOTE cell does possess one of these.

The first two domains, Archaea and Bacteria, do not have organelles, but try not to think of them as closely related, nor that either are predecessors to eukaryotes (Eukaryota is the third domain). The reality is much more complex, and no final model has been accepted. Some examples of the fog include:[38]

- Bacteria use one class of protein to control transcription initiation, while both archaea and eucarya use a completely different type.
- Bacteria wrap their DNA in a variety of basic proteins, while eukaryotes and many archaea both use histones (nucleoproteins found in chromatin).
- Eukaryotes and bacteria make their membranes from one type of lipid, whereas archaea use a completely different type.

Some researchers reject outright the term prokaryote and instead use non-eukaryote.[39] The point they make is that grouping a life form into a category based on what it does not have is like calling baldness a hairstyle (my own analogy). I will continue with prokaryote and leave that battle for others to fight.

## 4.4.5 SOME KEY CELL COMPONENTS

Many of the following concepts will be readdressed in the discussion about the emergence of biological cells. Some key cell components include the BIOLOGICAL MEMBRANE, CYTOPLASM, RIBOSOME, and ENDOPLASMIC RETICULUM.

## 4.4.6 THE CELL-DIVISION CYCLE

I will be spending significant space on the emergence of replication, so this will be interesting reading.

The cell-division cycle is the series of events that lead to the duplication of cellular DNA and, in eukaryotes, the division of cytoplasm and organelles to produce two daughter cells. Before naming names, DNA replication has four basic steps:

1. A replication-origin sequence within the genome is recognized by protein components.
2. The initiation of replication occurs through the recruitment of proteins at the origin.
3. The general replication reaction duplicates both strands of DNA.
4. Replication terminates and the two daughter chromosomes are separated.

The key cell-division cycle processes are INTERPHASE (both eukaryotes and prokaryotes), MITOSIS (eukaryotes), CYTOKINESIS (eukaryotes), MEIOSIS (eukaryotes), and FISSION (prokaryotes and mitochondria/chloroplasts).

If you want to explore this topic in more detail, try "Principles and Concepts of DNA Replication in Bacteria, Archaea, and Eukarya."[40]

## 4.4.7 Two Types of Organisms

There are two types of organisms – autotrophs and heterotrophs. An autotroph (producer) is an organism that produces complex organic compounds from simple substances present in its surroundings (e.g., carbon dioxide or minerals). Autotrophs include photoautotrophs, which use energy from light (photosynthesis) – we call them plants – and chemoautotrophs, which use inorganic chemical reactions (chemosynthesis) and are mainly found on ocean floors where underwater volcanos can provide heat as an energy source.

A heterotroph (consumer) is an organism that does not produce its own food. Instead, it takes nutrition from other sources of organic carbon, mainly plant or animal matter. Heterotrophs include all animals and fungi, some bacteria and *protists* (a group of mostly unicellular eukaryotic organisms), and parasitic plants.

## 4.4.8 ENERGY STORAGE AND USAGE

Energy is required by cells for metabolic activities. During metabolic transductions, entropy increases as the potential energy of complex nutrient molecules decreases. Organisms extract energy and nutrients from the environment (sunlight, biomolecules), transduce some of it into energy to perform cellular work through the flow of electrons in oxidation-reduction reactions, and return some of it to the environment as heat and simple molecules ($CO_2$, $H_2O$). The nutrients can also be transformed into new biomolecules that are used by the organism.

There are distinct autotrophic and heterotrophic storage processes, including PHOTOSYNTHESIS (AUTOTROPHIC) and INGESTION, DIGESTION, ABSORPTION, AND TRANSPORT (HETEROTROPHIC). Storage molecules include MONOSACCHARIDES, POLYSACCHARIDES, LIPIDS, and COENZYMES, and the usage processes can be OXYGEN-INDEPENDENT, AEROBIC, or ANAEROBIC.

## 4.4.9 GENETICS

Here is a simple definition of genetic code:

"A mapping of genetic information encoded by one type of biological macromolecule, the nucleic acids, into another family, the amino acids, which constitute the building blocks of proteins. The scheme is simple enough to state: a dictionary of 64 possible code-words (codons), is associated with 20 amino acids plus a stop signal."[41]

A NUCLEOTIDE is the basic structural unit and building block for DNA, which is one of the two nucleic acids (RNA is the other).

CHROMATIN is a complex of unpaired DNA, RNA, and proteins found in eukaryotic cells, while CHROMOSOMES are single-stranded base pairings of condensed chromatin that consist of a long strand of DNA and contain many genes. A CHROMATID is either of the two strands of a replicated chromosome. A GENE is a sequence of nucleotides in DNA or RNA that encodes the synthesis of a gene product, either RNA or protein, and RNA, the other nucleic acid, which is essential in various biological roles in coding, decoding, REGULATION, and EXPRESSION OF GENES, helping to synthesize, regulate, and process proteins.

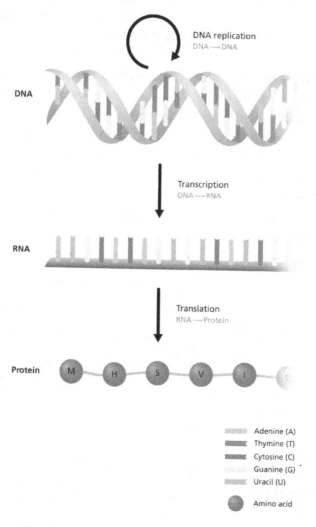

*Figure 3 – The Central Dogma of Molecular Biology*

The Central Dogma of molecular biology explains that the information flow for genes is from the DNA genetic code, to an intermediate

RNA copy, and then to the proteins synthesized from the code (see Figure 2 above). Regulation of gene expression gives control over the timing, location, and amount of a given gene product (protein or ncRNA) present in a cell that determines cellular structure and function. It is the basis for cellular differentiation, development, and morphogenesis.

It is essential to reiterate what a PROTEIN is and how it functions. In essence, it does the work. A protein is a biomolecule that binds to substrates. This way, these substrates are held in the right place so they can undergo a chemical reaction. This reaction is often facilitated by a cofactor (e.g., vitamin), which is also held in place by the protein and serves as the catalyst. Examples of protein functions include antibodies, contraction proteins, enzymes, hormones, messengers, structural components, transport/storage, and removing toxins.

Below is a chart comparing DNA, RNA, and proteins.[42]

|  | DNA | RNA | Proteins |
|---|---|---|---|
| Encodes genetic information | Yes | Yes | No |
| Catalyzes biological reactions | No | Yes | Yes |
| Building blocks (type) | Nucleotides | Nucleotides | Amino Acids |
| Building blocks (number) | 4 | 4 | 20 |
| Strandedness | Double | Single | Single |
| Structure | Double helix | Complex | Complex |
| Stability to degradation | High | Variable | Variable |
| Repair systems | Yes | No | No |

*Table 1 – DNA, RNA, Proteins Comparison*

To support the later abiogenesis discussion, it is important to note that the RNA-DEPENDENT RNA POLYMERASE (RDRP) is an enzyme that primarily catalyzes the transcription and replication of genomes from the RNA template in RNA viruses. RdRPs are also found in cells involved in RNA interference in which RNA molecules inhibit gene expression or translation by neutralizing targeted mRNA molecules.

The GENOTYPE is the genetic makeup of an organism, while the PHENO-TYPE is its observable characteristics. The hologenome is the combined genome of all bionts (host and symbiotic microbiota) in the holobiont.

## 4.4.10 NEURONS

An overview of the entire nervous system is unnecessary for our purposes, so I will just focus on neurons because of their fundamental relationship to the Real Matrix and its monopoly on sensing and response.

In vertebrates, neurons are found in the central nervous system (CNS) and the peripheral nervous system (PNS). The CNS consists of the brain and spinal cord. The PNS consists mainly of nerves, which are enclosed bundles of the long fibers or axons that connect the CNS to every other part of the body. From a functional perspective, the types of neurons are SENSORY and MOTOR NEURONS, and INTERNEURONS.[43]

## 4.4.11 CELL SIGNALING

Cell signaling is the one and only means by which organisms interact with their environment and with the internal pathways I discussed earlier. Thus, it is essential to understanding the later sections on sensory and response systems (4.5 and 4.6) and my entire premise of the Real Matrix.

There are two kinds of cellular communication – between cells (*intercellular signaling*) and within a cell (*intracellular signaling*). The four attributes of stimulus are modality, intensity, location, and duration.

Cells maintain a diversity of signaling receptors that are sensitive and respond specifically to received stimuli. These receptors are chemical structures composed of proteins that *receive*, *transduce*, and *respond* to signals. They enable cells to act in concert to maintain homeostasis by responding rapidly to changes in incoming environmental signals, while the crosstalk between signaling pathways allows coordinated responses to multiple different and sometimes opposing signals.[44]

*First messengers* are the signaling molecules that reach the cell from the extracellular fluid and bind to their specific receptors. *Second messengers* are the chemical relays that enter the cytoplasm from the membrane and act within the cell to trigger a response.

Different types of signals are grouped according to the distance they travel to reach their targets. The types of signals include INTRACRINE, AUTOCRINE, JUXTACRINE, PARACRINE, and ENDOCRINE.

### 4.4.11.1 INTERNAL RECEPTORS

Nuclear, intranuclear, or nuclear hormone receptors are activated by lipid-soluble molecules, such as estrogen and progesterone, and lipid-soluble signals, including retinoic acid, oxysterols, and thyroid hormones (types of LIGANDS) that alter DNA and RNA expression. This results in an alteration of the production of cellular proteins. Unlike most intercellular messengers, the ligands cross the cellular membrane and directly interact with NUCLEAR RECEPTORS inside the cell. Once activated, nuclear receptors directly regulate the transcription of genes that control a wide variety of biological processes, including cell proliferation, development, metabolism, and reproduction.[45]

CYTOPLASMIC RECEPTORS are found in the cytoplasm or nucleus that binds signaling molecules and triggers changes that influence the behavior of cells. The major groups are the steroid hormone receptors and the thyroid hormone receptors.

### 4.4.11.2 CELL-SURFACE RECEPTORS

Cell-surface receptors are transmembrane proteins embedded in the plasma membrane that maintain communication between the internal processes within the cell and various types of extracellular signals.[46]

Cell-surface receptors have an extracellular (recognition) domain that binds ligands and is exposed to the outer surface of the cell, which is a membrane-spanning region made up of hydrophobic protein molecules and an intracellular (coupling) domain that is in contact with the cytoplasm. The primary types of cell-surface receptors are ENZYME-LINKED (CATALYTIC), G PROTEIN-COUPLED, and ION-CHANNEL-LINKED RECEPTORS, as well as INTEGRINS.

## 4.4.12 VIRUSES, VIROIDS, VIRUSOIDS, SATELLITES, AND PRIONS

### 4.4.12.1 VIRUSES

A virus is a biological entity that only replicates inside the cells of an organism. When infected by a virus, a host cell produces thousands of copies of the original virus. Viruses contain DNA or RNA, giving them the ability to mutate and evolve. They depend on the host cell for almost all their life-sustaining functions. They cannot synthesize proteins because they lack ribosomes for the translation of their mRNA into proteins. Viruses must use the ribosomes of their host cells to translate viral mRNA into viral proteins.

Viruses also derive their metabolic functions from the host cell since they cannot generate or store energy in the form of ATP. They use the nucleotides and amino acids of the host cell to synthesize their nucleic acids and proteins.[47]

Viral particles are the most abundant biological entities on Earth. There are millions of different types of viruses, although only about 5,000 types have been described in detail. Every cellular organism is infected by many viral species. Viruses possess genes, evolve by natural selection, and reproduce by creating multiple copies of themselves through the use of their host's cellular machinery.

The Baltimore classification scheme groups viruses into seven categories based on how mRNA is produced during the replicative cycle[48] (Covid-19 is a Group IV virus).

| Group | Characteristics | Mode of mRNA Production | Example |
|-------|-----------------|-------------------------|---------|
| I | Double-stranded DNA | mRNA is transcribed directly from the DNA template | Herpes simplex (herpesvirus) |
| II | Single-stranded DNA | DNA is converted to double-stranded form before RNA is transcribed | Canine parvovirus (parvovirus) |
| III | Double-stranded RNA | mRNA is transcribed from the RNA genome | Childhood gastro-enteritis (rotavirus) |
| IV | Single-stranded RNA (+) | Genome functions as mRNA | Common cold (picornavirus) |
| V | Single-stranded RNA (-) | mRNA is transcribed from the RNA genome | Rabies (rhabdovirus) |
| VI | Single-stranded RNA viruses with reverse transcriptase | Reverse transcriptase makes DNA from the RNA genome; DNA is then incorporated in the host genome; mRNA is transcribed from the incorporated DNA | Human immunodeficiency virus (HIV) |
| VII | Double-stranded DNA viruses with reverse transcriptase | The viral genome is double-stranded DNA, but viral DNA is replicated through an RNA intermediate; the RNA may serve directly as mRNA or as a template to make mRNA | Hepatitis B virus (hepadnavirus) |

*Table 2 – Virus Group Characteristics*

While not infecting a cell, viruses exist in the form of independent entities, or *virions* (see the next section) made up of:

- the genetic material (DNA or RNA) that encodes the structure of the proteins by which the virus acts.
- a protein coat, the *capsid*, which surrounds and protects the genetic material and is made up of *capsomeres* (made from proteins encoded by the viral genome).
- in some cases, an outside envelope of lipids derived from the host cell membrane.

The life cycle of viruses differs greatly between species, but there are SIX BASIC STAGES: attachment, penetration, uncoating, replication, assembly, and release.

The only universal gene among RNA viruses is the gene encoding the RdRp (see Section 4.4.9). RNA genomes dominate the world of viruses because of RdRp's ability to perform rapid changes via mutations caused by their high rate of error during the copying process, which is a result of the lack of proofreading. The increased rates of mutation can result in some of the variants being selected under the fitness pressures imposed by the host defense mechanisms and other environmental factors.[49]

## 4.4.12.2 VIROIDS

Viroids are like viruses, but they are composed solely of a short strand of circular, single-stranded RNA that has no protein coating. Viroids are the smallest infectious pathogens known. All known viroids are inhabitants of higher plants and most cause diseases.

The viroid's replication mechanism uses a host cell's enzyme RdRp, which catalyzes the synthesis of new RNA using the viroid's RNA as a template. Unlike other polymerases, the RdRp have high mutation rates that generate the variability of RNA viruses.

Interesting characteristics of the viroid[50] include:

- a non-coding, non-translatable RNA.
- the small size of their genome.

- their circularity, which enables them to circumvent the problems of linear genome replication.
- their lack of capsid or outer envelope.
- their lack of protein manufacturing.

### 4.4.12.3 VIRUSOIDS

Virusoids are circular, single-stranded RNA(s) dependent on viruses for replication and encapsidation, and they only affect some plants. Virusoids are essentially viroids that have been encapsulated by a helper virus coat protein. The genome of virusoids consists of several hundred nucleotides and does not code for any proteins but instead serves only to replicate virusoid RNA. Virusoids require that the cell also be infected with a specific helper virus. It is the helper virus that performs protein coding.

### 4.4.12.4 SATELLITE RNAS AND SATELLITE VIRUSES

Satellite RNAs are short RNA molecules that depend on helper viruses for replication, encapsidation, movement, and transmission. They share little or no nucleotide sequence similarity with their helper viruses. In contrast, satellite viruses are satellite RNAs that encode and are encapsidated in capsid proteins.[51]

### 4.4.12.5 PRIONS

For completeness, I include prions, which are misfolded proteins that can transmit their abnormal three-dimensional structure onto normal variants of the same protein, conferring infectious properties. The role of a protein that contains no nucleic acids as an infectious agent contrasts with all other known infectious agents, such as viruses, bacteria, fungi, and parasites, all of which contain DNA, RNA, or both. Prions are extremely difficult to destroy because they are resistant to heat, chemicals, and radiation.

## 4.5 Sensory Systems

*The only things we perceive are our perceptions.*
George Berkeley

The only way we experience the world is through our senses. Therefore, the senses that organisms have are fundamental to their perception. Even more deeply, our understanding of the world is truly our understanding of what we can sense, not of *the world*. Whatever perception processes occur, perception is 100% reliant on the senses, which are the interface between an organism and its environment.

The central premise of the movie *The Matrix* is that a virtual reality program hijacked human sensory systems and made humans think that what they were sensing was the true reality, when it was instead the program. My central premise is that the Real Matrix performs the equivalent function, as well as controls our responses. Therefore, it is especially important to discuss an organism's sensory function in much more detail than other biological systems. It is the perceptions constructed by, and within, the Real Matrix that are experienced by all life.

### 4.5.1 Sensing System Components

A sensing system has eight components:

1. **Distal stimulus/emitter/object** – the agent that emits what may eventually be received by receptors. This is what exists (reality) and is independent of observation – i.e., Immanuel Kant's "Das Ding an sich" (the thing in itself). I will not be addressing the concept of the *Observer Effect* in the quantum world, thank you.
   - I do not like the term "stimulus" found in the literature when this is the thing that emits the stimulus before there is any representation of what received it. "Emitter" is a little more

general, but it is still defining the thing in the context of the receiver. "Distal" just means not nearby. I am going to drop everything here except for the **distal object**, something that does not necessarily need to emit nor create a stimulus.

2. The next component is what is being emitted by the distal object and received by sensory receptors. This can be either information-bearing, i.e., **stimulus and signal,** or not information-bearing, i.e., **noise**.

   - I do not like any of these terms at this early stage in the sensing process because we do not know yet what is information or noise until it is processed by *perception,* and because doing so too early can sloppily imply intent (or worse, teleology) of the distal object. Only the perception of a signal determines if it is information or noise.

   - When I researched signal and noise, I discovered conflicting definitions. In some places, noise is an unwanted signal;[52] in others, noise is separate from signal (e.g., signal-to-noise ratio, or SNR).

   - My baggage-less term – **energy**. Notice that by expanding the term to energy, I am preparing you for the fact that not everything that is emitted is necessarily detected, nor is everything detected necessarily information.

   - The energy emitted by the distal object exists in Reality and is completely independent of the sensing function.

3. **Sensory receptor/organ** – a structure that receives and trans-duces energy. *Reception* is the process of activating a sensory receptor by a stimulus.

   - I am dropping "organ" because it adds too much overhead to the term, and I am not ready for biology yet. When does a receptor become an organ? Just a transition issue. It is sufficient to call it the **sensory receptor**.

   - A receptor's *receptive field* is determined by the distance it can be from the distal object and still receive its energy.

4. **Sensory (proximal) stimulus** – a signal detected by a sensory

receptor. Proximal means nearby, while distal (earlier) means not nearby.

- I am fine with using **sensory stimulus**, but I must make a few things clear. The energy emitted by the distal object does not become sensory stimulus if it cannot be sensed by the sensory receptor. Also, it is too early in the process to know whether the energy sensed is information or noise, which is 100% dependent on perception. The term *signal* has too much information-bearing baggage to be of use yet.
- The magnitude of a receptor's *potential* is dependent on the strength of the sensory stimulus.
- Sensory receptors and stimuli are usually treated separately in the literature, but this is a false distinction. A stimulus only exists if a receptor also exists that measures it.

5. **Sensory/signal transduction** – the process of converting a sensory stimulus into a receptor potential.
   - Since the transduction process may result in information or noise, depending on perception, I am going to remove the term "signal" and call it **sensory transduction**.
   - For simplicity, I am including within transduction the stimulation and transformation steps. The first is the initial exciting of the receptor, and the latter is the conversion of receptor potentials into action potentials.

6. **Sensory input** – what comes out of transduction and is available to perception. This is also called conduction or transmission.

7. **Perception** – the organization, identification, and interpretation of sensory input. This can include processing low-level information to higher-level information and processing based on restorative/selective mechanisms and concepts/expectations.

8. **Sensory information/noise** – sensory input that has been processed as either information or noise. Most discussions focus on information while avoiding noise. I think that both are equally important.

- A signal is an information carrier. Noise is an unwanted effect on signals.[53] These are conclusions only reached after perception has occurred, and yet, many articles identify them as such at the source with no reference to perception.

I intentionally excluded any biology from this sensing system discussion, which will make it easier to apply the sensory system to later discussions when comparing the movie Matrix and the Real Matrix. Now, I will associate the sensing system above to biological entities.

## 4.5.2 BIOLOGICAL SENSORY SYSTEMS

I will start with Wikipedia's biological definition of a "sense":

> A system that consists of a group of sensory cell types that responds to a specific physical phenomenon, and that corresponds to a particular group of regions within the brain where the signals are received and interpreted.

I have several problems with this definition. It throws in an ambiguous term (*physical phenomenon*), a fuzzy term (*corresponds to*), a too-specific term (*the brain*), and what one might call an anthropomorphic term (*interpreted*). My cleaned-up definition of a "sense" is:

> A system that consists of a group of cells that responds to specific *energy* by *emitting signals* to regions *within an organism* where the signals are received and *processed.*

Now, for the definition of a sensory nervous system from Wikipedia:

> A system that is part of a nervous system responsible for processing sensory information. A sensory system consists of sensory

*neurons (including the sensory receptor cells), neural pathways, and parts of the brain involved in sensory perception.*

*Exteroceptive senses* are those that look outward to the environment. *Interoceptive senses* are those that look inward to the organism.[54]

Here is a comprehensive list of biological sensory systems, some of which have not been observed in humans:

- VISUAL SYSTEM
- AUDITORY SYSTEM
- CHEMORECEPTION
- PROPRIOCEPTION
- SOMATOSENSORY SYSTEM
- VESTIBULAR SYSTEM
- EQUILIBRIOCEPTION
- INTEROCEPTION
- THERMORECEPTION
- NOCICEPTION
- ELECTRORECEPTION
- MAGNETORECEPTION
- CHRONOCEPTION
- ACTIVE SENSORY SYSTEM
- SPATIAL ORIENTATION AND NAVIGATION
- NUTRIENT SENSING
- QUORUM SENSING

Evolutionary selection acts on the sensory systems that receivers use to perceive external stimuli. If the benefits of perception to one sex or the other are different, sex differences in sensory systems can arise.

### 4.5.3 Biological Sensory Components

Now, I will go back to the sensing system components and discuss the equivalent *biological sensory components*. I go into this detail because an organism's senses are its window to Reality.

#### 4.5.3.1 Sensory Receptors

Receptors are protein molecules inside a target cell (intracellular or cytoplasmic receptors that act as regulators of mRNA synthesis) or on its surface (cell-surface or transmembrane receptors that perform signal transduction, in which an extracellular signal is converted into an intercellular signal) that receive a chemical signal. Chemical signals are released by ligands that bind with receptor proteins. All receptors receive distinct stimuli and transduce the signal into an electrical action potential. Viruses act like ligands in that they bind with receptor proteins to gain entry to cells.[55]

Sensory receptors are transmembrane receptors that convert energy from both external and internal environments into electrical impulses in a process called induction. They can be grouped to form a sensory organ or scattered in the skin and internal organs. These sensory, or *afferent*, neurons conduct receptor impulses inward to the brain or spinal cord. The opposite, *efferent* (motor) neurons, conduct impulses away from the brain and spinal cord and transfer them to the PNS.

For sensory receptors, the electrical action potential travels along afferent neurons to specific brain regions, where it is processed and interpreted. There are usually three neurons in this sensory pathway – the *first-order neuron* from the stimulation point to the CNS, the *second-order neuron* from entry into CNS to the thalamus, and the *third-order neuron* from the thalamus to the perception site.

The primary types of sensory receptors include MECHANORECEPTORS, THERMORECEPTORS, OLFACTORY RECEPTORS, NOCICEPTORS, CHEMORECEPTORS, PHOTORECEPTORS, HYGRORECEPTORS, OSMORECEPTORS, ELECTRORECEPTORS, and SOMATIC, PATTERN RECOGNITION, DERMAL PRESSURE, and VOMERONASAL receptors.

Some human sensory receptors in unexpected places include olfactory receptors, found in sperm (maybe to help find the egg), lungs, liver, skin (promote healing), heart, intestines, muscle (muscle migration), kidney (blood pressure monitoring), and cancer cells; photoreceptors, found in blood vessels (photorelaxation); and taste receptors, found in the stomach (immune response), testes, sperm, and upper airway (defense against bacteria).[56]

### 4.5.3.2 SENSORY STIMULUS

As mentioned previously, here are the four characteristics of a stimulus:[57]

- **Stimulus type (modality)** – Receptors of a sensory neuron are sensitive to the same type of stimulus.
- **Stimulus intensity** – An increased stimulus results in a larger receptor potential, leading to a higher frequency of action potential and recruitment of a larger number of receptors.
- **Stimulus location** – The response is highest at the center of the receptive field.
- **Stimulus duration** – Rapid adapting receptors respond at the onset of stimulus but slow down during the remainder of a stimulus and are important in signaling rapid changes. Slow adapting receptors maintain their response at, or near, the initial level of firing through the duration of the stimulus and are important in signaling slow changes.

### 4.5.3.3 SENSORY TRANSDUCTION

Sensory transduction is the process by which a chemical or physical signal is transmitted through a cell as a series of molecular events, which ultimately results in a cellular response. The changes elicited by the sensing in a receptor give rise to a biochemical cascade, which is a chain of events known as a signaling pathway.

At the cellular level, *signal transduction* is the generally accepted term that refers to the movement of signals from outside a cell to inside. Changes in protein level, protein activity, protein localization, and protein-protein interactions are all aspects of signal transduction, allowing cells to respond specifically to stimuli and to vary the sensitivity, duration, and dynamics of the response.[58] Remember that I do not like the term *signal*, since, to me, it implies information, and it is too early in the process to make that distinction.

### 4.5.3.4 SENSORY INPUT

Signals that reach the CNS are classified as sensory input or senses. These are transmitted along afferent neurons to specific areas of the CNS in a process called synaptic transmission.

The multiple areas of the brain in which sensory input is received to be processed are called the *sensory cortices*, which are one functional part of the cerebral cortex. The other two cortices are *motor* and *associative*. The primary sensory cortices are multimodal, showing clear sensory connectivity and direct influences of one modality upon the primary sensory cortex of another.[59] The sensory cortexes include the VISUAL, AUDITORY, PRIMARY OLFACTORY, GUSTATORY, and PRIMARY SOMATIC SENSORY cortexes.

*Multisensory* or *multimodal integration* is the integration of information by the nervous system from the different sensory modalities (such as sight, sound, touch, smell, self-motion, and taste). This integration facilitates perception and behavioral reactions by organisms to their environment.

Unlike visual stimuli, auditory information is not spatially represented, but once one has the spatial mapping from the visual information, multisensory integration brings the information from both the visual and auditory stimuli together to make a more robust mapping. A dynamic neural mechanism exists for matching the auditory and visual inputs from an event.

Eye-hand coordination is the tactile sensation in the context of the visual system. The visual system is very static, but the tactile sensory collection is dynamic. This sensory collection is included in the mapping of both the tactile and visual sensations.

### 4.5.3.5 PERCEPTION

Perception is the central processing of sensory stimuli into a meaningful pattern by an organism. The brain receives sensory stimuli through a sensory pathway. Then, action potentials from sensory receptors travel along neurons to dedicated parts of the brain for interpretation. I will cover this in much more detail in Section 6.1: Perception.

### 4.5.3.6 SENSORY INFORMATION/NOISE

Sensory information is a sensory input that is perceived as meaningful. Sensory noise is a sensory input that is perceived as meaningless.

For example, I have a condition called tinnitus, whereby I have a constant high-pitched ringing in my ears. Is that sound information or noise? I would say that it is noise when I ignore it and information when I pay attention to it. I can recreate that noise frequency with a phone app, and I have found that it is about 10,000 Hz. When I play that frequency to someone else to educate them on what I hear all the time, the usual reaction is, "Please, turn that off!" Now, in that case, I would say for the subject that the sound started as information and turned into noise.

## 4.5.4 COGNITIVE MAPS AND SENSORIMOTOR INTEGRATION

CNS neurons found in the superior colliculus and lateral occipital-temporal cortex in mammals are primary sites of multisensory convergence. In non-mammalian vertebrates, the homologous structure is known as the optic tectum or optic lobe. In insects, it is the central complex. These structures demonstrate an architecture that facilitates efficient sensorimotor transduction. Its visual, auditory, and somatosensory sensory representations are laid out in a map-like manner with all the maps in overlapping spatial register with one another. The different maps are constituted by neurons that have modality-specific receptive fields in register with one another. The *sensory maps* overlap with a common *motor map*, which involves many of the same multisensory neurons and through which the orientation of the eyes, ears, head, and limbs can be initiated. It is through this structure that an environmental event excites a localized region of the map (or maps) to register an appropriate sensory report and initiate a response.[60]

The posterior parietal cortex is another area important for sensorimotor integration. Among its functions is the forming of high-level cognitive plans for movement. It contains a map of intentions, including the planning of eye movements, reaching movements, and grasping movements. The map specifies the goals of movements rather than the exact muscle activations required to execute the movement. These operations are facilitated using a distributed space representation that is independent of both sensory input and motor output.[61]

Different types of neurons build up the geographical cognitive map:[62]

- **Place cells** – provide an animal with a sense of location and geographic mapping that includes a temporal aspect.
- **Head-direction cells** – support the sense of direction.
- **Grid cells** – periodic firing patterns provide odometric (distance) information and seem to represent space at different scales.
- **Border cells and boundary vector cells** – mark out environmental boundaries.

## 4.5.5 Time Perception

There are many papers on the brain anatomy of time perception that I will not address here. As I have said before, I am not interested in "where" but in "how" and maybe "why." Also, all the brain anatomical studies are full of monkey and rat brain dissections and electrode hookups, and that just makes my skin crawl since I am a tree-hugging, animal-loving vegetarian. In turn, many of the articles on time perception get lost in ambiguities.

### 4.5.5.1 Rhythms

A very heavily mathematical paper[63] takes me partway to where I want to go. Before it gets way too advanced for me, it introduces two types of rhythms associated with biological organization: external and internal. External rhythms are directed by phenomena exterior to the organism that physically impose themselves upon the organism. They are identified with physical time determined universally. Examples include seasonal rhythms, the 24-hour cycle and their harmonics; tidal cycles, the rhythms of chemical reactions that oscillate at a given temperature, etc. These rhythms are associated with a "shadow" rhythm inside the system.

Internal rhythms are specific to physiological functions of the organism that depend on biological functional specifications and are not associated with external rhythms. Examples include heart rate, respiratory rate, the mean life span, cerebral frequencies, etc.

### 4.5.5.2 Time Tracking

- **The past** – the internal clock keeper, a form of memory that somehow tracks seconds, minutes, hours, days, etc., stretching back from the present.
  - o Examples (without referencing a clock): how long someone has been gone on an errand, how long I have been driving,

and what time it is now (i.e., how much time has passed since I last checked a clock).

- **The future** – projecting time estimates into the future.
  - o Examples: when our meeting will start, if I can get to work on time, if I can clean the yard in time for breakfast, and when I need to start making dinner.

## 4.5.6 Non-Human Sensory Capabilities

*Since we 'see' the world with our own particular sensing devices, it is difficult to understand fully how other animals 'see' it. What picture of the details of the world is perceived by the bee that sees in the ultraviolet, the snake that is deaf to airborne sounds but detects infrared, the shrew that cannot see color, the electric fish that detects changes in the electric field about it?*
V. G. Dethier, *The Physiology of Insect Senses*

Along with every other biological system, the Real Matrix is an organism's sensory system. The sensory system is the entry point at which it reveals its total control.

Humans are wired to think that what we perceive is reality. Far from it. I want to give an overview of sensory capabilities found in non-human organisms. My objective is to give you a body blow to force you to realize how limited human sensation tools are. I have assembled the most extensive list you will find of non-human sensory capabilities. For context, I sometimes compare them to their human equivalent. This list supports the much later discussion in Section 6.1: Perception.

- **Visual system**
  - o The human eye can sense between 380 and 760 nanometers (nm) of the electromagnetic spectrum, being trichromatic (three colors).
  - o About 6% to 8% of humans today are red-green color blind.

Most of them are men. However, people with this condition are at an advantage in differentiating slight variations in khaki colors.[64]

o Birds, dragonflies, and bees can see into the ultraviolet (300-400 nm).

o The eye of a housefly contains 3,000 lenses that are formed by thousands of small panels, capable of perceiving movement up to 200 frames per second.[65]

o Worker honeybees have 5,500 lenses (ommatidia) in each eye.[66]

o Foraging insects can see wavelengths that flowers reflect (300-700 nm).

o The mantis shrimp eye holds 12 color-receptive cones, whereas humans only have three.[67] The variety of cones enables them to perceive an enhanced array of colors as a mechanism for mate selection, avoidance of predators, and detection of prey.

o The box jellyfish is named for the cube-like shape of its bell, which is about 10 mm in diameter in adult animals. On each side of the bell are sensory structures that accommodate in total 24 eyes of various types, looking 360-degrees not outside but inside of the medusa. The transparency of the bell allows the jellyfish to see in all directions. The sensory structures maintain the same natural orientation independent of the orientation of the bell with the help of the crystal structure in the bottom, called statolith, which acts as a weight, while the flexible stalk on top connects them to the bell.[68]

o The swordfish eye can generate heat to better cope with detecting their prey at depths of 2,000 feet.

o The warnowiid dinoflagellate, a single-celled micro-organism, has eye-like ocelloids, with analogous structures to the lens and retina of the multi-cellular eye.

o The chiton marine mollusk has an armored shell covered

with hundreds of aragonite crystalline eyes, named ocelli, that can form images.

o Many fan worms have evolved compound eyes on their tentacles, which they use to detect encroaching movement.

o Scallops have up to 200 small (about 1 mm) eyes arranged along the edge of their mantles. These eyes rely on a concave, parabolic mirror of guanine crystals to focus and retro-reflect light instead of a lens as found in many other eye types. Additionally, their eyes possess a double-layered retina, with the outer retina responding most strongly to light and the inner to abrupt darkness. This results in exceptional contrast definition, and the ability to detect changing patterns of light and motion.

o Most mammals have eyes that are sensitive to short and middle wavelength visible light that includes blues and greens. Having this form of limited color vision capability is known as *dichromacy* ("two colors").[68]

o Nocturnal owl monkeys are *monochromatic* ("one color"). They see only black, white, and intermediate grays.[68]

o Apes (including humans) and Old-World monkeys normally have three types of cone cells and are therefore *trichromats*.

o *Tetrachromacy* is the condition of possessing four independent channels (four types of cone cells) for conveying color information in the eye. Organisms with tetrachromacy are called *tetrachromats*. In tetrachromatic organisms, the sensory color space is four-dimensional, meaning that to match the sensory effect of arbitrarily chosen spectra of light within their visible spectrum requires mixtures of at least four primary colors. Tetrachromats include:

§ Goldfish and zebrafish
§ Reindeer
§ Most birds
§ Foraging insects
§ Some humans – possibly 15-50% of women and 8% of men

o With marmosets, tamarins, squirrel monkeys, and spider monkeys, all males only see blues and greens. About 40% of the females are also dichromatic, but the other 60% are trichromatic.[68]

o The bluebottle butterfly has 15 types of photoreceptors. One type of cone is stimulated by ultraviolet, another by violet, three by varying shades of blue, one blue-green, four by green, and five by red light. A similar system is found in a six-photoreceptor butterfly – the Asian swallowtail.[71]

o In most invertebrates, eyes consist of a cup of dark pigment with anywhere from a few to a few hundred photoreceptors. In most pigment cup eyes, there is no optical system other than the aperture through which light enters the cup. This aperture restricts the width of the cone of light that reaches any single photoreceptor, providing a limited degree of resolution.[69]

o The nautilus has pinhole eyes with millions of photoreceptors. They also have muscles that move the eyes and pupils that can vary in diameter with light intensity.[73]

o Lens eyes have increased refractive index of the material in the chamber due to denser material, such as mucus or protein that converges incoming rays of light. This results in a lens capable of forming an image focused on the retina. Most lenses in aquatic animals are spherical because this shape gives the shortest focal length for a lens of a given diameter, which, in turn, gives the brightest image. Lens eyes focus an image either by physically moving the lens toward or away from the retina, or by using eye muscles to adjust the shape of the lens.[73]

o Land vertebrates' eyes have a cornea, a refracting surface that is an image-forming lens, but the lens is flattened and weakened compared with a fish lens.[73]

o Corneal eyes are found in spiders, many of which have eyes with excellent image-forming capabilities.[73]

- o *Apposition eyes* were the original type of compound eye and are the oldest fossil eyes known. Some clams have numerous tiny compound eyes, each with up to a hundred ommatidia (individual optical unit of a compound eye) situated around their mantles. Each *ommatidium* consists of a photoreceptor cell and screening pigment cells. The eyes have no lenses and rely on shadowing from the pigment tube to restrict the field of view.[73]
- o Penguins have a flat cornea that allows for clear vision underwater.[70]
- o Many lepidosaurs (a reptile subclass that includes snakes and lizards) have a photosensory organ on the top of their heads called the parietal eye, which has a rudimentary retina and lens that cannot form images. It is sensitive to changes in light and dark and can detect movement.
- o Starfish and some worms have light-sensitive but not color-sensitive patches on their skin called eyespots.[71]
- o Four-eyed fish (!) have only two eyes that are on the top of the head, and the fish floats at the water's surface with only the lower half of each eye underwater. The eye has two pupils, connected by part of the iris. The upper half of the eye is adapted for vision in air, the lower half in water. The lens of the eye also changes in thickness to account for the difference in the refractive indices of air versus water.
- o Some deeper water fish have tubular eyes with big lenses and only rod cells that look upward, which allows the fish to pick out prey that is silhouetted against the gloom above. Some fish have a retroreflector (which boosts light availability to photoreceptors) behind the retina. Flashlight fish (!) have this, plus photophores (a glandular organ that appears as luminous spots), which they use in combination to detect eyeshine in other fish.
- o Cats also have a retroreflector, a membrane called the tapetum lucidum, that gives them excellent night vision.

o The brownsnout spookfish uses a mirror instead of a lens to focus an image in its eyes.

o The giant squid's retina can contain up to 1 billion photoreceptors, and the octopus' retina can contain up to 20 million.[70]

o Certain protozoa that contain chlorophyll for photosynthesis possess a mass of bright red photoreceptor granules (carotenoid pigments) called the *stigma*. The photoreceptor plus the stigma enable protozoa to orient themselves so that their photoreceptors are exposed to light for photosynthesis.

o Some fish have eyeshine, which is the result of a light-gathering layer in the eyes that reflects white light. It allows fish to see well in low-light conditions and in stained or rough, breaking waters.

o In insects, two compound eyes are the principle visual organs. Compound eyes are composed of many facets, called the *ommatidia*, which are the units of vision. The number of ommatidia varies considerably from species to species – some worker ants have fewer than six, while some dragonflies may have more than 25,000.[70]

o Cephalopod eyes evolved independently from vertebrate eyes. Their eyes move the lens to focus rather than changing lens shape as in the vertebrate eye, and the nerves are behind the photoreceptor cells. In contrast, vertebrate eyes have an "inverted" retina, where blood vessels and nerves are in front of them.[71]

o **Polarized light** – many animals are sensitive to the e-vector orientation of linearly polarized light. This capability is known as "polarization sensitivity" to celestial and non-celestial clues. For celestial, e-vectors in the sky are all oriented along parallel circles centered on the sun's (and moon's) position, whether the sky is clear or cloudy. Photoreceptors in the retina distinguish between light traveling in different e-vector planes. Animals use this sensitivity for navigation, for spatial orientation, and for finding large bodies of water. These animals include terrestrial and marine invertebrates, fish, amphibians, and birds. Light's polarization can rotate clockwise or counterclockwise, giving it what is called a circular polarization.[72,73]

§ Mantis shrimp have patterns in the circularly polarized light that only other mantis shrimp can distinguish.

§ Underwater light has a polarized component that octopuses can detect. When this light travels through the body of a transparent animal, its polarization changes, and the octopus can distinguish its prey.

§ Observations of ants and bees suggest that these animals use celestial cues to monitor their foraging trips.[74]

§ Locusts use celestial cues to navigate during migration.[78]

§ The African dung beetle uses the polarization of a moonlit sky to orientate itself so that it can move along a straight line.[75]

§ Non-celestial polarization vision has been shown in different insect species (dragonflies, butterflies, beetles, bugs, and flies).[76] This comes from the reflection of sunlight off shiny surfaces (water, leaves, or body surfaces). Such polarized reflections can be used to either seek out or avoid localized water sources, to follow the course of a continuous stream, to provide information for evaluating the quality of certain environments, and to identify both conspecifics (i.e., an animal of the same species, e.g., during courtship), as well as prey (e.g., blood-sucking insects).

- **Auditory system**
  o Humans, on average, can detect sounds as pitched when they contain periodic or quasi-periodic variations that fall between the range of 30 to 20,000 Hz. As stated earlier, frequencies capable of being heard by humans are called

*audio*. Frequencies higher than audio are called ultrasonic, while frequencies below audio are called infrasonic.

- § Fun trivia – In the Beatles' song "A Day in the Life," the band included a whistling noise at a frequency of 15,000 Hz right after the last chord of the song, designed to be heard by canine Beatles fans. In 2014, activists from Pussy Riot rigged an electric piano to play music designed specifically for cats.[77]

o The primate tarsius can hear up to 90,000 Hz.

o Bats can hear ultrasonic sounds with frequencies up to 110,000 Hz.

- § When you gently rub your thumb and index finger together, the friction creates an ultrasonic signal. Pet bats can be trained to respond to the sound and fly toward it.[81]

o Dogs can hear ultrasound. They are also capable of perceiving sounds up to 30 kilometers away, while the average human hearing ability reaches less than 10 kilometers.[69]

o Cats can hear in the range between 100 and 60,000 Hz.[70]

o Snakes sense infrasound through their jaws.

o Mice can hear frequencies between 1,000 and 100,000 Hz.[70]

o Baleen whales, giraffes, dolphins, and elephants emit and hear infrasound (as low as 14 Hz) for communication.

o Sharks can hear infrasound. They may track sounds over many miles, listening specifically for distress sounds from wounded prey.[78]

o Some fish can hear sensitively due to a bony connection between the ear and their swim bladder.

o Certain caterpillar species have evolved hair that resonates with the sound of buzzing wasps, warning them of the predator's presence.

o Mosquitoes have hair on their antennae that resonate with the flying sound of homogeneous females, enabling the males to detect potential sexual partners.

- o Crickets can hear using their legs. Sound waves vibrate a thin membrane on the cricket's front legs.[70]
- o Several groups of flying insects that are preyed upon by echolocating bats can perceive the emitted ultrasound emissions using a tympanal organ that covers air-filled chambers on the legs to enable ultrasound avoidance.
- o In cephalopods, like squids, *statocysts* provide a cochlea-like mechanism to hear. A statocyst is a sac-like structure that contains a mineralized mass (statolith) and numerous innervated sensory hairs (setae).
- o Recordings of the munching noises produced by caterpillars caused plants to flood their leaves with chemical defenses designed to ward off attackers.[79]
- o *Phonoreceptors*, found in insects, arachnids, and centipedes, respond to sound. Crickets, grasshoppers, and cicadas possess phonoreceptors called tympanic or tympanal organs.[80]

- **Olfactory system**
  - o Humans can discriminate between about 10,000 different odorants.
  - o Dogs have an olfactory sense that is approximately ten thousand to one hundred thousand times more acute than humans'. Scenthounds can smell one to ten million times more acutely, and bloodhounds can smell ten to one hundred million times more acutely.
  - o Bears have a sense of smell seven times stronger than that of bloodhounds and can detect the scent of food from up to 18 miles away.
  - o The sense of smell is nonexistent in cetaceans.
  - o A male silkworm moth can sense a single molecule of the sex pheromone bombykol.
  - o Salmon utilize their sense of smell to identify and return to their home waters.
  - o Catfish use their sense of smell to identify other individual catfish and to maintain a social hierarchy.

o Many fish use their sense of smell to identify mating partners or be alerted to the presence of food.

o Some plants can either smell approaching insects or smell volatile signals released by neighboring plants in response to them.[83]

o Studies of two species of soil bacteria showed that both colonies can detect airborne ammonia.[81]

o As a shark moves, water flows through two forward-facing nostrils and moves past folds of skin covered with extremely sensitive sensory cells. Most sharks can detect blood and animal odors from many miles away. Smells coming from one side of a shark will arrive at that cavity just before it arrives at the other. In this way, a shark can sense where a smell is coming from.[82]

o The African bush elephant has about 2,000 olfactory receptors in its trunk/sniffer compared to around 1,000 sensors found in dogs and 400 in humans.[82]

o In insects, olfactory receptors are thin-walled pegs, cones, or plates with pores through which airborne molecules diffuse. Dendrites of sensory neurons branch abundantly within these pores. Olfactory receptors are most plentiful on the antennae but can also be found on the mouthparts or external genitalia.[83]

o The jewel beetle can smell and detect a burning pine tree that is ten miles away (compared to an average human who can only detect one at hundreds of feet).[86]

o There is a set of specialized olfactory receptors in mosquito sperm. These are the same as the sensors that play a central role in the mosquito's olfactory system, which is found on the insect's antennae. The receptors in the sperm are expressed along their tails, where they drive the rapid increase in the beating of the sperm tails.[84]

o The silkworm moth can detect pheromones up to 11 kilometers away. It can detect pheromones in concentrations as low as one molecule per $10^{17}$ molecules of air.[70]

- o The *vomeronasal organ* (VNO) is an auxiliary olfactory sense organ located in the soft tissue of the nasal septum found in all reptiles and most mammals but not humans. The sensory neurons of the vomeronasal organ detect non-volatile chemical cues, which requires direct physical contact with the source of the odor. Some mammals, particularly cats and ungulates (which includes horses, cattle, and pigs, among other species), use a distinctive facial movement called the Flehmen response to direct the inhaled compounds to the VNO. The animal lifts its head after finding the odorant, wrinkles its nose while lifting its lips, and ceases to breathe momentarily.
    - § Snakes use this organ to sense prey, sticking their tongue out to gather scents and touching it to the opening of the organ when the tongue is retracted.
    - § Primates such as lemurs and lorises have the organ.
    - § Elephants transfer chemosensory stimuli to the vomeronasal opening in the roof of their mouths using a prehensile structure, sometimes called a finger, located at the tips of their trunks.
    - § Painted turtles use this organ as a sense of smell underwater.
    - § Garter snakes use the organ to detect the presence of prey or predator by gathering the chemical cues in the environment through the flicking behavior of their forked tongue.
    - § Mice use their vomeronasal pathway to detect odors from a sick animal's urine that then mediates sick con-specific avoidance.[85]
- **Gustatory system**
  - o Some rodents can taste starch (but humans cannot).
  - o Carnivores cannot taste sweetness.
  - o Octopuses have chemoreceptors on the suckers of their tentacles.[70]

o At least 15 different whale and dolphin species have lost the ability to sense up to four of their ancestral five taste senses. Only the genes connected to salty detection remain functional. It is theorized that they may have other taste genes not yet known to science.

o Flies and butterflies have taste organs on their feet, allowing them to taste anything they land on.

o In insects, gustatory receptors are like thick-walled hairs, pegs, or pits, where the dendrites of several sensory neurons are exposed to the environment through a single opening. Each neuron responds to a different range of compounds (e.g., sugar, salt, water, protein, acid, etc.). Taste receptors are most abundant on the mouthparts but are also found on the antennae, feet, and genitalia.[87]

o Catfish have taste organs across their entire bodies and can taste anything they touch, including chemicals in the water.

o Plants can detect pathogens and microbes that initiate the plant's immunity for a defense response.

o Protozoa avoid strong acids, alkali, and salt.[86]

o Specific chemicals attract predatory ciliates (a single-celled protozoan animal having cilia or ciliary structures) to their prey.[90]

o In arthropods, the chemoreceptors called sensilla are found on the antennae, mouthparts, and legs.[90]

o An earthworm's body is entirely covered in chemoreceptors.[70]

o Invertebrates can detect humidity, access pH, track their prey, recognize food, and identify mates.[90]

o In bacteria, chemoreceptors detect a variety of signals and feed this information into chemosensory pathways. They differ in topology, sensing mode, cellular location, and the type of ligand-binding domain (LBD). Although signals can stimulate chemoreceptors in a variety of different ways, diverse LBDs appear to employ a universal transmembrane signaling mechanism.[87]

o Using something like taste, *chemotaxis* is a mechanism by which bacteria sense and respond to changes in the chemical composition of their environment, approaching chemically favorable environments and avoiding unfavorable ones. This behavior is achieved by integrating signals received from receptors and modulating the direction of flagellar rotation.[88]

- **Mechanoreception**
  o More than 30,000 fish species have a sensory system called the lateral-line system. Appearing as distinct pores that run along the flanks and dot the heads. The lateral line is composed of mechanoreceptors called *neuromasts* (clusters of hair cells) that relay information about the velocity and acceleration of water flow.[84] The lateral-line system can also alert the fish to any potential prey or predators in the area.[82]

  o An elephant's feet and trunks are sensitive enough to pick up vibrations created by other elephants as far as 10 miles away. From this signal, they can tell if the other is a friend or a stranger and use subtle differences in what each foot feels to triangulate the source.[76]

  o Hairs on the flight membranes of bats act as airflow sensors.[89]

  o The butterfly has hairs on its wings to detect changes in air pressure.[70]

  o Crabs have hairs on claws and other parts of the body to detect water current and vibration.[70]

  o Insect mechanoreceptors:[90]

    § **Trichoform sensilla** – tactile hairs (setae) that are innervated by a sensory neuron. Dendrites of the neuron attach near the base of the hair and generate a nerve impulse when they detect movement.

    § **Campaniform sensilla** – flattened oval discs that serve as flex receptors in the exoskeleton. They respond whenever mechanical stress causes the exoskeleton to bend.

§ **Stretch receptors** – multipolar neurons that accompany muscle or connective tissue. They are commonly embedded in intersegmental membranes and the muscular walls of the digestive system.

§ **Pressure receptors** – provide sensory information about an aquatic insect's depth in the water. These receptors are usually associated with a cushion of air against the body or within the tracheal system. Increasing water pressure deflects hair-like processes within the receptor.

o Plants have mechanoreceptors that perform mechanoreception and can also act as auditory systems,[91] including:

§ Pollen from anthers is released only against a specific sound frequency produced by a specific pollinator.

§ Plant roots can locate a water source by sensing the vibrations generated by moving water.[92]

§ Sound vibrations of certain frequencies can influence processes, such as seed germination, root elongation, callus growth, and cell cycling.

§ Plants may generate acoustic emissions, although the exact mechanism for this unknown.

• **Thermoreception**

o Pit vipers, pythons, and boa snakes can sense infrared radiation emitted by warm objects using pit organs that are usually located on the snake's face between its eyes and nostrils and contain thousands of infrared-sensitive receptors.[71] These are a type of transient receptor potential channel, which is a temperature-sensitive ion channel. It senses infrared signals through a mechanism involving warming of the pit organ rather than a chemical reaction to light. They can work out which part of the pit is hottest and, therefore, the direction of the heat source. By combining information from both pits, the snake can also estimate the distance of the object.

o The common vampire bat has specialized infrared sensors in its nose-leaf. The infrared sense enables the bat to localize homeothermic (warm-blooded) animals within a range of about 10 to 15 cm and to find the warm blood vessel under its prey's skin.

- o Dogs can detect weak thermal radiation with their noses.
- o Darkly pigmented butterflies use specialized heat detectors to avoid damage while basking.
- o Paramecia collect in areas where the water temperature is moderate and avoid temperature extremes.[84]

- **Vestibular system**
  - o Cats use the inner ear and tail to maintain balance.
  - o The statocyst is also a balance and gravity sensory receptor present in some aquatic invertebrates, including gastropods (snails and slugs), bivalves (clams, oysters, cockles, mussels, and scallops), echinoderms (starfish, sea urchins, sand dollars, and sea cucumbers), cephalopods (squid, octopus, and nautilus), and crustaceans (crabs, lobsters, crayfish, shrimps, prawns, krill, woodlice, and barnacles). Any movement causes the statolith to brush against the setae, which, in turn, sends a message to the brain to correct its balance.

- **Somatosensory system**
  - o Horses and mules are so sensitive to touch that they can feel a fly land on a single hair.[93]

- **Proprioception**
  - o Plants use a form of proprioception along with gravisensing to help right themselves when tilted.
  - o Arthropods have proprioceptors in their appendage joints and body extensor muscles that can be specialized muscle cells, elastic connective tissue fibers, or various membranes that span joints.
    - § In the insect femur, a large chordotonal organ contains hundreds of mechanosensory neurons connected to the tibia by a stiff tendon. The dendrites of femoral chordotonal neurons detect mechanical stretch as the tibia moves relative to the femur.[94]

§ Some insects possess spindle-like receptors known as muscle receptor organs, complete with efferent innervation and length/velocity encoding.[98]

§ In mammals, the load on a limb is detected by Golgi tendon organs—proprioceptors that lie at the interface between muscles and tendons.[98]

§ Insects and mammals both possess proprioceptive organs that detect when a joint reaches a certain threshold.[98]

- **Substrate vibrations** – vibrations carried in a substrate (i.e., an underlying layer like the ground, a hive, a spider web, a leaf, or even water or air) can provide a communication channel for biological organisms that can be used alone or in combination with other information channels in multimodal signaling. The sensory organs are generically known as somatosensory mechanoreceptors.

o Although just as important and more complex, I will not address the signaling, communication, and response of organisms. More than 150,000 insect species use substrate-borne vibrations to communicate, and at least 45,000 other insect species use vibrational signals, along with other mechanical methods of signaling. Arachnids (spiders and scorpions), crustaceans, worms, mammals, birds, reptiles, amphibians, and fish also signal this way. Additionally, many plants sense substrate vibrations created by nearby insects.[95]

o Techniques for sensing these vibrations include:

§ Many vertebrate animals can detect vibrational events in the skin and joints, from which they are carried as action potentials through the CNS.[99]

§ Vertebrates can also use receivers centralized in the cochlea of the inner ear. Vibrations are carried from the substrate to the cochlea through the body in a pathway that bypasses the eardrum and, sometimes, even the middle ear. Vibrations then project to the brain, along with information from airborne sound received via the eardrum.[99]

- § In insects, substrate vibrations are detected mainly by sense organs found at different sites in the legs.
- § The wandering spider can differentiate vibrations created by rain, wind, prey, and potential mates.[99]
- § Snakes receive signals by sensors in their lower jaw or body.
- § Invertebrates have sensors in their legs or body (e.g., earthworms).
- § When mice perceive vibrations in their forepaws, neurons in the somatosensory cortex are activated similarly to those in the sound-reactive auditory cortex.[96]
- § Birds have sensors in their legs (e.g., pigeons) or bill-tip (e.g., shorebirds, kiwis, and ibises).
- § Some mammals have sensors in their feet or lower jaw (e.g., mole rats).
- § Kangaroos have sensors in their legs.
- § The star-nosed mole has an elaborate nose structure that may detect seismic waves.
- § Specialized (and varied) skeletal features in amphibians, blind mole-rats, golden moles, elephants, and possibly extinct ground sloth species allow efficient conduction of vibrations from the soil to the inner ear.[99]
- § Elephants have acoustic fat in their feet that promotes better coupling with the substrate while receiving substrate-borne vibrations.[99]
- **Teleceptive active sensory system**
  - o Bats, dolphins, toothed whales, oilbirds, swiftlets, shrews, and humans (primarily blind people) all use echolocation (using sound waves reflected off objects in their path/echoes to understand the environment, navigate, and find prey). They find their target based on the length of time it takes the pulse to return (determining distance and location), and the Doppler shift of the sound (determining speed and direction).
  - o Fireflies use bioluminescence (self-generated light) to find

mates, while deep ocean barbeled dragonfish produce near-infrared light to see in the dark.

o Organisms with slow locomotion (such as the slime mold) utilize chemical signals to probe the environment.

o In all these cases, prey and predators have also evolved to eavesdrop or protect from eavesdropping on active sensing signals – insects for echolocation, dolphins for orca ultra-sonic clicks, and barbeled dragonfish use infrared that its prey cannot see. Electric fishes change their discharge frequencies to avoid frequency interference.

- **Contact active sensory system** (mechanosensory)
  o Humans use their extremities to explore the environment.
  o Insects use antennae to probe the environment during locomotion.
  o Nocturnal animals use whiskers to navigate by gathering information about the position, size, shape, orientation, and texture of objects.
- **Gravitropism** – the coordinated process of differential growth by a plant or fungus in response to gravity pulling on it.
  o Growth of a shoot upward is called negative gravitropism; growth of the roots downward is called positive gravitropism.
- **Electroreception** – there is evidence that electroreception existed in the last common ancestor of all vertebrates that lived over 500 million years ago.[97] Most vertebrates lost this ability, but it remains in others.
  o Many fish have a specialized electroreceptor called the ampullae of Lorenzini. They include cartilaginous fish (sharks, rays, and chimeras), reedfish, sturgeon, and lungfish. This sense organ provides these fish with an additional sense capable of detecting electric and magnetic fields, as well as temperature gradients.
  o Other animals have secondarily derived forms of electroreception without having the ampullae of Lorenzini, including catfish, South American knifefish, freshwater elephantfish,

monotremes, and cetaceans.

o Monotremes (echidnas and the platypus) and some dolphins[98] use electroreception to locate prey solely by the electric fields generated by their muscle contraction. Using these electroreceptors, they can detect the direction of the source and the strength of the signal.

§ The bill of the platypus has sensory cells able to detect the weak electrical fields put out by animals as they move. The bill also contains cells sensitive to disturbances in the water. This combination of electroreception and mechanoreception enables the platypus to locate its prey while underwater with its eyes closed.[99]

o Electric fish, such as eels, use electrosensory detection to probe the environment and create active electrodynamic imaging. They also modulate their electric discharge during courtship to "sing" a mating song.

o Amazonian catfish may use their electroreceptive sense to hunt and prey upon other active electroreceptors.

o Spiders can detect electric fields.

o Bumblebees can detect electric fields around plants and use them to decide whether to visit flowers. They accumulate a small positive charge as they fly, and flowers have a negative charge. Mechanosensory hairs on a bee's legs respond to the attraction between these opposite charges, guiding it to a bloom. A flower's charge changes once a bee stops by, which is something other bees can sense.[76]

o Bees use electric cues from other bees to evoke behavioral responses during their dancing. Electric fields induce a range of behavioral responses in ants, cockroaches, mosquitoes, fruit flies, and bees.[100]

- **Photoreception other than visual**
  o **Photosynthesis** – there are seven types of photoreceptors involved in photosynthesis,[101] but I will not be reviewing their names and details here.

o **Photomorphogenesis** – plants possess two types of photoreceptors: photosynthetic pigments that harvest light energy for photosynthesis, and photosensory receptors that mediate non-photosynthetic light responses (primarily structural development). *Photomorphogenesis* is the growth and development of plants in response to light using *phytochromes*, a class of photoreceptors sensitive to red and far-red light and *cryptochromes/phototropins*, photoreceptors sensitive to blue light. It occurs in three stages of plant development: seed germination, seedling development, and the switch from the vegetative to the flowering stage.

   § Phytochromes regulate the germination of seeds (photoblasty), the synthesis of chlorophyll, the elongation of seedlings, the size, shape, number, and movement of leaves, and the timing of flowering in adult plants (i.e., *photoperiodism* – response to the timing and duration of day and night by comparing the ratio of night to day over several days).

   § Cryptochromes regulate entrainment of the circadian clock by light in plants and animals, including humans. They help mediate phototropism and are also thought to be essential for sensing magnetic fields and providing magnetic orientation.[102]

o **Phototropism** – a directional response that allows plants to grow toward or away from light.[103] These photoreceptors ultimately induce the light-controlled switch from *skotomorphogenesis* (the development of a seedling in the dark) to photomorphogenesis because they determine if there is any light at all.

o Some plants possess at least 11 types of photoreceptors, compared to a human's four.[83]

o There are many *biofluorescent* animals, including reptiles, amphibians, chameleons, corals, jellyfish, fish (over 180 species), sharks, scorpions, butterflies, budgies, parrots, penguins, puffins, sea turtles, and flying squirrels. They emit a fluorescent glow (usually green or red) after absorbing higher-energy photons (blue or ultraviolet), using fluorescent molecules called fluorophores that are both photoreceptors and emitters.

o In squid and cuttlefish, components, including photoreceptors needed for vision in the eye, are present in the skin and color-changing organs (*chromatophores*) that they use to create color patterns on their skin. They may use this information from both their eyes and their skin to determine their body color patterns.[104]

- **Magnetoreception**
  o Some of the animals shown to use magnetoreception include magnetotactic bacteria, salmon, salamanders, toads, sea turtles, sharks, spotted newts, lobsters, honeybees, fruit flies, domestic hens, mice, bees, mole-rats, bats, pigeons, roundworms, and migratory birds.
  o Salmon possess both a magnetic "compass" that allows them to use the Earth's magnetic field as a directional cue and a magnetic "map" that allows them to gauge their position within an ocean basin.[105]
  o Retinal cryptochromes may be involved in the avian magnetic sense. The same protein is found in the human eye and may serve the same function.

- **Sex differences in sensory systems**
  o Male sphinx moths rely on female released sex-pheromones to guide flight behaviors used to locate mates. Enhanced pheromone detection has only evolved in the olfactory system of male sphinx moths.
  o Sex differences in the visual system of flies are extremely common, with males generally possessing specialized eye features. Some male flies possess large dorsal eyes that are absent in females. Male dorsal eyes may be specialized for the detection and capture of females.

o The auditory systems of frogs can detect species-specific vocalizations, and behavioral responses to these vocalizations often differ between the sexes. Sex differences in auditory systems underlie these gender-specific behaviors in multiple species.

- **Dermal pressure receptors**
  o Crocodiles' entire bodies are equipped with dermal pressure receptors, while alligators have dermal pressure receptors on the scales around their jaws.

## 4.5.7 SPECIALIZED EQUIPMENT SENSORS

I will not detail them here, but Wikipedia lists over 400 specialized manmade equipment sensors.[106] They make for interesting reading. I mention them here because these sensors respond to stimuli the same way that biological receptors do. Some of the stimuli can be perceived by humans, some by other organisms, and the rest have no known biological receptor equivalent. In almost all cases, the purpose of the equipment is to transform the incoming energy into an outgoing signal that humans can sense.

The sensor types include:

- Acoustic, sound, vibration
- Automotive
- Chemical
- Electric current, electric potential, magnetic, radio
- Environment, weather, moisture, humidity
- Flow, fluid velocity
- Ionizing radiation, subatomic particles
- Navigation instruments
- Position, angle, displacement, distance, speed, acceleration
- Optical, light, imaging, photon
- Pressure
- Force, density, level

- Thermal, heat, temperature
- Proximity, presence
- Sensor technology
- Speed sensor

## 4.6 Response Systems

*The fixity of the milieu supposes a perfection of the organism such that the external variations are at each instant compensated for and equilibrated.... All the vital mechanisms, however varied they may be, have always one goal, to maintain the uniformity of the conditions of life in the internal environment.... The stability of the internal environment (**Milieu Intérieur**) is the condition for the free and independent life.*
Claude Bernard, 1865

In the previous section, I discussed sensory systems. The processes of these systems are enabled by afferent proteins and nerve fibers that direct impulses into the nervous system and brain. I was about three-fourths done with that section before I realized that I was not accounting for an organism's reaction to this sensory input. These reactions in any mode or capacity are enabled by efferent neurons that direct impulses through the nervous system away from the brain but, at the same time, are tightly integrated with sensory input and perception by interneurons in the brain.

It became obvious to me in writing this section that the response systems are fundamental to my central premise concerning the Real Matrix. Recall what I mentioned earlier – the Matrix in the movie may have also been directing response and motivation along with sensing and perception.

I am going to separate my discussion into processes and systems.

# 4.6.1 PROCESSES

Homeostasis and allostasis definitions and interactions are hotly debated in the literature (much more for allostasis). I have selected and edited those definitions that make the most sense to me.

## 4.6.1.1 HOMEOSTASIS

Homeostasis is the ability of an open system to regulate its internal environment to maintain stable conditions through multiple dynamic equilibrium adjustments controlled by interrelated regulation mechanisms. It includes many variables being kept within certain limits (homeostatic ranges) that are regulated despite, and in response to, changes in the environment and level of activity. Within animals, these variables include body temperature, blood pressure, fluid balance, pH of extracellular fluid, blood sugar level, and concentrations of sodium, potassium, blood glucose, carbon dioxide, oxygen, and calcium. Each of these variables is controlled by one or more homeostatic control mechanisms, which together function to sustain life.

Homeostatic control mechanisms have the following interdependent components:[107]

- **Stimulus** – physiological variable to be regulated.
- **Receptor** – the sensing component that receives and measures the stimulus (see Section 4.4.11: Cell Signaling).
- **Set-point mechanism** – a means for establishing the "normal range" of values for the regulated variable.
- **Detector** – something that compares the signal being transmitted by the sensor with the set point. The result is a signal that is interpreted by the controller.
- **Control center** – what reacts to the detector signal by sending action potentials to a control center. The control center responds to the receptor signal by determining a response and sending new signals to an effector.

- **Effector** – what responds to signals from the control center, thus providing a response to the stimulus. Examples include one or more muscles, an organ, or a gland. When the signal is received and acted on, negative feedback is provided to the receptor that stops the need for further signaling.

You remember my pet peeve – the homeostasis literature is full of *teleological sloppiness* with phrases like:

- "The ultimate goal of homeostasis"
- "Purpose of homeostasis"
- "A natural resistance to change"
- "Equilibrium is maintained"
- "When a change occurs in an animal's environment, an adjustment must be made"
- "Animal's ability to maintain homeostasis"
- "This optimal state can be maintained by set point"
- "The tendency of an organism or cell to regulate its internal environment and maintain equilibrium"
- "The body is in homeostasis when its needs are met"
- "The true object of all the vital mechanisms is not 'constancy' but survival to reproduce"
- "Organisms are designed for efficiency"
- "Wisely defend bodily parameters critical to an animal's wellbeing"
- "These systems strive to achieve homeostasis"

### 4.6.1.2 ALLOSTASIS

Allostasis is the next level up from homeostasis. Think of homeostasis as something that happens at the cellular and organ level, while allostasis takes place at the level of the organism. Here is my simple allostasis definition, derived from my reading:

> Allostasis is the process of compensatory responses to events to attain some desired balance within some physiological system through behavioral actions.

In effect, it is behavior initiated in *the brain* to serve physiology.

Much of the literature on allostasis focuses on allostatic load, overload, stress, stress mediators, stress response, behavioral therapy, and psychoanalysis. I will not be addressing any of them here. These discussions are important but also gloss over the larger impact of allostasis.

Through allostasis, the brain continually anticipates the body's needs and prepares to meet those needs before they arise. Allostasis is defined in terms of prediction, and recent theories propose that the prediction of interoceptive signals is necessary for successful allostasis. Such theories have proposed the existence of a distributed intrinsic allostatic-interoceptive system in the brain.[108]

Allostasis accounts for a wide variation in function, adaptation, and brain involvement in physiological regulation. Biologically, genes are activated and express diverse neurochemical signaling systems in the brain that affect diverse behavioral regulatory systems essential for bodily viability, including thirst, hunger, sex drive, and sodium appetite.[109] The goal of allostatic regulation is not a steady state; rather, it coordinates variation to optimize performance at the least cost through cognitive predictive regulation.[110]

I plan to address my concerns with this definition and application thoroughly in Section 6.3: Ubiquitous Allostasis.

### 4.6.1.3 SENESCENCE

> *If you do not know how to die, do not worry; Nature will tell you what to do on the spot, fully and adequately. She will do this job perfectly for you; do not bother your head about it.*
> Michel de Montaigne

Nothing is more fundamental to life than death. Senescence or biological aging is the gradual deterioration of life's functional characteristics. It can refer either to cellular or organism senescence. Organism senescence involves an increase in death rates and/or a decrease in fertility in the latter part of an organism's life cycle.

Nine hallmarks of aging that are common between organisms with emphasis on mammals are GENOMIC INSTABILITY, TELOMERE ATTRITION, EPIGENETIC ALTERATIONS, LOSS OF PROTEOSTASIS, DEREGULATED NUTRIENT SENSING, MITOCHONDRIAL DYSFUNCTION, CELLULAR SENESCENCE, STEM CELL EXHAUSTION, and ALTERED INTERCELLULAR COMMUNICATION.[111]

There is a database that lists primarily animal *maximum longevity*. It includes about 4,000 animals and is called *An Age Database of Animal Ageing and Longevity*.[112] It can be downloaded and imported into MS Excel so that you can fool around with it. I have included a table of animals that beat out humans.

|  | Maximum Longevity in Years |
| --- | --- |
| Hexactinellid sponge | 15,000 |
| Epibenthic sponge | 1,550 |
| Ocean quahog clam | 507 |
| Greenland shark | 392 |
| Bowhead whale | 211 |
| Rougheye rockfish | 205 |
| Red sea urchin | 200 |
| Galapagos tortoise | 177 |
| Shortraker rockfish | 157 |
| Lake sturgeon | 152 |
| Aldabra tortoise | 152 |
| Orange roughy | 149 |

| Warty oreo | 140 |
| Eastern box turtle | 138 |
| Mediterranean spur-thighed tortoise | 127 |
| Human | 122 |

*Table 3 – Animal Maximum Longevity*

## 4.6.2 SYSTEMS

An insightful paper (unfortunately filled with teleological language, I assume because the authors come from departments of science philosophy) categorizes response systems into two levels:[113]

- **Dynamic stability response** (first-order control) – a collective network response to stimuli. These systems both sense and respond.
- **Regulatory response** (second-order control) – a dedicated and operationally distinct subsystem that activates the response of a different system.

Homeostatic systems would fall under first-order, with allostatic systems under second-order. The systems described below do not neatly fall into one or the other, but the concept is still helpful. There may also be a third-order control level sneaking around that controls the regulatory systems that control the response systems.

### 4.6.2.1 MOTOR CONTROL SYSTEMS

Motor functions are controlled by the PRIMARY MOTOR CORTEX, PREMOTOR CORTEX, SUPPLEMENTARY MOTOR AREA, POSTERIOR PARIETAL CORTEX, DORSOLATERAL PREFRONTAL CORTEX, and the BASAL GANGLIA.[114]

## 4.6.2.2 Sensorimotor Control Systems

Sensorimotor control is the coupling of the sensory system and motor system that allows an organism to use sensory information to make motor actions. Motor response to sensory input (adaptive behavior) relies on neural processing in multiple interacting networks of both systems.

One such interaction employs CNS signals that predict the sensory outcomes of a specific behavioral action, enabling self-generated and external sensory information to be isolated from each other. In the absence of this isolation, an incorrect perception of the environment would occur because the organism does not discriminate between sensory inflow resulting from external events and sensory inflow from stimulation by the motor action itself. To predict the sensory effects of their own behavior and enable behaviorally relevant stimuli to be processed, motor systems implement intrinsic representations of the actual movement command. These signals are sent to various levels of sensory processing and other motor systems (motor-to-motor signaling), where they serve to weaken or remove the self-generated component.[115] Researchers use the fancy terms *corollary discharge* and *efference copy*, but I will group them and call them "ancillary signals."

To generate efficient actions, the motor system must compensate for CHARACTERISTICS inherent in sensorimotor control, including nonlinearity, nonstationary, delays, redundancy, uncertainty, and noise. [116]

## 4.6.2.3 Homeostasis Support Systems in Mammals

I do not think I need to go into the biology of every system in mammals that contributes to homeostasis, so I will just provide an incomplete list of homeostasis support systems for you to follow up on if interested. They are regulated primarily by negative feedback to maintain hormonal levels within a narrow range.

- Autonomic nervous system
- Parathyroid gland
- Juxtaglomerular apparatus
- Hypothalamic-pituitary-adrenal axis
- Hypothalamic-pituitary-thyroid axis
- Hypothalamic-pituitary-gonadal axis
- Hypothalamic-neurohypophyseal system
- Renin-angiotensin system

### 4.6.2.4 Endocrine System

I will be discussing specific hormones later in Section 6.3: Ubiquitous Allostasis, so I will introduce the system that produces them here. The glands that secrete hormones that enter the bloodstream comprise the *endocrine system*. They include the pineal gland, pituitary gland, pancreas, ovaries, testes, thyroid gland, parathyroid gland, hypothalamus, and adrenal glands.

## 4.6.3 Non-Human Sensorimotor Control Systems

In the area of sensorimotor control, it is easier to study non-human animals than humans, I guess because the non-humans cannot complain as much when they get caged, hooked up to electrodes, shocked, and dissected.

- *Nocifensive behaviors* are those that are evoked by stimuli that activate the nociceptive sensory apparatus. Responses to noxious stimuli in animals may include behaviors resembling responses to pain in humans, such as limping, flinching, vocalization, and reflexive withdrawal. Other specific pain-related responses in animals include tail and paw flicks, licking, and scratching.[117]
- The following are summarized from "A New Perspective on Predictive Motor Signaling":[119]

o During the escape behavior of crayfish, ancillary signals act to prevent mechanosensory hair cells from becoming habituated during a tail flip so that they maintain their responsiveness.

o During chirping in crickets, an interneuron inhibits central auditory signal processing in time with the animal's singing. Consequently, central auditory sensitivity is diminished during each phase of the self-generated chirp cycle so that the peripheral sensor remains receptive to the auditory environment.

o In weakly electric fish, neural motor copies of their electric organ discharge are subtracted from concurrently occurring electroreceptive sensory inputs, thereby enabling the detection of electrical sensory cues from the environment.

o In primates, fast eye movement causes a correspondingly rapid movement of the visual scene across the retina, which would be perceived as blurred if not for ancillary signals. The mechanism uses neuronal copies of the motor commands that encode the overall spatio-temporal parameters. These ancillary signals are integrated with incoming visual inputs to prevent the perception of illusionary object motion during fast eye movement.

o During supersonic call emission in echo-locating bats, predictive vocal signals inform neurons along the peripheral and central auditory pathways about the occurrence of self-generated sound.

o Activity in marmoset and squirrel monkey cortical auditory neurons is suppressed during vocal activity. However, this suppression only blocks an expected neuronal discharge modulation, thereby allowing unexpected alterations in the self-generated sound to be detected.

o During self-motion in mice, such as locomotion, head movements, and grooming, the motor-related signal, which precedes movement onset, is conveyed via long-range motor-to-auditory circuitry to activate local interneurons that, in turn, inhibit auditory cortical excitatory neurons and thus suppress sound-evoked responses during subsequent movement.

o Self-generated electric fields in weakly electric fish directly activate electroreceptors along the animal's body, affecting the detection of environmental electric fields. To extract these small perturbations from the overall sensory signal, mirror images of the unperturbed electric field are subtracted from the combined signal. This subtraction results in a representation of the external electrical disturbance.

o The coupling relationship between locomotor and respiratory motor systems is readily observable in animals when exertion is associated with an increase in their respiratory rate to meet the increased oxygen demand. The locomotor rhythm-generating centers in the lumbar spinal cord generate ancillary signals that are then transmitted to the parafacial respiratory group that contributes to breathing rhythm generation.

o Animals require activation of gaze-stabilizing eye movements to compensate for the disruptive effect that head/body motion has on visual perception. To maintain visual acuity, retinal image drift is minimized by counteractive image-stabilizing eye motion. Additionally, feed-forward copies of the motor commands responsible for generating locomotor movements are used as an internal prediction of the effects of head/body movements for visual processing.

## 4.7 Systems Chemistry

### 4.7.1 Definition

Systems chemistry is the study of networks of interacting molecules to create new functions from a set of molecules with different hierarchical levels and emergent properties. I give you a very brief introduction to the subject here because it will appear many times when I get into the details of abiogenetic mechanics.

Systems chemistry is the study and modelling of chemical phenomena through examining their complexity and inter-dynamics. Complex chemical systems operate under kinetic and thermodynamic control and give rise to unique properties, some of which are emergent.

The behaviors of complex chemical systems can be divided into the following:[118]

- Behaviors associated with individual components that are observed in parallel within a large system.
- Behaviors that can be observed only in the context of the complex system but can be predicted by understanding the properties of individual components.
- Behaviors that can be observed only in the context of the complex system and can only be predicted by an understanding of the system and not by its components (i.e., emergent phenomena).

### 4.7.2 Prebiotic Systems Chemistry

As you will see in the abiogenesis section, significant progress is being made toward demonstrating the abiotic generation of biological components and entities through the application of abiotic systems chemistry. These include studies exploring the dynamic behavior and the synergistic effects of nucleic acids, peptides, lipids, and other prebiotic small molecules.[119]

The huge personal challenge I discovered is that, instead of lab experiments, the literature presents theoretical models that are not intellectually accessible to me. On the one hand, physical experiments can be very satisfying and instructional when successful but frustrating and inadequate when they fail. On the other hand, abstract models, using a lot of theorems, statistics, and probability, can be extraordinarily complex but can construct a theoretical abiotic world hopefully understood by others in the field. An example of that theoretical complexity pulled out of context[120] includes the following diagrams, formulas, and theorems:

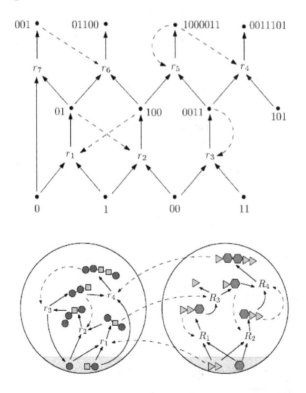

$$\overline{\mu} := \frac{1}{|X|} \sum_{x \in X} \mathbb{E}[\,|\{r \in \mathcal{R}^+ : (x, r) \in C\}|\,]$$

$$= \frac{1}{|X|} \sum_{x \in X} \sum_{r \in \mathcal{R}_+} \mathbb{P}(\mathcal{E}(x, r)).$$

(a) If $\overline{\mu} \le \lambda \cdot \frac{|\mathcal{R}^+|}{|X|}$ then the probability that there exists
an RAF for $Q$ is at most $\phi(\lambda)$, where
$\phi(\lambda) = 1 - (1 - \frac{\lambda}{k})^\tau \to 0$ as $\lambda \to 0$, and where $\tau$ is a
constant dependent only on $k$ and $t$.

(b) If $\overline{\mu} \ge \lambda \cdot \frac{|\mathcal{R}^+|}{|X|}$ then the probability that there exists
an RAF for $Q$ is at least $1 - \psi(\lambda)$, where
$\psi(\lambda) = \frac{k(ke^{-v\lambda/K})^t}{1 - ke^{-v\lambda/K}} \to 0$ exponentially fast as $\lambda \to \infty$.

$$\mathbf{P}^T \begin{bmatrix} |X_1| \\ |X_2| \end{bmatrix} = \begin{bmatrix} p_{11} & p_{21} \\ p_{12} & p_{22} \end{bmatrix} \begin{bmatrix} |X_1| \\ |X_2| \end{bmatrix} = \begin{bmatrix} c_1 \\ c_2 \end{bmatrix}$$

## And my favorite!

For part (ii) we have from (4):

$$q_r \le \prod_{x \in X}(1 - p(x, r))) + \left(1 - \prod_{x \in X}(1 - p'(x, r))\right).$$

and since

$$\prod_{x \in X}(1 - p(x, r))) \le \exp\left(-\sum_{x \in X} p(x, r)\right) \le \exp(-c_l)$$

and

$$1 - \prod_{x \in X}(1 - p'(x, r)) \le \sum_{x \in X} p'(x, r) \le \epsilon$$

(by (C2) and (C3)) we obtain the claimed inequality in part
(ii).

As you can see, modeling abiogenesis is extraordinarily complex.
Abiotic systems chemistry is an approach that can build and test
models of that complexity, and you will see me reference and try

to summarize papers from that field. For example, the same above paper concluded (among other things) that:

> due to the utility of polymers in modern life, much of the theoretical and experimental work on the origin of life problem has focused on system of polymers, and it was shown in [13] that the level of catalysis need only increase linearly as the number of molecules increases, in order to maintain a high probability of RAF (**Reflexively Autocatalytic and Food-generated**) sets occurring. We have presented a generalization of this result, showing that under mild assumptions, the same linear bound applies to a system in which the molecules are not necessarily polymers. Furthermore, partitioned systems were shown to support the development of RAF sets similarly to typical systems containing only one type of polymer, and the effect of the pattern of catalysis on the emergence of RAF sets was explored. Previous research into template-based catalysis [14,20] and recent work incorporating more realistic patterns of catalysis [35] have indicated that the emergence of RAF sets is quite robust to the structure of the underlying reaction system, a conclusion which this paper supports.

I understand no more than 50% of the above, which is why I am grateful we have scientists who do and keep pushing the envelope.

## 4.8 ABIOGENETIC MECHANICS

> Everything existing in the universe is the fruit of chance and necessity.
> Democritus

Now, let us apply what we have learned to the mechanics (and implications) of abiogenesis.

The challenges of determining abiogenetic mechanics have to

do with the ahistoric nature of the processes that must have led to biological complexification (i.e., life). Everything I discuss below had to happen at some point, or we would not all be here today. What is not certain is the actual sequence that resulted in our biology and what labels to put on these precursors to our biological concepts/ entities. The debate lies here, and I will try my best to avoid it.

I set you up for this by saying in Section 4.1 that evolution kicks in after abiogenesis ends. That is a handy way of stating it, but it is false. Abiogenesis has no *intent*; therefore, it does not drive toward biology, and its mechanics did not end at the first IDAs or LUCA but are built into the fabric of chemistry and biochemistry. The obvious implication is that abiogenesis mechanics are still operating and are, of course, observable. Look at all the lab experiments I will be referencing that were intended to test out abiogenesis using these same mechanics.

I will begin by asking what are the core enabling building blocks that abiogenesis could not function without and, therefore, life could not emerge without. Here is my personal definition:

> Abiogenetic mechanics consist of autocatalytic entities in a dynamic steady state. These entities exist within matter and energy and receive, retain, and release matter and energy from, and to, a time- and resource-constrained environment. This environment is within a thermodynamic/kinetic framework, with error-prone intermolecular detaching, recombining, self-replicating, self-maintaining, and self-assembling capabilities that can result in subsequent variant entities.

I will spend significant space on each of these characteristics. First (especially you biologists), notice that a few things are missing from this definition:

- Chemical complexity
- Biology
- Biochemistry

- Biomolecules
- Genes/genetics
- Cells
- Organisms
- RNA/DNA
- Reproduction
- Selection
- Adaptation
- Evolution
- Life

I will now break down my definition with the fundamentals of that mechanism. Then, I will describe it in the prebiotic world trending to biology. Note that *everything* I will discuss is 100% accepted science or mainstream peer-reviewed theory and research.

## 4.8.1 AUTOCATALYTIC

### 4.8.1.1 FUNDAMENTALS

Biologists will notice my starting with the use of the word "autocatalytic" instead of "metabolic." This was intentional. I chose autocatalytic over metabolic because there was a time before living organisms emerged when autocatalysis was acting.

### 4.8.1.2 AUTOCATALYTIC TO METABOLISM

Since we were not there, it is impossible to know how metabolism emerged from simpler autocatalytic reactions. We have theories and lab results that, in turn, contribute to theories. Some of the theories I have come across (that I will not specifically address here) include:[121]

- The Retrograde hypothesis
- The Granick hypothesis

- The Patchwork hypothesis
- Semi-enzymatic origin of metabolic pathways

I briefly mentioned reflexively autocatalytic and food-generated (RAF) sets earlier in Section 4.7.2 with respect and a little fear. They are a class of *mathematical objects* in which each reaction is catalyzed by a molecule from within the network, and all molecules can be produced from a set of food molecules by the network itself.[122,123] The authors theorized that if autocatalytic sets enabled the origin of metabolism, lineages with physiology very similar to that of the first protocells should contain early sets.[124] In a complex way that I, as a non-scientist, never quite understood, they investigated different levels of ancient metabolism preserved in modern cells. Some interesting conclusions included the following:

- NAD+ is strongly embedded in the ancient RAF sets.
- ATP was not the primordial energetic currency, which points to other energy currencies.
- RAF sets generated amino acids and bases using small-molecule catalysis (pre-metabolism) prior to the emergence of nucleic acids (pre-RNA) and peptide polymers (pre-proteins).

I found an interesting paper concerning the emergence of metabolism using marine cyanobacteria (e.g., Prochlorococcus) as a stand-in. Prochlorococcus is the smallest known cyanobacteria. These bacteria belong to the photosynthetic picoplankton and are probably the most abundant photosynthetic free-living or endo-symbiotic-plastid organism on Earth. By producing and releasing oxygen (as a byproduct of photosynthesis), cyanobacteria converted the early oxygen-poor atmosphere into an oxidizing one, causing the *Great Oxygenation Event.*

In the study, "Metabolic evolution and the self-organization of ecosystems,"[125] the researchers played around with (performed *reconstructions* of) Prochlorococcus and a co-occurring heterotrophic bacterium SAR11. They found that:

- The organisms formed a co-evolved mutualism that maximized their collective metabolic rate by recycling organic carbon through complementary excretion and uptake pathways.
- Their metabolic codependencies were like those of chloroplasts and mitochondria within plant cells.
- Theoretically, these adaptations lowered the minimal subsistence nutrient concentration of cells, which resulted in a drawdown of nutrients in oceanic surface waters.
- This led to an increase in total ecosystem biomass and facilitated the coevolution of all cells in the ecosystem.

The phenomenon where one species lives off the products of another species is called *syntrophy*.

Two other excellent papers that I will not cover here[126,127] discuss symbiosis and the evolution of the plastid.

## 4.8.2 ENTITY

### 4.8.2.1 FUNDAMENTALS

If you look it up, a typical definition of "entity" is "a thing with distinct and independent existence." My definition is a little different: *a thing that has a boundary between itself and its environment that exists over time.* It is basically the same definition, but instead of calling the thing "distinct," I prefer calling it something with an inside and outside (environment). If an entity does not have an "inside," then it cannot be an entity, and if it does not have an "outside" with which it interacted, then it also cannot be an entity. Instead of saying it has an "independent existence," I say that the boundary exists over time, i.e., to be an entity, it must persist.

The "boundary" between inside and outside is difficult to precisely define. The boundary is better thought of as a relationship between the inside and outside or a set of rules for anything that occurs between them, as opposed to a physical boundary. That time can be seconds or centuries.

These concepts of an entity and inside/outside are just that – something in our minds to help us understand things. This is a "mind concept" for an organization of matter and energy in space and time and through space and time. You will see later how our "mind" is always involved when we think we are dealing with reality. We can maintain that concept and fill in the gaps over time because it simplifies our perception of reality.

I am bringing this up now because I want to flag both the error of teleology and our labeling of reality being confused with Reality.

- **Error of teleology** – as I stated earlier, when you read any biology literature, you will constantly be bombarded with phrases like, "the cell does this, the gene does that, DNA does this, a chromosome does that." All these statements are factually incorrect because they imply intent (which implies a level of intelligence), or teleology, and are only used as a conceptual facilitator for easier understanding. None of these things "do" anything – they do not "act." It is the combination of their constituent parts that *enables* things to happen.
- **Labeling of reality** – in the thought experiment first discussed in *Plutarch's Lives* called "The Ship of Theseus," Plutarch supposes "that the famous ship sailed by the hero Theseus in a great battle has been kept in a harbor as a museum piece. As the years go by, some of the wooden parts begin to rot and are replaced by new ones. After a century or so, all the parts have been replaced. Is the "restored" ship still the same object as the original?" The ship is the stand-in for the "entity" I introduced above, and the constant replacement of parts is the entity continuously changing over time. I will just go far enough to say that even though the ship/entity is constantly changing, our

label for it can remain unchanged. Or, as Herakleitos wrote, "One cannot step into the same river twice."

So, the entity is what is on the inside of the boundary, its environment is on the outside, and the boundary itself exists as part of the entity and the environment.

### 4.8.2.2 VESICLE TO PROTOCELL TO CELL

We need entities that then result in variant entities – the fundamental end process of abiogenesis and evolution. What were the first chemical entities? The autocatalytic set that I introduced earlier is the term most often found in the literature that best represents these earliest entities during the period of abiogenesis.

The autocatalytic set is fundamental to the concept of an entity with its boundary, and its emerging formation during abiogenesis is referred to as *compartmentalization*. Such compartmentalization is a characteristic of all forms of life. An interesting theory is that the earliest "boundary" of an entity may not have been an actual compartment but simply a spatial separation.[128] The more *defined* an entity's boundary is from its environment, the greater its *autonomy*.[129]

Regardless of its nature, this boundary is essential in physically separating the system from its environment, while allowing nutrients and (low-entropy) energy to enter and waste, (high-entropy) heat, and other products to leave – a necessary disequilibrium.

For biomolecular products to emerge through autocatalysis, a true compartment would be necessary to provide a higher concentration of simpler molecular reactants and catalysts. For that to happen, early simple products would have to be molecules that are non-soluble in water (lipid-like) to provide the ability to persist as an entity's barrier in a water world.

Amphiphilic molecules, such as fatty acids, have been synthesized under simulated prebiotic conditions and have been isolated from carbonaceous chondrite meteorites. Such molecules can form bilayer membrane vesicles with the ability to entrap macromolecules and highly charged small molecules, while remaining permeable to smaller polar solutes. Such vesicles played an important role in the prebiotic world by providing both a spatially limited environment for protometabolic reactions and a mechanism for the spatial confinement of genetic polymers, thus enabling recombination and self-replication.[130]

The protocell's boundary layer must be somehow maintained by the autocatalytic set itself or it will cease to exist. In a discussion on how this compartmentalized entity may have developed,[131] Konikoff et al. described a potential pathway to a functioning entity with a lipid-based boundary and autocatalytic contents. They then studied it using cryogenic transmission electron microscopy (cryo-TEM) combined with video-enhanced light microscopy (VELM). In other words, they looked at it *very closely.*

From their laboratory work, they were able to delineate a sequence of microstructural developments that occur during the earliest stages of cholesterol nucleation (formation of cholesterol crystals that can lead to gallbladder stones). They looked inside biliary lipid aggregates (human bile), and they found several different microstructures:

1. **Micelles** – the predominant aggregates with a size of 3-5 nm and a spheroidal shape.
2. **Discoidal membrane patches** – 50-150 nm, resembling "primordial vesicles" but are, in fact, flat membranes before they close to form vesicles (see later). Their transient nature preceding the abundance of vesicles indicates that they are short-lived (one hour), intermediate structures in the transformation from micelles to vesicles.
3. **Uni-, oligo-, and multilamellar vesicles** (i.e., liposomes)

They watched them over time and found that larger and larger liposomes were forming from the available spheroidal micelles and transient membrane patches. What they observed is a reasonable hypothesis for what happened during abiogenesis to go from micelles to liposomes – inorganic micelles to organic protocells.

I described how early abiogenetic autocatalytic reactions could have taken place in spatially close areas. Biochemistry takes place within spatially confined areas or compartments. Metabolisms are processes occurring in this space, with the diffusion and transport of compounds across diverse boundaries. The relationship between the inside (metabolism) and the outside (environment) is a central aspect of biological organization.

In another study, "Viability Conditions for a Compartmentalized Protometabolic System: A Semi-Empirical Approach,"[132] the researchers had as their objective "to determine the conditions for viability of cyclic reaction networks (e.g., coupled autocatalytic loops with potential for self-maintenance) within vesicles made of prebiotically plausible amphiphilic molecules." They looked at the balance between the compartment's nutrient accessibility, the limits placed on the reactive process rates, and the system's longevity and found that even highly permeable compartments could enable a restriction on the timescale of a protometabolism, depending on the size and type of compounds that this requires as starting materials. Their broader conclusion was that the properties of compartments and the chemistries that take place within and around them are joined at the hip and emerged in common through abiogenesis.

Another set of experiments[133] found that using a system consisting of RdRP and DNA template entrapped in submicrometer-sized liposomes, the membrane could be made sufficiently permeable to allow access of molecules as large as nucleoside triphosphates to RdRP through passive diffusion. The encapsulated polymerase transcribed the template-specific base sequences of the DNA to the RNA that was synthesized. These experiments show that genetic information (DNA) can be associated with RdRP in a single compartment and that transcription of DNA fragments can be achieved by relying solely on passive diffusion to supply nucleoside triphosphate substrates. It also implies that active cellular membrane transport likely emerged later than when the central dogma suggests.

Keeping the protocell front and center, researchers[134] identified dynamic, functionally integrated protocell systems as the units of prebiotic evolution. What I think they meant to say was what I said earlier: that these protocell systems were the IDAs. They posit that "both for reactive processes to become proto-metabolic and for vesicles to become proto-cellular, their mutual, dynamic engagement could well be an early, unavoidable requirement."

The researchers further posit three hypothetical stages of development toward IDAs (not LUCA), with the correlation between protocell organization and evolutionary potential depicted at each stage:

a) Self-assembled fatty acid vesicles grow and divide in an unregulated and error-prone way, relying on environmental conditions and stimuli.

b) After a Major Transition, the first self-producing protocells appear that can internally synthesize membrane lipids and other components.

c) After another Major Transition, protocells reach IDA complexity levels.

For those who need and can understand even more complex works (is that even possible?), I am including reference to a comprehensive paper, titled "From Self-Assembled Vesicles to Protocells,"[135] which analyzes vesicles in abiotic conditions from a *systems biology* perspective. The researchers review:

- *The importance of vesicles during the origins of life, fundamental thermodynamics, and kinetics of self-assembly, and experimental models of simple vesicles, focusing on prebiotically plausible fatty acids and their derivatives.*
- *Recent work on interactions of simple vesicles with RNA and other studies of the transition from vesicles to protocells.*

- *Current challenges in understanding the biophysics of protocells, as well as conceptual questions in information transmission and self-replication.*

### 4.8.3 DYNAMIC STEADY STATE

#### 4.8.3.1 FUNDAMENTALS

A system is in a dynamic steady state when it has values that oscillate between maxima and minima around a central mean value. In other words, the steady state is *not constant* but continually fluctuating around "something." This dynamic steady state represents what is happening inside entities and their relationship with the outside. An entity persisting over time would be impossible without this *dynamic* steady state that allows for *ongoing* interaction between that entity and its environment.

A required characteristic of a dynamic steady state is a *sensing function* that interacts with environmental conditions to enable the entity to maintain this dynamic steady state.

With regards to abiogenetic mechanics, we need to respect the extreme complexities, uncertainties, and lack of intention of "steady state," "dynamic," "mean value," and the sensing function, both in the moment and over time, taking place inside entities.

#### 4.8.3.2 HOMEOSTASIS

As defined earlier, homeostasis is the dynamic state of steady, internal physical and chemical conditions maintained by living systems. Although the term "homeostasis" was coined in a biological context, there must have been steady state (proto-homeostasis) mechanisms that developed before the advent of full biological homeostasis. I could not find any journal articles that hypothesized on what those steps may have been, but they happened, nonetheless.

### 4.8.3.3 ALLOSTASIS

I introduced allostasis back in Section 4.6.1.2 and had no expectations to include it within the abiogenesis section, since allostasis requires *behavior* that I would not have thought would have operated until long after the *Initial Darwinian Ancestor*. Then, when I thought I was effectively finished with the book, I discovered a provocative paper[136] that gave me my third or fourth epiphany – a concept the authors called *behavioral metabolution*.

Their conclusions were based on a minimal model of metabolism-based chemotaxis. If you remember from back in Section 4.4.2, *chemotaxis* is a mechanism by which bacteria sense and respond to changes in the chemical composition of their environment, approaching chemically favorable environments and avoiding unfavorable ones. The model demonstrated how changes to metabolic pathways can lead to improvement of behavioral strategies and how behavior can contribute to the exploration and retention of new metabolic pathways, operating during both abiogenesis and evolution, through:

- Increasing exposure to environmental differences.
- Making more probable the retention of beneficial metabolic pathways.
- Enabling behavioral adaptation to change in the environment and the organism (i.e., *allostasis*).
- Increasing the likelihood of speciation, since new behavior can expose a subset of the population to a new environment that could involve different selection pressures.

Again, this was a model with no supporting lab work, and the authors pointedly say that this opens an interesting area and much more work needs to be done.

## 4.8.4 THERMODYNAMIC FRAMEWORK

### 4.8.4.1 FUNDAMENTALS

The *Second Law of Thermodynamics* is formulated for closed, single-phase systems. A closed system is not affected by any outside action during the observed period. A single-phase system consists of only one type of matter. The Second Law states that such a system tends toward greater entropy (disorder is a metaphor for entropy) and reaches its maximum entropy when the system reaches an equilibrium state. Entropy is a macroscopic quantity or measurement that refers to the whole system and is not a dynamical variable and, in general, does not act as a local potential that describes local physical forces.[137]

Some argue that the Second Law supports an external "designer" since we see increased order in living organisms that seems to violate the law. A simple response is that living organisms are not closed nor single-phase systems, so the Second Law is not violated by an increase in order. The expected decreased order (increased entropy) is not ubiquitous across the system – it is the sum total, and decreased entropy can exist within an entity (the "open system"), while increased entropy exists outside of it (the "surroundings") in a *maintained disequilibrium* with no violation. Although the universe's entropy increases with time, the entropy of any part of the universe can decrease with time so long as that decrease is compensated by an increase in some other part of the universe. For example, as a hot cup of coffee left on a tabletop decreases in entropy (cools), the room's entropy increases (warms up) as they reach equilibrium.[138]

So, what are some examples of increased "order" in open systems on Earth? A hurricane is an example of a physical system, and life is a good example of a biochemical system that exhibits increasing "order." Do these violate the Second Law and require an external designer? No. Remember that the law refers to a "closed system," and Earth by itself is not closed. Order can be created in an open system by a decrease in order of the system's surroundings (still part of the overall system). Part of our surroundings includes the Sun (and meteorites, electromagnetic radiation, gravitational waves, neutrinos, etc.). The Sun (and the universe) is becoming more disorderly as it emits its energy as light, some of which the Earth receives. The total disorder of the Sun and the Earth increases, even though orderly hurricanes (earthbound thermal non-equilibrium) and life (earthbound biochemical non-equilibrium) are generated using the Sun and Earth's energy (total equilibrium).

This is the thermodynamic framework that abiogenesis/biological mechanics operate within. The Earth receives energy from the Sun in *low-entropy* form (directed photons), some of which entities process, enabling the low entropy within the entity. The rest is returned to the environment in a *high-entropy* form (mostly heat).

From a thermodynamics perspective, the inside of an entity is in disequilibrium with the outside, thus maintaining the two sides of the boundary. In other words, *disequilibrium defines the entity*. With no disequilibrium, there is no entity.

This is all at the organism or cellular level, but what about the molecular level? These thermodynamic laws apply to macroscopic systems, where entropy and temperature have a clear meaning and measurement. At the microscopic level, they may be statistically applied to many molecules but not to individual molecules where temperature and pressure are neither well-defined nor measurable. At the molecular level, other "laws" come into play, including the *Boltzmann distribution* that describes how the relative amount of molecules' specific energy depends on both energy and temperature and quantifies the compromise between minimizing energy and maximizing entropy.[139]

### 4.8.4.2 Out-of-Thermodynamic Equilibrium

Abiogenesis could not have resulted in life without an emerging capability to maintain the protocells in an *out-of-thermodynamic-equilibrium* state – sustaining more order on the inside, while decreasing order on the outside. As Erwin Schrödinger stated in 1944 in his famous and oft-cited book, *What Is Life? The Physical Aspect of the Living Cell*, "Living matter evades the decay to equilibrium."[140]

A *dissipative structure* is a thermodynamically open system operating far from thermodynamic equilibrium that exchanges energy and matter with its environment, creating both spatial and temporal ordered structures.[141,142,143,144,145] The buildup of the system's internal complexity is always accompanied by the production of positive entropy (less order), which must be dissipated out of the system as waste or low-grade energy, resulting in a net increase of negative entropy (more order). Otherwise, the accumulation of positive entropy will eventually bring it to thermodynamic equilibrium, in which the system cannot maintain its order and organization. Over the 50 years since this concept was proposed,[146] a tremendous amount of work has been done to understand the basis of nonequilibrium self-organization in biological systems. A paper entitled "Dissipative structures in biological systems: bistability, oscillations, spatial patterns and waves"[147] shows that there are many physical, chemical, and biological examples of dissipative structures. Its conclusion is instructive but too complex for me to try to simplify, so I am including it here:

> Why are dissipative structures so common in biological systems? If life is such a rich source for multiple attractors, oscillations, and spatio-temporal organization, it is because life is inherently nonlinear. This nonlinearity is prone to give rise to instabilities, and originates from the cooperativity of allosteric proteins such as enzymes, ion channels or receptors, and from the multiple feedback loops which control the operation of biological systems at all levels, from cells to tissues, organs and animal populations. Life depends on feedback regulation. Positive feedback is required for bistability, while negative feedback is associated with oscillatory behaviour. Both types of feedback are often intertwined. The examples of the cell cycle and the circadian clock illustrate well how positive and negative feedback loops cooperate to confer on

*a complex regulatory network the capability of temporal self-or-*
*ganization in the form of sustained oscillations. The occurrence*
*of nonlinear interactions capable of giving rise to bistability or*
*oscillations might in fact be more widespread than envisaged on*
*the basis of identified feedback loops.*

Applying this to abiogenesis, an excellent article[148] demonstrates that a replicator can be maintained out-of-equilibrium by the continuous consumption of chemical energy. The system is driven by the autocatalytic formation of a surfactant whose products are converted back into building blocks by a chemical fuel. The consumption of fuel allows the replicators to persist at a steady, but out-of-equilibrium, state, much like a simple metabolic cycle.

As discussed earlier, these protocells maintain a thermodynamic disequilibrium with their environment. To maintain this disequilibrium, the protocell uses the acquired external nutrients (free low-entropy energy) to fuel its metabolism for self-assembly and self-maintenance that externally increases entropy. Taken from "Evolution and the second law of thermodynamics: effectively communicating to non-technicians"[149]:

*Cells maintain a relatively higher degree of order compared with*
*their environment by continually importing free energy in the*
*form of nutrients and exporting entropy as disordered wastes*
*and heat. Cells selectively import ordered nutrients from a largely*
*chaotic world via its semipermeable cell membrane, composed*
*of substrate-specific protein channels and transporters (colored*
*cylinders) embedded in a relatively impermeable phospholipid*
*(dotted lines) membrane. A cell's metabolism converts nutrients*
*into usable forms of energy (ATP) and into diverse biomolecules*
*that are used for self-maintenance, reproduction, and growth.*
*The costs of converting nutrients into these useful low entropy*
*forms for self-preservation are the production of high entropy*
*wastes and heat. The constant export of entropy from cells via*

*the cell membrane ensures the cells maintain higher internal
order compared with their external environment.*

### 4.8.4.3 Time Constrained

I am spending a lot of time on resource constraints in the sections
on entities and environments, but I will not be thoroughly addressing the critical constraint of *time*. I have not found any literature
that attempts to demonstrate the emergence of time-dependent
processes in the prebiotic world, but, obviously, this had to take
place. Instead, I will extend the dissipative structures that I introduced earlier to include a dimension of time[151] and give biological
processes as examples.

Biological rhythms can be considered as *temporal* dissipative
structures. These rhythmic behaviors exist because of the feedback
processes that control the dynamics of abiological and biological
systems at the biochemical, entity/cellular, and entity/supracellular
levels. Today, they occur at all levels of biological organization, with
periods that cover more than 10 orders of magnitude.[150]

I find this definition circular (pun intended!). It says that rhythmic
*cyclical* behavior exists because cycles exist. From my perspective,
and I have not found this in the literature, more fundamentally, this
behavior exists because *everything takes time*, including abiogenetic
mechanics. Energy and matter requirements being equal, the less
time an entity-related beneficial process takes, the more competitive
that entity will be in an environment of other entities (the measure
of fitness, introduced later in Section 5.2). Another paper beyond my
education level, "Chaotic flow: The physics of species coexistence,"[151]
provides a hydrodynamical explanation for the *spatial and temporal* heterogeneity of resources and populations in the presence of
imperfect chaotic horizontal mixing that provides an alternative
explanation for information integration (genetic recombination) in
early evolutionary systems – physics leading to biochemistry.

## 4.8.5 KINETIC FRAMEWORK

### 4.8.5.1 FUNDAMENTALS

Any chemical reaction has both thermodynamic and kinetic aspects. Kinetics is about what happens during a reaction (the *time course*), while thermodynamics is about the state at the end of the reaction. Thermodynamics addresses the energy differences between reactants and their products *after* the reaction takes place. Kinetics addresses both the rate of reactions and the pathway of the reaction to equilibrium *during it*.[152]

Reactants are *unreactive* under certain conditions. The reaction must have some sort of energy input before it can proceed. Otherwise, the reactants cannot cross the activation energy threshold and convert to products. Kinetics measures how fast a chemical reaction reaches equilibrium, assuming the reactants were supplied with enough activation energy to enable the reaction to proceed in the forward direction – reactants to products.[156]

In biochemistry, enzymes, ribozymes, and ribosomes are catalysts that speed up the rate of chemical reactions without being used up in the process. They achieve their effect by temporarily binding to a substrate and lowering the activation energy needed to convert it to a product.

### 4.8.5.2 KINETIC FRAMEWORK

The groundbreaking work of Addy Pross, Robert Pascal, and John D. Sutherland[153,154,155,156,157] introduced and developed a stabilizing framework other than thermodynamics that they have termed *dynamic kinetic stability* (DKS). I will do my best in this limited space to describe it, but I will not do it justice. I strongly recommend you go to the noted sources above to get all the facts and implications.

DKS applies to persistent replicating systems (both chemical and biological) and populations of replicators. It comes into operation under the following conditions:

- The replication reactions must be persistent and irreversible.
- The system must be maintained in a far-from-equilibrium state.
- It must be open and continually fed activated component building blocks.

Since DKS applies to both chemical and biological replicators that express similar reaction characteristics, the authors concluded that the abiotic (chemical) phase leading to the simplest life and the biotic (biological) phase are one continuous physicochemical process. In this framework, the driving evolutionary force is "the drive of replicating systems towards greater stability." And, just as important, abiogenesis is based on "the spontaneous emergence of a simple (unidentified) replicating system, initially fragile, which complexified and evolved towards complex replicating systems exhibiting greater DKS."

## 4.8.6 INTERMOLECULAR DETACHING, RECOMBINING, AND ASSEMBLING

### 4.8.6.1 FUNDAMENTALS

I mentioned above that entities can physically interact and exchange matter. Biomolecules received by entities can be processed in two fundamental ways:

1. To use the received biomolecules to create new molecules through chemical reactions (primarily through breaking intramolecular bonds). This would be the equivalent of using these biomolecules as food. I am going to cover this process under Section 4.8.9: Receives and Releases Matter and Energy.
2. To use the received biomolecules or entire entities without fundamental change (primarily through breaking and reforming intermolecular bonds or through symbiosis). These

biomolecules/entities would have to stick around and become a lasting part of the receiving entity. This is what I mean by detaching, recombining, and assembling.

A feature of recombination is that blocks of this complex matter are exchanged among entities rather than by combining much simpler and smaller components. Whatever happens in recombining, the resultant is a modified (variant) entity. The two types of intermolecular recombination are:

1. **Horizontal** – when the two different exchanging entities exist before and after the recombination. The entities could also maintain their identity but enter a horizontal symbiotic relationship.
2. **Vertical** – when the "child/descendent" entity emerges with the recombined biomolecules from the "parent/ancestor" entity.

Horizontal recombining impacts and changes already-existing entities, while vertical recombining results in a new entity that continues to exist. Horizontal recombining had to emerge before vertical because it would have a smaller and more random impact on the receiving entity, while vertical requires much more control of the process (e.g., templated replication) and a 100% impact on the new entity.

Self-assembling is enabled by the chemistry of the intermolecular assembly process using covalent bonds and noncovalent interactions discussed earlier. Covalent bonds, an intramolecular force, also appear in some of the intermolecular structures. For noncovalent interactions, we do not need to worry about which types exist between these molecules, just that they are individually weak but collectively strong. Two things must exist for noncovalent interactions to hold together these intermolecular structures:[158]

- A substantial number of noncovalent interactions.
- A surface topography (3D structure) that enables substantial areas of two interacting surfaces to approach each other favorably.

### 4.8.6.2 INTRAMOLECULAR SELF-ASSEMBLING

I am going to distinguish between "intra" and "inter" molecular recombining and self-assembling. I will address intramolecular first in the abiotic world.

First, many biomolecules such as amino acids have been found in carbon-containing meteorites. These compounds have isotopic compositions that date their formation before the birth of our sun. The selective abundance of biomolecule precursors suggests their possible contribution to biomolecular evolution.[159]

Second, researchers have formed hundreds of organic compounds in the lab. "These compounds include more than 10 of the common amino acids, a variety of mono-, di-, and tricarboxylic acids, fatty acids, adenine, and formaldehyde. Under certain conditions, formaldehyde polymerizes to form sugars containing three, four, five, and six carbons. In addition to the many monomers that form in these experiments, polymers of nucleotides (nucleic acids) and amino acids (proteins) also form. The sources of energy that are effective in bringing about the formation of these compounds include heat, visible and ultraviolet light, x-rays, gamma radiation, ultrasound, shock waves, and alpha and beta radiation."[160]

Also, intramolecular self-assembly entails anabolic reactions forming polymers from monomers (i.e., polymerization, an anabolic pathway). If you go back to our list of monomers and polymers, this can be combining monosaccharides to form polysaccharides, fatty acids to form triglycerides, amino acids to form proteins, and nucleotides to form nucleic acids. These processes use the energy generated by catabolic reactions.[161]

Now, how might this have emerged? A nice discussion on this can be found in "Self-Other Organization,"[162] but only after you weed through the (possibly required) obtuse/complex scientific exposition. I do think that the author sets up a strawman argument in describing natural selection in a very restrictive way and then knocks it down as the mechanism for abiogenesis. I am not as interested in the overall argument but in some of the early framing, so I am going to pick and choose and make understandable my area of interest.

The capability of template-based (coded, DNA-like) replication that we are familiar with *had to* emerge from a world without it. For this to be correct, two things must be true: 1) coded replication would be too complex to emerge first, and 2) non-coded replication had to be feasible as the starting point. The paper's model (relying on many other papers) is simply that life arose through monomers, followed by polymers, acting as catalysts in autocatalytic reactions that generate an increasing number of different polymers. As the diversity of polymers increased, so did the probability of a catalytic pathway to every member polymer.

Another paper[163] posits a reasonable emergence of nucleic acids from monomers prior to the existence of enzymes (the RNA world hypothesis). The logically proposed sequence (all backed up by theories, formulas, chemical equations, and experimental observations) was:

1. **Self-condensation** – where nucleotide monomers aggregated by themselves into supramolecular assemblies and then linked together to create nucleic acid polymers.
2. **Template-directed** – where the template backbone was a pre-existing nucleic acid polymer that determined the nucleobase sequence of the polymer product.

This is an intramolecular, covalent model.

To continue with the earlier paper, some of these larger polymers could have spontaneously adhered to one another (intermolecular, noncovalent interactions), forming a spherical vesicle that was prone to fission or budding. Thus, you have a very rough model of a highly random, non-coded, protocell-enabled replication. These new vesicles "inherited" polymers from their parent vesicles, and if they lasted long enough in their environment, the process continued (fitness, discussed later in Section 5.2).

### 4.8.6.3 INTERMOLECULAR SELF-ASSEMBLING

The success of intermolecular self-assembling is determined by five characteristics of the system:[164]

- **Components** – a self-assembling system consists of a group of macromolecules that interact with one another. These macromolecules may be the same or different. Their interaction leads from some less ordered state to a more ordered state.
- **Interaction** – self-assembly occurs when macromolecules that are complementary in shape interact with one another through a balance of attractive and repulsive interactions. These interactions are generally noncovalent, but weak covalent bonds can also be involved.
- **Adjustability** – for self-assembly to generate ordered structures, the bonds must be adjustable or even reversible.
- **Environment** – self-assembly normally takes place in a solution or at an interface to allow the required motion of the components.
- **Mass transport** – for self-assembly to occur, the macromolecules must be mobile, typically through thermal motion.

Intermolecular self-assembling requires a protected, stable space to do its assembling. During abiogenesis, that would be the protocell. Working in the lab, a group of researchers[165] attempted to replicate this environment and observe the results. They started with a model composed of lipid vesicles, a membrane-impermeable receptor, and a membrane-permeable ligand. They showed how compartmentalization modulated the interaction between the receptor and its ligand. This confinement stabilized complex self-assembled inter-molecular structures and the formation of long-range assemblies. The effect rendered complex self-assembled biomolecules robust and persistent. The formation of these assemblies did not require the prior confinement of all components but only of the key building blocks that could not pass out through the impermeable membrane. The necessary additional reagents required for this self-assembly passed into the protocell through the selective membrane. They believe that this confinement effect would have played a role in the increase in complexity within protocells during abiogenesis.

The emergence of vesicles and protocells discussed back in Section 4.8.2 is the intermolecular self-assembly of biomolecule aggregates.

### 4.8.6.4 INTERMOLECULAR RECOMBINING

Many papers I reviewed stated that one cannot have evolution without reproduction (vertical, parent/child), but I can envision a world that is solely driven by self-assembly and horizontal recombining of biomolecules between protocells that then spontaneously split into *variant* protocells. This is enough for the other abiogenesis mechanisms to operate before vertical-transfer mechanics emerged. This is also a defining process for prokaryotes.

Earlier, I introduced horizontal and vertical intermolecular recombining. In this section, I will move closer to biology by discussing horizontal and vertical gene transfer at a basic level.

*Horizontal Gene Transfer*

Horizontal gene transfer is the transmission of DNA between different genomes. The transfer can take place through *transformation* (spatial locality), *conjugation* (direct connection), and *transduction* (viruses). More broadly, this *horizontal evolution* can occur through species hybridization in eukaryotes, horizontal gene transfer in prokaryotes, recombination and reassortment in viruses, viral integration in eukaryotes, and fusion of genomes of symbiotic species.[166] Examples of gene transfer between species include:

- Bacteria to fungi
- Bacteria to plant
- Plants to plants
- Fungi to insects
- Humans to protozoan
- Bacteria to insects
- Viruses to plants
- Human genome – perhaps 100 out of 20,000 genes
- Bacteria to animals
- Plants to animal
- Plants to fungi

A research paper[167] concluded that thousands of foreign genes are expressed in all the animals, including humans, obtained through horizontal gene transfer.

How heavily horizontal recombining dominated abiogenesis directly impacts scientists' best efforts to describe evolution through the tree of life metaphor that no longer fits the research. At the same time, it challenges the concept of the last universal common ancestor (LUCA) at the root of that tree. Better metaphors would be of a mosaic to describe the histories combined in individual entities and of a net to visualize the effects of horizontal recombining. Instead of a tree or network, in an advanced paper[170] the authors propose "a set of higher-dimensional objects with well-defined topological properties."

I am introducing *symbiosis* and related concepts here because these processes probably existed before LUCA. Let me break down the terms:[168]

- **Symbiosis** –any type of close and long-term biological interaction between two different biological organisms.

- **Symbiont** – an organism in a symbiotic relationship with another organism.
- **Symbiogenesis** – the genesis of a new species or kind of life through the merger of two or more existing species.
- **Endosymbiosis** – the symbiogenetic process and the resulting state in which one partner (species) lives inside another.
- **Endosymbiont** – an organism that exists in an endosymbiotic relationship inside another organism.
- **Endosymbiogenesis** – the origin of a new lineage because of endosymbiosis.

A great example of symbiosis is *biological nitrogen fixation* (BNF) – a process by which molecular nitrogen in the air is converted into ammonia in the soil. The bacteria responsible for nitrogen fixation are called *diazotrophs*. These bacteria have symbiotic relationships with plant groups, especially legumes. BNF is essential to life because nitrogen compounds are required for the biosynthesis of all nitrogen-containing organic compounds, such as amino acids and proteins, nucleoside triphosphates, and nucleic acids. Atmospheric nitrogen is a nonreactive molecule that makes up most of the atmosphere (78%) and is metabolically useless to all but a few microorganisms, while ammonia is metabolized by most. After photosynthesis, BNF is the second most important biological process on Earth.

Endosymbiosis includes a broad range of interaction types, from harmful (parasitic) to beneficial (mutualistic) and applies to organisms living anywhere within the host body, such as within tissues or cells. The endosymbiont can be transmitted horizontally (each new generation acquires free-living symbionts from the environment) or vertically (the symbiont is transferred directly from parent to offspring).

It is a well-established theory that mitochondria and plastids evolved from free-living bacteria (an alpha-proteobacterium) that merged into a symbiotic relationship with a vesicle (originally a prokaryotic cell) – symbiogenesis. It eventually became an organelle in what was emerging to become a eukaryotic cell. Since the discovery of the hydrogenosome,[169] one can add it to that list, although the actual evolutionary path is still hotly debated.[170]

Endosymbiogenesis has substantial evidence,[171] including the following:

- Mitochondria and plastids each have DNA that is separate from the DNA in the cell's nucleus and is only passed down through females because sperm do not have mitochondria.
- Mitochondria and plastids' DNA are circular, like bacterial DNA.
- New mitochondria and plastids only arise from binary fission, which is the same way that bacteria asexually reproduce. This fission occurs inside the host, independent of, but coordinated with, the host's replication.
- The genome of mitochondria and the Rickettsiales proteo-bacteria are so similar that it suggests that mitochondria are closely related to these bacteria.
- Plastids appear to be related to nitrogen-fixing filamentous cyanobacteria.

The latest study searching for a possible "missing link" between prokaryotic and eukaryotic cells has generated a lot of excitement in the field of evolutionary biology.[172] From deep marine sediment, the authors isolated and grew an archaeon/prokaryotic organism called Prometheoarchaeum that is anaerobic, extremely slow growing (dividing once every 14-25 days, taking them 12 years to get enough!), and lives off amino acids. Based on data obtained from that cultivation, genomics, and literature interpretations, the authors proposed a model for *eukaryogenesis* named the entangle–engulf–endogenize (aka E3) model. It is more sophisticated than the model where, in a single step, a prokaryotic cell ingested and endosymbiotically held onto a mitochondrion and became a eukaryotic cell.

The E3 model suggests that prokaryotes first consumed amino acids and provided H2 to attached sulfate-reducing bacteria and O2 to attached aerobic bacteria (*entangle*). Then, any beneficial interaction (primitive endosymbiosis and carriers of biomolecules) would have increased over time, resulting in engulfment and eventual ATP/ADP carriers (*engulf*). Finally, there would be an internal delegation of catabolism and ATP generation to the endosymbiont and establishment of a symbiont-to-host ATP channel (*endogenize*), resulting in eukaryotes. All of this would have been driven by abiogenesis mechanics.

An interesting discovery in the study was that although Prometheoarchaeum had no nucleus, it did have many of the proteins found only in today's eukaryotes, meaning that these proteins existed and had functions in prokaryotes before they provided the same and other functions in eukaryotes.

Once this process began, what happened to the *engulfed* ancestor of mitochondria under evolutionary mechanics? This has been explored in an in-depth study, "From Endosymbiont to Host-Controlled Organelle: The Hijacking of Mitochondrial Protein Synthesis and Metabolism."[173] The bacterial-like metabolism of this early alpha-proteobacterium endosymbiont differed substantially from that of modern mitochondria. The authors compared a reconstructed set of genes representing the mitochondrial ancestor and compared it with those of modern mitochondria. They found that pathways for protein synthesis and those involved in energy conversion have been retained in the mitochondrion, whereas those involved in replication, transcription, cell division, transport, regulation, and signal transduction have been replaced by eukaryotic proteins.

A summary with nice pictures of the leading theories can be found in "Hypothesis and the Origin of Eukaryotic Cell."[174] A rich analysis that distinguishes between gradualist and symbiogenesis theories of horizontal transfer is in "Symbiogenesis, gradualism, and mitochondrial energy in eukaryote evolution."[175]

Another potential source of horizontal gene transfer is temporary symbiogenesis,[176] whereby species joined together, resulting in increased fitness (Section 5.2), then later separated.

*Vertical Gene Transfer*

Vertical gene transfer is a general term that includes all forms of replication. As I stated earlier, I do not think this was mandatory (it all depends on your definitions) for the emergence of biological evolution. This position lends support to the "metabolism first" abiogenesis theory.

In an interesting paper titled, "Emergence of Self-Reproduction in Cooperative Chemical Evolution of Prebiological Molecules,"[177] Fishkis (2010) developed a theoretical model proposing that amino acid and nucleotide monomers were available in the prebiotic environment. Subsequently, polymerization of amino acids and nucleotides occurred on mineral surfaces, the oligonucleotides served as templates for self-replication and translation of peptide compositional sequences, and some peptides served as weak catalysts. The model output was the emergence of self-replicating molecular systems consisting of oligonucleotide templates and peptide catalysts. The model points to a prebiotic emergence of simple biomolecular replication, which could have then continued through complexification to full reproduction.

### 4.8.6.5 INTERMOLECULAR DETACHING

For these complex molecules to be available for recombination, there must be a process of intermolecular "detachment." Whether the process is based on a loose intermolecular association that more easily separates or a tight connection that is severed in a controlled manner, this material must be made available for recombination.

This detaching alone can act as a rudimentary form of replication, where an entity can reach a limiting size and then split apart, perhaps when some critical ratio of surfactants (its boundary) versus core volume (its internal biomolecules) is passed, resulting in two entities with individual boundaries and similar contents. This would not require that the original entity carry any information about its *descendants*, as template-based replication would.

As discussed earlier, if you combine autocatalytic intermolecular growth with intermolecular detachment, then you get an early form of replication that does not require that the biomolecules carry any descendant information.

A journal article[178] presents a theory of an information-free protocell based on a micellar system and a single autocatalytic reaction that serves as metabolism. The protocell was driven away from equilibrium by the supply of precursors, which had higher internal energy than the surfactants that build up the micelles. The metabolism transformed precursor molecules into new surfactants of the protocell. The number of surfactants increased while, at the same time, the volume of the hydrophobic core became smaller. When a critical ratio of surfactants versus core volume was passed, the aggregates became unstable and divided into two daughter protocells.

## 4.8.7 INTERMOLECULAR SELF-REPLICATING

### 4.8.7.1 FUNDAMENTALS

Before the ability to self-replicate through controlled division emerged, random detachment and recombination of biomolecules and entities were the only ways that entities could change. Eventually, self-replicating would have emerged as the second way.

A molecule that is self-replicating is the reactant in a chemical reaction that has as a product molecule that is of identical composition to the reactant. When the newly formed product continues in the same process with the same results, the self-replicating system is autocatalytic. Paraphrased from "A self-replicating ligase ribozyme"[179] but with all the sloppy teleology removed.

I think there is still a language problem here in that intermolecular self-replicating does not mandate that the reactant is one molecule nor that the replicant is identical to the reactant. The reactant could be a somehow interrelated molecular set, and the product could be only *like* the reactant. That would be messier but sufficient to get things going on their variant-entity way.

Abiogenesis and evolution must include intermolecular replicators. If not, then there are no "results" to add to, no success to be continued, no progression. It cannot start from the beginning every time – it must build on the material created from previous steps. These replicators must have three parts:[180]

1. A *coded representation of the replicator* – representation of the copy to be copied.
2. A *mechanism to copy the coded representation* – the instructions to copy the copy.
3. A *mechanism for affecting construction within the host environment of the replicator* – the ability to build the copy based on the instructions using available materials.

This definition is correct but a little misleading at first glance. The "copy" that is the result of the "copying" may or may not be an identical "copy," i.e., replicating is not necessarily producing a replicant. The instructions may be making a copy that is different from the source. Think of replication as a mechanism for information storage and propagation. More on that later. We will also discuss replication that takes place with and without a *template*.

Keep in mind that this intermolecular "replicator" has no "intent." All it does is work on what is there, not even accurately. It cannot direct its process with any goal in mind, i.e., it *does not respond* to its environment.

## 4.8.7.2 Intermolecular Self-Replicating

A *self-replicating molecule* directs the covalent assembly of component molecules to form a product that is of identical composition to the parent. When the newly formed product can also direct the assembly of more identical product molecules, the self-replicating system is *autocatalytic*. The prebiotic replication of information-coding molecules is an essential pre-requisite of the *Initial Darwinian Ancestor* (IDA).

All biological systems self-replicate through a division of labor between the template storage of genetic information (DNA) and the application of genetic information (RNA) to produce catalysts (proteins) – *vertical gene transfer*. Only self-replication can enable heredity. This could not have emerged in full bloom but had to follow incremental emergent steps.

Let me give you a taste of some of the different hypotheses concerning the emergence of life that include this replication process.

## RNA-First Hypothesis

The RNA world hypothesis is that RNA once functioned as the principal catalyst and informational storage molecule before DNA and dedicated proteins. This hypothesis proposes that many of the roles played by RNA today existed in the prebiotic period. Proteins with higher catalytic efficiencies superseded RNA's early enzymatic activities, and DNA, with its greater chemical stability, largely assumed RNA's informational role.[181]

RNA can be both genetic material (like DNA) and a biological catalyst (like protein enzymes). The existence of both genetic material and ribozymes would have allowed for evolutionary mechanics to act on these enzymes, later being replaced by protein-based enzymes. The argument is that you need pre-RNA to support any replication. Supporting this, researchers have produced RdRp in the lab that can catalyze their synthesis from activated monomers.[182]

The evolution of RdRp is linked with the evolution of RNA viruses because it is responsible for the replication of RNA viral genomes. In a recent paper, de Farias et al. (2017)[183] the researchers performed a comparative analysis of ancestral structural models and modern proteins for RdRp using the Protein Database.[184] The results suggest that a ribozyme with polymerase activity could have bound with a simple cofactor, performing the functions of replication of some information stored on RNA molecules. The RdRp were then formed by translation of the junction of proto-tRNAs.

RNA molecules can function both as GENOTYPE and PHENOTYPE, hence raising the possibility of Darwinian selection and protocellular evolution at the RNA level in the absence of DNA or proteins (perhaps a component of the IDA). Some studies have proposed that the pre-RNA molecules could share the properties of intron-derived ribozymes. In a study back in 1989, "Circular RNAs: Relics of precellular evolution?"[185] the researchers proposed that an alternate starting point – viroids and satellite RNAs – and introns could have emerged from circular RNAs. The authors wrote, "Their small size and circularity would have enhanced probability of their survival in error-prone, primitive self-replicating RNA systems and assured complete replication without the need for initiation or termination signals."

A proposed pre-RNA candidate[186] was asymmetrical (chiral) polymers constructed from nucleoside (nucleotides without a phosphate group) analogs working within a non-cyclical system that would have evolved to RNA, and finally DNA.

Studies of RETROVIRUSES led to the first demonstrated synthesis of DNA from RNA templates. These retrovirus transcription processes may have first caused DNA to be used as genetic material, leading to cellular organisms using the more stable DNA instead of RNA. It is thought that viruses originated before DNA when cells still had genomes made of RNA.[187] So, the emergence sequence proposed is RNA, then retroviruses, then DNA.

There are many other papers that support or build on the RNA world hypothesis.[188,189,190,191,192,193,194,195,196,197,198,199,200,201]

*Metabolism-First Hypothesis*

In this hypothesis, metabolism emerged before genetics. This hypothesis says that 1) enzymes driving metabolic reactions emerged before RNA, and 2) these enzymes also exhibited replicating functions that led to more complex informational molecules.

On the first point, one of the conclusions in "The RNA world and the origin of metabolic enzymes"[202] is that "metabolic reactions similar to those used in modern cells did not necessarily originate from the evolutionary selection of complex catalysts, but instead that they are able to occur under the chemical conditions that prevailed in the Archaean sea." Archaea include the extremophilic microorganisms that live only at extremes of temperature, pH, salts, pressure, or a combination of these. (I did not need to add that last sentence, but I just loved typing the word *extremophilic*.)

On the second point, research that was just published in 2018 tells a story about a potential candidate/process for abiogenetic replication based on peptides alone. In "A prebiotic template-directed peptide synthesis based on amyloids,"[203] amyloids (fibrous aggregates of short protein fragments, or peptides) were shown to have the ability to self-replicate in the lab. Previous research showed that amyloid structures can spontaneously form from simple amino acids that probably already existed under prebiotic conditions. Under diverse and feasible reaction conditions, amyloids are a candidate for abiogenetic replication. This may have been an early step along the way to RNA and, eventually, DNA. This has been laid out more rigorously in "Organoautocatalysis: Challenges for experiment and theory."[204]

Before writing this book, I was familiar with the biological taxonomy of "Domain, Kingdom, Phylum, Class, Order, Family, Genus, Species." If you need any help remembering the terms, then memorize "Dreamy kids play chess on fat green spiders." Did you know that proteins also have a taxonomy? It is "Class, Fold, Superfamily, Family, Protein Domain, Species, Domain." That, I have not memorized. As I introduced much earlier, proteins are three-dimensional structures of chained amino acids. Detailed analysis of the fold of a protein is often required to reveal its evolutionary history.

Kim and Caetano-Anolles (2012) avoided the lab and performed a statistical analysis of 2,397 protein fold families in 420 proteomes (all the proteins in an organism at a given moment) of free-living organisms to develop phylogenomic trees.[205] These trees defined timelines of domain appearance, with time spanning from the origin of proteins to the present. Timelines were segmented into five different evolutionary phases, according to patterns of sharing of fold families among domains: (1) a primordial protein world, (2) the rise of Archaea, (3) the rise of Bacteria from the common ancestor of Bacteria and Eukarya, (4) the rise of Eukarya, and (5) Eukarya diversification.

The researchers concluded that metabolic domains evolved earlier than informational domains involved in translation and transcription, supporting the metabolism-first hypothesis rather than the RNA-world scenario. They further suggested that the archaeal ancestor is more ancient than the ancestors of other domains. The findings in the paper, "Systems chemistry of ⊓-amino acids and peptides," support this hypothesis,[206] and findings in the paper "Lack of evolvability in self-sustaining autocatalytic networks constraints metabolism-first scenarios for the origin of life," bashes it.[207]

In a paper that seems to take all this previous work into account,[208] Liu and Sumpter (2018) developed a more comprehensive model for chemical reaction systems (using a systems chemistry approach) that accounts for energetics, kinetics, and the conservation law of thermodynamics. They found that:

1. Some systems are collectively catalytic, while others are self-replicating.
2. Many alternative chemical universes often contain one or more such systems.
3. It is possible to construct a self-replicating system where the entropy of some parts spontaneously decreases.
4. Complex self-replicating molecules can emerge spontaneously and easily from simple chemical reaction systems through a sequence of transitions.

Their model showed that complexity can evolve from simplicity stage by stage. It gives insights into three issues related to the emergence of life.

1. The first RNA molecule was likely produced by this incremental procedure, which provides theoretical support to "metabolism-first" theories.
2. Prebiotic Earth went through many stages in which different self-replicating systems existed using different material compositions.
3. Collectively-catalytic and self-replicating systems generate many more types of new molecules. These new molecules in turn make more catalytic and autocatalytic reactions feasible.

*Both-at-the-Same-Time Hypothesis (co-evolution of polynucleotides and polypeptides)*

Another hypothesis acknowledges the challenges of independent and time-boxed emergence of proteins and nucleic acids – integrated emergence. Self-replication has its own three building blocks that may have emerged in an integrated fashion (within some form of a protocell) due to their tight interdependencies:[209,210]

1. Genetic code (the nucleotides) – the map, eventually emerging as DNA.
2. Protein synthesis (the amino acids and peptides) – the production, eventually emerging as RNA.
3. Nucleic acid replication – the future variants.

The paper, "Evolution of the genetic code, protein synthesis and nucleic acid replication," seems to address this challenge but at a level of biochemistry and genetics beyond my ability to fully understand it. Basically, it shows that nucleotides, peptides, polynucleotides, and polypeptides would have emerged in a parallel way – some acting as catalysts and others as stabilizers. Protein synthesis would have then enabled nucleic acid replication, and the self-replication engine would have begun to function.

In a later paper, "Formamide and the origin of life,"[211] researchers demonstrated a similar, integrated path from a commonly available molecule – formamide. They wrote,

> The most abundant three-atoms organic compound in the interstellar environment is hydrogen cyanide HCN, the most abundant three-atoms inorganic compound is water H2O. The combination of the two results in the formation of formamide H2NCOH. We have explored the chemistry of formamide in conditions compatible with the synthesis and the stability of compounds of potential pre-genetic and pre-metabolic inter-est. We discuss evidence showing (i) that all the compounds necessary for the build-up of nucleic acids are easily obtained abiotically, (ii) that essentially all the steps leading to the spon-taneous generation of RNA are abiotically possible, (iii) that the key compounds of extant metabolic cycles are obtained in the same chemical frame, often in the same test tube.

In an even later paper, "A prebiotic template-directed peptide synthesis based on amyloids,"[208] the authors showed in the lab that amyloids (special aggregates of proteins composed of short peptides) can direct the sequence-selective, regioselective, and stereoselec-tive condensation of amino acids. The sequential addition of amino acids to a peptide in a self-replicative manner is a prerequisite for the development of life. Amyloid fibers have been shown to arise spontaneously from amino acids under prebiotic conditions, which supports the possibility that peptides, acting as both informational and catalytic entities, preceded life on Earth.

In an interesting paper, "The ribosome as a missing link in the evolution of life,"[31] on how the metabolism-first and/or genes-first worlds may have evolved into IDAs, Meredith and Robert Root-Bernstein (2015) suggest that a ribosome-like entity was one of the key intermediaries between prebiotic and cellular evolution.

The ribosome is a self-organizing complex composed of both polynucleotides and proteins, and it performs a series of chemical reactions that translate genetic information into proteins. Ribosomes are not thought to carry genetic information or the genetic information required to encode their structures and functions. In the above-mentioned paper, the researchers tested the hypothesis that the ribosome evolved before cellular life and that ribosomal RNA (rRNA) had the capability of genetically encoding its own transcription and translation apparatus. This represented a primitive genome that encoded the genetic information needed to direct ribosomal replication, translation, and self-organization. Therefore, rRNA should encode the tRNAs and proteins necessary to ribosomal function.

To get technical, the authors show evidence that:

- The entire set of tRNAs for all 20 amino acids are encoded in the rRNAs of a strain of E. coli.
- Nucleotide sequences that could encode key fragments of ribosomal proteins and many enzyme types are also found in the rRNAs.
- Every sequence of bases in rRNA has information encoding more than one of these functions, in addition to acting as a structural component of the ribosome.

rRNA is not just a structural scaffold for proteins but the remnant of a primordial genome that may have encoded a self-organizing, self-replicating, auto-catalytic intermediary between macromolecules and cellular life.

The evolution of replicating ribosomes assumes that the necessary precursor molecules (sugars, bases, nucleosides, nucleotides, amino acids, etc.) were either readily available through inorganic, prebiotic reactions or by the simultaneous evolution of other protocells capable of catalyzing these prebiotic reactions.

The Root-Bernstein's work does not explain the evolution of DNA, but it provides hints about how and why DNA storage of information may have evolved. They suggest that DNA was a by-product of RNA replication since many of the RNA-encoded protein sequences have DNA-related functions.

I have found many other papers that propose similar hypotheses that I will not detail here.[212,213,214,215,216]

*Pre-Enzyme, Pre-Compartment Autocatalytic World*

I am including this possibility to stretch your mind the way that it stretched mine. I was fortunate that I read this paper – "Modern views of ancient metabolic networks"[217] – after digesting maybe 500 others. Of the many observations it makes, I am going to focus on just a few that were novel to me. I will then risk stating a conclusion that the authors do not. They start by clarifying that no molecule in a cell self-replicates in reality; rather, replication is actually *collective auto-catalysis*. They write that "the capacity for an ensemble of chemicals to enhance or catalyze the synthesis or import of its own components, enabling a positive feedback mechanism that can lead to their sustained amplification." They then challenge cellular self-reproduction as the level at which life and its emergence should be understood and propose that autocatalytic/metabolic networks may have existed in a broader chemical space, effectively generating molecular ecosystems before the emergence of spatially and chemically well-defined protocells. These metabolic reactions were possibly catalyzed by small organic molecules, metal ions, minerals, short RNA polymers, prebiotic amino acids, or peptides that could have been incorporated into protein enzymes as catalytic cores or cofactors.

The authors do not address it explicitly, but these non-compartmental metabolic networks would have been *captured* within a vesicle, resulting in increased concentration, protection from parasites, etc. Most importantly, these entities would then have their own identity as discussed in Section 4.8.2. What I propose is that *those protocells were the first IDAs!* I would love to get the reaction of the scientific community on my conclusion. Another paper, "The Origins of Cellular Life,"[218] focuses on the various processes that could have led to the emergence of membranes and genetic polymers and their assembly into encapsulated nucleic acids. The processes that allowed for their replication seems to start from that point. A third paper, "The Behavior-Based Hypercycle: From Parasitic Reaction to Symbiotic Behavior,"[219] begins with the premise that "the formation of a pre-biotic individual system does not necessarily require a special compartment; some dissipative structures are able to self-organize their spatiotemporal individuation, for instance in the form of chemical gradients. These kinds of individuals can exhibit adaptive behavior in an incompletely mixed spatial medium, especially selective self-movement in a chemical gradient." The authors then go on to build a working sustainable, evolvable model of such an environment.

*Virus World*[220]

To continue with the pre-compartment world, the virus world hypothesis is based on an abiogenetic model in which the emergence of genetic diversity predates the emergence of biological cells, enabling widespread gene mixing in *genetic pools*. Modern viruses and other selfish agents are inferred to descend from these genetic elements. Several genes coding for key proteins are shared by many types of viruses but are absent in cellular organisms. RNA viruses would evolve first, followed by retroviruses and DNA viruses that then became intracellular parasites once bacteria and archaea emerged. Selection against parasites that would kill off the host would lead to the emergence of more temperate viruses and defense mechanisms. Eukaryotic viruses then emerged from the recombination of genes from BACTERIOPHAGES, archaeal viruses, plasmids, and eukaryotic genomes.

Noncoding DNA sequences (introns) are evidence of a major infiltration of the virus world into the cellular world. The selfish nature of introns and their place in the virus world are evident, and eukaryote introns are believed to have migrated from the mitochondrial endosymbiont at the dawn of eukaryotic evolution. In complex eukaryotes, such as mammals, introns comprise about 30% of the genome, while about 60% of the genome consists of noncoding regions that are full of mobile elements in various stages of decay. Thus, most of our genome is derived from this ancient Virus World.

## 4.8.8 AN ENVIRONMENT OF OTHER ENTITIES

### 4.8.8.1 FUNDAMENTALS

Environment merits being repeated but in a different context. The environment (or system) has the matter and energy that the entities receive/release, but it also contains other entities that can receive/release this finite matter and energy. The environment's matter and energy received by entities are now either:

- No longer available to an entity if received by other entities.
- Available to an entity by "receiving" it from other entities.
- Available to other entities by their "receiving" it from an entity.

The matter received/released can be simple (e.g., oxygen, water, hydrogen, nitrogen, potassium, carbon dioxide, iron) or complex (e.g., sugar, protein). Some of the simple and most of the complex matter was somehow the result of chemical reactions taking place within entities or the entities themselves (see symbiosis later). Examples of energy are sunlight (low entropy) and heat (high entropy).

### 4.8.8.2 AN ENVIRONMENT OF OTHER ENTITIES

Protocells have selectively permeable membranes that can receive and retain larger biomolecules to feed their autocatalytic reactions while releasing smaller ones as waste. But how do protocells exist in an environment of other protocells under diverse competitive dynamics?

In a paper in synthetic protocell biology, researchers demonstrated that prebiotic vesicles could take lipids from each other.[221]

This process is a result of asymmetries in the composition of the vesicle membranes, and, when lipid resource is limited, this process translates into competition amongst the vesicles. This demonstrates a basic form of protocell-level selection. Another paper[222] showed that under a model of efficient or uninhibited autocatalysis, all of a protocell's components follow an exponential catalytic growth independent of the replication efficiency of the involved subsystems. These results suggest that protocell assemblies become the main selective unit.

In Section 4.8.7.2, I discussed some hypotheses as to how life emerged – polynucleotides first, polypeptides first, and co-evolution of polynucleotides and polypeptides. Here, I include my favorite theory that throws the rest out the window and emphasizes self-assembling.[223] The authors hypothesize that:

- Life began in a prebiotic environment of co-evolving populations of composomes (assortments of micelle-like or gel-like macromolecular aggregates).
- The diverse set of a composome's macromolecules resulted from molecular complementarity among available prebiotic compounds generated by abiotic mechanisms.
- Composomes varied in properties and functions, such as stability, interaction with other composomes, buffering their local environment, catalysis, fission, fusion, and selective accumulation of molecules from solution.
- Composomes were affected by natural selection.
- Fission permitted molecular replication based on composition. The division did not need to yield identical daughters to preserve the range of phenotypes.
  o Genetic information (and inherited genotypes) arose only after compartmentalization of structure/function in composomes that allowed polymerization reactions to be carried out.
- Fusion contributed to composomal variability and diversity.

- Catalytic functions eventually resulted in autocatalytic and mutually catalytic networks that led to metabolism.

Compartmentalization leading to membrane formation arose by three mutually reinforcing processes. As micelles grew, those composed of appropriate subunits spontaneously encapsulated aqueous materials. Internal compartmentalization happened within the lipid membrane due to self-assortment among different components. Molecular complementarity among composomes would have provided mechanisms for storage via precipitation, solubility, or permeability.

  o Such mechanisms maintained and segregated the composomal composition stably and robustly. Evolution resulted in the protein-studded lipid bilayers in contemporary cells.
  o Maintenance of these systems away from equilibrium would have emerged by the evolution of energy-trapping systems and polymerization.
  o Given a flow of usable free energy, composomes functioned as non-equilibrium structures.
- The existence of chemical interfaces created templates upon which self-replicating molecules (polynucleotides, peptides, or proteins) were synthesized, permitting the evolution of informational replication by molecular templating.

Many lab studies that were mentioned in the journal article show how these composomes could have self-assembled and grown. (These studies were primarily performed by the paper's many contributing authors) Such binding formed larger aggregates that were stabilized against degradative processes, conferring a survival advantage so that they could accumulate. Results of the lab studies included:

- Specific interactions between small molecules in aqueous solutions lead to self-assembly.

- Lipids will spontaneously form micelles.
- Nucleotides and polynucleotides will bind to lipids.
- Fission occurs spontaneously in liposomes in the presence of a supply of amphiphilic constituents.
- Polynucleotides, amino acids, and lipids will associate to form regular structures with some similarity to a bacteriophage.
- Micelle-to-vesicle transitions are promoted by the presence of peptides and proteins.
- Partial incompatibility of molecules enhances self-assembly.
- Peptides can self-assemble into non-covalently bound polymers and can self-aggregate through complementarity.

Shenhav, Oz, and Lancet (2007) offer a sufficient supporting article.[224]

## 4.8.9 RECEIVES AND RELEASES MATTER AND ENERGY

### 4.8.9.1 FUNDAMENTALS

This brings us back to the concepts of inside and outside. The discussion of thermodynamic frameworks leads to the conclusion that entities (inside) receive matter and energy from the surrounding system (outside) to create their autocatalytic reactions. The entities are not closed systems, and a mechanism must enable their increased order from the external environment. This can only happen via the boundary between what is internal and external to the entity. The receiving of this matter and energy through the boundary is what results in the increase in order (negative entropy) within the entity. The release of matter and energy is also required to make possible the dynamic steady state discussed earlier.

From a thermodynamics perspective, these entities receive and utilize matter and low-entropy energy and release high-entropy heat and waste. This maintains the thermodynamic disequilibrium between inside and outside when the entity's self-organizing and self-maintaining processes are operating. When these mechanics stop operating, a thermodynamic equilibrium between the entity and the environment is reached through a breakdown in the boundary.

From a kinetic/complexification perspective, these entities must be able to release biomolecules into the environment through their barrier. This requires macromolecular detachment within the entity, followed by those biomolecules somehow traversing the barrier through its membrane.

## 4.8.9.2 RECEIVES AND RELEASES MATTER AND ENERGY

*The Protocell Boundary*

Earlier, I focused on the maintenance of thermodynamic disequilibrium, and separately, I discussed the boundary of a protocell. Now, I am going to shift to how the functionally protective lipid barrier that defines the protocell's boundary also allowed for the flow of nutrients and waste products. Most of this is taken from "Nutrient Uptake by Protocells: A Liposome Model System."[225]

All contemporary living cells and many of their organelles are defined by lipid-bilayer membranes (i.e., liposomes). These liposomes are relatively impermeable, and complex protein transport systems have evolved to tunnel through the membrane. Since these sophisticated transport systems were initially absent in protocells, passive diffusion across bilayer membranes had to be sufficient to take up nutrients and chemical energy from the environment. These protocell barriers must have had a selective permeability that permitted diffusion of smaller biomolecules (monomers and waste products) while retaining the polymers produced by metabolism.

In studies referenced in the aforementioned paper, small solute molecules, such as water, glycerol, urea, and glucose, could cross the membrane barrier. In their lab, the researchers were able to show that "under certain conditions molecules as large as nucleoside triphosphates can permeate across bilayers composed of an intermediate-chain length lipid (DMPC). Furthermore, the selectivity of these membranes is very high: oligonucleotides as small as dimers are unable to permeate under the same conditions."

Roughly translated, building blocks of DNA, such as ATP, could passively diffuse through the membrane, while larger short DNA/RNA molecules (i.e., oligonucleotides) could not. So, the barrier could pass some smaller complex biomolecules but not the larger, more complex ones. This would enable the retention of increased complexification necessary for the emergence of life.

*Hypercycle Abiogenesis*

Remember all those "world hypotheses" back in Section 4.8.7.2? They focus on which biomolecules came first (e.g., proteins versus RNA) and do not explicitly consider that life comprises high levels of diverse biomolecular interactions. Abiogenesis is not restricted to the emergence of molecular heredity mechanisms and kinetic control over chemical reactions. A semi-empirical (lab, plus model) systems chemistry paper[226] looks at how these diverse molecules may interact and couple, becoming part of more intricate networks and biomolecular assemblies with correspondingly more intricate structural, dynamic, and evolutionary properties. The researchers consider the constraints related to the spatial organization of those processes, like the presence of interfaces, diffusion barriers, semi-permeable compartments, gradients, and osmotic forces. The paper shows how a protocell that produces heterogeneous lipid components spontaneously taken up by a permeable membrane can simultaneously enhance metabolic activity and lead to faster reproduction cycles of the protocells. I think of it as a systems-based "lipid world" hypothesis, first introduced about 20 years earlier.[227]

Although the paper does not reference it, this is a type of abstract model of organization called a *hypercycle* – a special case of the replicator equation. Its key properties include autocatalytic growth competition between cycles, once-for-ever selective behavior, utilization of small selective advantage, rapid evolvability, increased information capacity, and selection against parasitic branches.

### Emergence of Anaerobic Respiration

How was energy stored in protocells? The following is taken from "Small-Molecule Systems Chemistry."[113] Life is a metabolic reaction. Because many metabolic reactions have a net energy consumption (uphill, endergonic), the biochemical pathways of a cell require an energy-releasing (downhill, exergonic) reaction that generates an energy storage medium, usually ATP. Hydrolysis of ATP to ADP and phosphate (Pi) releases energy that pulls the reaction up that hill. This process is universal to life today, but at the onset of metabolism, the biochemistry needed to be simpler.

What came before ATP? The authors discussed a study that modeled the removal of all the reactions from metabolism that were ATP-dependent or involved phosphate-containing cofactors to see if anything remained and whether it was still metabolism. The results revealed ancient but less productive forms of anaerobic chemical energy in a connected reaction network of small carbon compounds, a prevalence of thioesters (common intermediates in many biosynthetic reactions), and enrichment of iron-sulfide-dependent enzymes. They believe that such a sequence might trace the emergence of non-ATP biochemical energy currencies at the evolutionary onset of metabolic networks.

### Emergence of Photosynthesis

The emergence of light-energy-utilizing metabolism was a critical event in prebiotic chemistry. Recent lab work[228] explored a precursor to chlorophyll as a possible mechanism for proto-photosynthesis on primordial Earth. The study provides insight into the emergent functionality of light energy conversion within a hierarchical architecture through the interaction and reaction of prebiotic molecules.

In the lab, a primitive pigment model was built based on the adaptive self-organization of amino acids and metal ions, followed by chemical evolution under hydrothermal conditions. The resulting hybrid microspheres were able to capture ultraviolet and visible light and use it in various photochemical reactions.

Cyanobacteria are sometimes called blue-green algae, even though they are prokaryotes. They are a diverse phylum of bacteria capable of carrying out photosynthesis and are gram-negative, meaning that they have two cell membranes. Plant chloroplasts are considered endosymbiotic cyanobacteria. Both chloroplasts and cyanobacteria have a double membrane, DNA, and ribosomes.

Somewhere around one to two billion years ago, a free-living cyanobacterium entered an early eukaryotic cell, either as food or as an internal parasite, but managed to escape the phagocytic vacuole it was contained in. The new cellular resident quickly became an advantage, providing food for the eukaryotic host, which improved its fitness. Over time, the cyanobacterium was assimilated, and many of its genes were lost or transferred to the nucleus of the host.

Chloroplasts are believed to have arisen after mitochondria since all eukaryotes contain mitochondria, but not all have chloroplasts. This is called serial endosymbiosis – an early eukaryote engulfing the mitochondrion ancestor and some descendants of it then engulfing the chloroplast ancestor, creating a cell with both chloroplasts and mitochondria.

*Emergence of Aerobic Respiration*

The first life forms on Earth came into existence in a world devoid of free oxygen. They used anaerobic processes to provide themselves with energy. At some point, still early in Earth's history, organisms evolved that employed photosynthesis to produce sugar molecules using carbon dioxide obtained from the atmosphere and water. The sugar served as a source of energy, and the process produced oxygen as a by-product. Oxygen was toxic to many anaerobic organisms, but some evolved to use it in a new kind of respiration that provided much more energy than the anaerobic process.

## 4.8.10 INTERMOLECULAR SELF-MAINTAINING

### 4.8.10.1 FUNDAMENTALS

According to my earlier definition, one characteristic of an entity is that it exists over time. This existence is not only about maintaining the "dynamic steady state" of disequilibrium but also about maintaining the entity's chemical composition (a form of identity) through self-regulation. Processes occur, and things break down. Without self-maintenance, the entity would cease being itself.

### 4.8.10.2 INTERMOLECULAR SELF-MAINTAINING

Researchers developed a model of a self-maintaining protocellular system.[229] The model provided a framework to allow the production of a wide variety of components that were potentially useful for metabolic-like organizations, i.e., some components were products of reactions catalyzed by other components whose formation depended recursively on the action of the network. The modeled entities generated new types of components (some being copies) without losing their basic organization and acquired a degree of independence from varying external conditions.

The model contained the following elements:

- Structural membrane elements to assure suitable concentrations of the substrates that have two kinds of components:
    o Structural components capable of self-assembling and physically enclosing the system.
    o Functional components capable of performing tasks like catalysis, transport, and energy transduction.
- Energy-rich biomolecules

- Precursors of each type of biomolecule
- An impermeable substance

In the model, the selective membrane played an important role in the maintenance of the cell and osmotic stability. Different kinetic parameters led to a wide range of stable steady states.

The model presented showed the protocell keeping its steady-state concentrations through self-maintenance, even when the external conditions varied widely. This maintenance was based on the overall properties of the model rather than on the kinetic properties of any single reaction step.

## 4.8.11 ERROR-PRONE

### 4.8.11.1 FUNDAMENTALS

There are three fundamental types of errors that can occur during these processes:

- **During recombination** – the biomolecules from external entities, in some fashion, become part of the entity's internal space, and the biomolecules within an entity can also recombine with each other. A lot of steps must happen to result in this, and random events and mistakes are probably much more prevalent here than in replication since the molecules are much more disparate.
- **During replication** – these are the intermolecular replication errors before DNA existed (abiogenesis) and the DNA replication errors during cell division (evolution). You could call these transcription errors.
- **Outside of recombination and replication** – these are changes caused by exposure to radiation, chemicals, and other environmental stressors that affect the entity.

It's funny that if this replication and recombination were perfect every time and these errors did not occur, then there would be nothing for abiogenetic/evolution mechanics to work on, and, therefore, there would be no abiogenesis/biological anything. All entities, including these variants, continue to be subject to the abiogenesis/biological mechanics, and some will or will not continue to recombine and replicate. Those that do will be the only entities around to maybe recombine and replicate again. Note that even the Matrix from the movie had eight iterations, probably entering the ninth by the end of the series.

### 4.8.11.2 ERROR-PRONE – THE SPECTRUM OF RANDOMNESS

The world before life emerged with its structured genetic instructions and processes had to be one of crazy randomness. Only this randomness, combined with self-replication within entities, enabled evolvability. Imagine a few scenarios:

- Before vesicles and replication, noncovalent successful detaching and combining happened between biomolecules that were in the same locality. The initial event (one could call it compatibility but that touches on teleology) was highly random, but each subsequent success meant that the random events were passing this compatibility on to subsequent variant entities and, therefore, was emerging as *less random.*
- The emergence of vesicles that bound groups of biomolecules meant that the groups were somehow sustaining the boundary, and the boundary was somehow sustaining the groups. Again, this vesicle environment could only emerge through successes that led to a reduction in randomness. This also reduced the randomness of the detaching and combining. Coming from the other direction, *success* was becoming less random as the environment became more complex, requiring that the events had to fit within this complexity or fail.

## 4.8.12 SUBSEQUENT VARIANT ENTITIES

As just mentioned, the only meaningful result of all these other mechanisms is *subsequent variant entities* that then can continue with these mechanisms to generate (or not) more subsequent variant entities. It seems obvious, but abiogenesis and evolution only act on what is available. If an entity and its complexities are no longer available, then the mechanics cease, except to pick up the released matter/energy for use by other entities. You and I are great (and vain) examples of subsequent variant entities.

There is an ongoing debate in the literature on how much of the "tree of life" is a tree versus a network, i.e., how much of the variation is due to vertical versus horizontal transfers. So, the term *subsequent* does not imply a predecessor/descendant (i.e., vertical) relationship. See more on this in Section 4.8.6.4.

## 4.8.13 EMERGENCE IN A PREBIOTIC WORLD

### 4.8.13.1 BIOMOLECULES OBTAINED IN PREBIOTIC EARTH EXPERIMENTS

I have been taking a divide-and-conquer approach to describing the creation and maintenance of biomolecules. Let me bring it back together by providing in one place a list of some of the classes of organic "biogenic" compounds and structures obtained in prebiotic-Earth simulation experiments (sourced from Follmann and Brownson):[230]

- Amino acids and related amino compounds
- Alcohols and carboxylic acids
- Carbohydrates (sugars)
- Hydrocarbons (lipids)
- Peptide bond formation
- (Poly)phosphates
- Purine bases – adenine and guanine

- Pyrimidine bases – in nucleic acids, three types of nucleobases are pyrimidine derivatives: cytosine (C), thymine (T), and uracil (U)
- Pyrimidine nucleotides
- Purine and pyrimidine polyribonucleotides
- Deoxyribonucleotides
- Sulphur compounds, thiols – the functional group of the amino acid cysteine
- Various metabolites – intermediate end products of metabolism

Their point here is this – "carbon atoms, the key element of organic and organismic chemistry, together with a few other light 'hetero' elements (hydrogen, nitrogen, oxygen, sulfur, and phosphorus) can exist in an almost unlimited number of molecular structures held together by stable carbon–carbon and carbon–heteroatom bonds in chains, rings, and heterocycles."

## 4.8.13.2 LUCA AND ITS ENVIRONMENT

In a breakthrough paper, "The physiology and habitat of the last universal common ancestor,"[231] the authors investigated all clusters and phylogenetic trees for six million protein coding genes from sequenced prokaryotic genomes to reconstruct the microbial ecology of LUCA. Among 286,514 protein clusters, they identified 355 protein families that trace to LUCA by phylogenetic criteria. Their functions and properties depict LUCA as:

- Anaerobic (requiring an absence of free oxygen).
- $CO_2$-fixing (electron acceptor) and $H_2$-dependent (electron donor) with a *Wood–Ljungdahl pathway* (a building block for biosynthesis that uses $CO_2$ and $H_2$).
- $N_2$-fixing (required for the biosynthesis of all nitrogen-containing organic compounds, such as amino acids and proteins, nucleoside triphosphates, and nucleic acids).
- Thermophilic (grows best at high temperatures).

- Iron-sulfur clusters (components of electron transfer proteins) and free-radical reaction mechanisms.

The 355 phylogenies are common and point to living clostridia (anaerobic bacteria) and methanogens (archaean that reduces $CO_2$ to methane), whose modern lifestyles resemble those of LUCA.

Not coincidentally, this LUCA archetype inhabited a geochemically active environment rich in $H_2$, $CO_2$, and iron. The data produced in the study support the theory of an autotrophic (fixing inorganic carbon into organic material) LUCA involving the Wood-Ljungdahl pathway in a hydrothermal setting.

## 4.8.14 INTEGRATION

To see if I kept my promise, here is my definition of abiogenetic mechanisms from Section 4.8:

> Abiogenetic mechanics consist of autocatalytic entities in a dynamic steady state. These entities exist within matter and energy and receive, retain, and release matter and energy from, and to, a time- and resource-constrained environment. This environment is within a thermodynamic/kinetic framework, with error-prone intermolecular detaching, recombining, self-replicating, self-maintaining, and self-assembling capabilities that can result in subsequent variant entities.

I have discussed every term in detail, backing it up with current research. If there are still gaps, drop me a note. If you understand everything, you can still drop me a note because I probably still have gaps in my understanding.

# 5 EVOLUTION

*(Evolution) general condition to which all theories, all hypotheses, all systems must bow and which they must satisfy henceforward if they are to be thinkable and true. Evolution is a light which illuminates all facts, a curve that all lines must follow.*
Pierre Eilhard de Chardin, *The Phenomenon of Man*

Now that we have reached the biotic world, wherever we may be with IDAs and LUCA, evolution has kicked in as the way variant entities continue to appear (and disappear). I am not going to cover every aspect of evolutionary theory or how each of life's characteristics (particularly the senses) specifically emerged under the Real Matrix – that is the purpose of textbooks and much of YouTube. What I will do is give you enough of the fundamentals to support my argument that all life is a result of non-directional, non-intentional, non-teleological processes built up by and consisting of the Real Matrix.

## 5.1 INITIAL COMMENTS

A few things you will not find in this section:

- The history of the development of the theory of evolution – everyone *loves* to talk about this subject. I admit that it is very cool, but we do not need to read it 10,000 times to appreciate it.
- Any proof, argument, or evidence for evolution – many, many books and articles spend much of their content on proving (or disproving) evolution. I will not be doing that here. As I said in the beginning, if you do not think evolutionary theory is valid,

then I cannot help you, and I am surprised that you got this far in the book!

- Every detail about evolution – there are plenty of textbooks for that. I am going to mostly limit the topic to support my argument concerning the Real Matrix.
- The timeline of the evolution of life – it had to happen. Exactly what happened and when does not contribute to my argument. You can find nice discussions in many places, including "The evolution of life"[232] and "Timeline of the evolutionary history of life."[233]
- The pairing of evolution with Earth's geological history – this would add unnecessary complexity. If this subject interests you, Kitadai and Maruyama's 2018 paper[234] is the most comprehensive (and technical) source that I discovered.
- The Extended Synthesis debate – empirical discoveries and conceptual advancements have led to the proposal of an extended synthesis theory of evolution. I will not spend time on this topic other than to give you citations of the major papers on the topic[235,236,237,238] and an incomplete list of the proposed revised concepts:[239]
  o Multilevel selection theory
  o Transgenerational epigenetic inheritance
  o Niche inheritance
  o Culture transmission
  o Facilitated variation
  o Evolvability
  o A distinction between micro-evolutionary and macro-evolutionary processes

A few things also really annoyed me when doing this research:

- I think because the theory of evolution has been, throughout its 160+ year history, in conflict with religious fundamentalists and their enablers, a lot of books and journals spend an inordinate number of pages reintroducing its development and the ensuing conflict and then defending it. I know it is not likely, but I would be happy if we could move on and spend our time on helpful things. Or, like I have said elsewhere in this book, since the history is not disputed, why not have everyone agree that one book gets published on the complete history of the development of the theory, and all the other books can then skip that part.

- I had to wade through a lot of creationism and intelligent design garbage. I read each one I came across from cover-to-cover, but it was tedious. The authors were so often deceitful, disingenuous, blinded, self-serving, and/or ignorant. Interesting that they often use "Darwinism" as it was first developed those 160 years ago as a pejorative term so that they can stand it up just to knock it down (in logic, it is called *the fallacy of incomplete evidence*). They have the dastardly habit of conveniently ignoring all the advanced scientific developments that have occurred since then and are continually being developed. It appears that it would be too difficult. What they do not understand (or do not want to), they can safely ignore, especially when it would challenge their point of view. "My mind is made up; do not confuse me with the facts."

- I was infuriated and gravely disappointed by so many authors for their casual and sloppy use of teleology. Maybe they did not realize what they were implying, genuinely believed that these inanimate or non-aware things were working from intent, or knew what they were doing and were following Ernst Mayr's approach to facilitating understanding (see back in Section 2.5) of which I am not a fan. It still drove me crazy, and a lot of my work was spent sifting through their choice of language to discern what was really going on.

- My final annoyance, which became one of my motivations, is that the vast majority of authors had minimal or no awareness of the premise of this book – that humans are all *inside evolution* and unable to look at it from the outside. They all want to appear so smart and above it all that they talk about "animals," "mammals," or "primates" in a way that you know means they think humans are something else! And this is not at all limited to the fundamentalist – it is our *nature*. One of the few exceptions would be Desmond Morris (the author of *The Naked Ape*), but he still often appears to stand on the outside looking into the human species rather than locating his perspective as coming from within it.

## 5.2 THE THEORY OF EVOLUTION

*One general law, leading to the advancement of all organic beings, namely, multiply, vary, let the strongest live and the weakest die.*
Charles Darwin, *On the Origin of Species*

*The chicken is only an egg's way for making another egg.*
Richard Dawkins

The power of the theory of evolution is not only that it is supported by every field of science but also that it is quite easy to understand the basics unless you are permanently prejudiced against it. Let me show you. Here is Wikipedia's definition:

*Evolution is change in the heritable traits of biological populations over successive generations.*

Even more simply, to use Darwin's term, evolution is "descent with modification."

Clear and simple! Let me break the first definition down the same way I did abiogenesis mechanics.

## 5.2.1 EVOLUTION IS CHANGE

The engine of evolution is *non-directional change* regardless of how it comes about. This is about "change," never "new." This change is at the level of the genome and gene expression. What are the sources of this change? Some examples include MUTAGENESIS, GENETIC RECOMBINATION, EXON SHUFFLING, GENE RETROPOSITION, and NETWORK EVOLUTION.

I searched far and wide, only to be surprised as to how little scientists understand the factors that can affect and change gene expression. This appears to be a nascent field of research.

## 5.2.2 IN TRAITS

Even though the underlying change is at the genome level, the observable change and the environmental impact are at the traits or phenome level, measured by *phenome fitness* – a phenotype's reproductive success, which is the average contribution to the gene pool of the next generation that is made by a population of individuals of a specific phenotype.

## 5.2.3 THAT ARE HERITABLE

Heredity is the passing on of genotypes/epigenotypes from parents to their offspring, measured by *genome fitness* (a genotype's replication success, which is the average contribution to the gene pool of the next generation that is made by a population of individuals of a specific genotype). Genotypes/epigenotypes can be passed through various mechanisms:

- Genetic information contained in DNA transmitted via homologous chromosomes – two pieces of DNA within a diploid organism that carry the same genes, one from each parental source.
- All the other ways are placed within the bucket of EPIGENETICS.

Before I move on, I want to point out that genome fitness is radically different from phenome fitness. On one level, evolution is all about successfully passing on traits (phenome) that present themselves to the environment. On another level, it is the DNA (genome) that physically gets passed to new generations. Go back and notice that in the definition of phenome fitness, I used the term *reproductive success*, while for genome fitness, I used *replication success*. This is because the phenome is at the organism level where reproduction occurs, and the genome is at the DNA level where replication occurs.

## 5.2.4 IN BIOLOGICAL POPULATIONS

This is the environment and all the biological entities in it, with all its competition and constraints.

A population or species of organisms typically includes multiple alleles (gene variations, e.g., blood type or eye color) at each gene location among various individuals. The diversity of alleles and genotypes within a population is called *genetic variance*. A population's allele and genotype frequencies can change through natural and sexual selection but also through *genetic drift*, which is simply the effect of chance over the other mechanisms – think of selection as discriminate and genetic drift as indiscriminate. This, of course, is a human interpretation of the process, where the outcome may be different from a prediction based solely on selection. *Gene flow* is the flow of alleles in and out of a population due to the migration of individuals.

## 5.2.5 OVER SUCCESSIVE GENERATIONS

Evolution continues only if the characteristics appear in an organism's descendants – phenotype fitness. Those that are not passed to descendants are no longer in the mix.

- **Natural selection** – acts on the phenotype, but the genotype basis of any phenotype that gives that phenotype a reproductive advantage may become more common in a population. Over time, this process can result in more fit populations within ecological niches and eventually result in the emergence of new species. Natural selection is a key process in the evolution of a population.

- o **Competition** – an interaction between organisms in which the fitness of one is lowered by the presence of another. Competition also acts at the level of the phenotype.
- **Sexual selection** – a mode of natural selection in which members of one biological sex choose mates of the other sex to mate with and compete with members of the same sex for access to members of the opposite sex. Some individuals will have better reproductive success than others within a population, resulting in stronger phenotype fitness.
- **Fertility selection** – the phenotype fitness advantage resulting from the preference of traits that increases the number of offspring.

There is an ongoing debate about which biological "level" is the actual unit of selection, as it can change based on context – which units are interacting, replicating, benefiting, or adapting.[240] Levels include:

- Genome[241,242]
- Phenome
- Hologenome[243]
- Group
- Species

I think that the term "unit of selection" is confusing. I prefer to differentiate between *what selection acts on* and *the selection result*. In evolutionary terms, selection acts on the phenome, and the selection result is the genome. More precisely, it is the *holophenome* (a term I just made up that represents all the traits of the holobiont) and the HOLOGENOME (the genome of the holobiont). Evolution occurs through the competition and survival of competing genes, with gene defined as all its replicas (alleles) existing in the world – *what selection acts on*. Alleles whose *phenotypic effects* benefit their own replication (but not necessarily the fitness of the organism) will be favorably selected relative to their competitor alleles within a population – *the selection result*.

- **Affecting the genome** – segments of DNA that specifically promote their own transmission in competition with other genes by moving within and between (horizontal gene transfer) genomes (mobile genetic elements) include transposons, bacteriophage, plasmids, and even mitochondria and chloroplasts.[244] They can be a recurrent source of coding sequences for the emergence of new genes.[44] *Horizontal genomics* is a new field in biology that is centered on the analysis of DNA sequences in prokaryotic chromosomes that seem to have originated through horizontal gene transfer.[252]
- **Affecting the phenome** – dysregulation can contribute to the appearance and pathology of many neurodevelopmental and neurodegenerative disorders.[245] These mobile elements can also carry genes beneficial for their hosts and/or the neighbors of their hosts.[246]

## 5.3 HIDDEN MULTICELLULAR EUKARYOTE BIASES

*Despite our monumental achievements in philosophy, technology and the arts, to bacteria humans are no more than an organic mass to be utilized for growth and reproduction.*
Sokurenko, Hasty, and Dykhuizen[247]

It in no way affects my conclusions concerning the Real Matrix, but my description so far is incomplete and also just plain wrong since it focuses on *classical* biology and evolution theory that is historically:

1. **Anthropocentric** – equates what is scientifically significant to what is important to the human organism.
2. **Based on petri dishes** – genomic data comes from a single cultured clone, making sequence assembly and annotation tractable.
3. **Observable** – focuses on macrobiotic multicellular organisms while ignoring microbiotic single-cell organisms.
4. **Emphasizing self-proliferation** – genetic vertical transfer along a tree of life.

The rest of this section will challenge those biases, but I must admit here that my proof of the Real Matrix is also fundamentally anthropocentric (i.e., it is most important to me that we humans are the ones locked in it) and focused on the observable (i.e., 95% of my argument emphasizes the roots of perception and behavior).

## 5.3.1 ANTHROPOCENTRIC VERSUS BIOCENTRIC MICROBE RESEARCH

So far, everywhere that I have mentioned the biosphere of microorganisms, it has been in the context of humans as the hosting holobiont. Like all biases, this anthropocentric one has historical roots. Before microscopes, microbes did not exist. Suddenly, they did! The discovered world of microbiology is both extremely complex and unobservable without the aid of advanced technology.

Scientists have primarily studied the metagenome from an anthropocentric perspective to the detriment of a biocentric one. As discoveries have been made in microbiology, research in this field has primarily been directed at benefiting human health and human interests – either focused on those microbes that are useful and need to be exploited, or those that are harmful and need to be controlled or exterminated – while avoiding those that do not interfere with humans.[248] We must move from applied research to pure research to obtain a full understanding of this new (to us) world.

## 5.3.2 CULTURED VERSUS UNCULTURED PROKARYOTES

This brief history is taken from "Environmental Shotgun Sequencing: Its Potential and Challenges for Studying the Hidden World of Microbes,"[249] which is also a good primer on environmental shotgun sequencing. With the invention of the microscope, the first way to identify microorganism species in a sample was to put it under a microscope and see what was there. Then, single cells of a microbial type were grown in isolation from other organisms (cultured) and then looked at. Then, they made billions of copies of every rRNA gene present in a sample and analyzed them. That was followed by what is called shotgun genome sequencing of cultured species. The latest approach is to directly isolate DNA from an environmental sample (uncultured) and then sequence it. With this development of *metagenomics*, a term first coined in 1998,[250] scientists now have the tools to study the *metagenome* (the collective genomes of all microorganisms in a sample/habitat – the complete microbiome), not just what grows in a dish (i.e., expanded to include uncultured microorganisms). In "Metagenomics - a guide from sampling to data analysis,"[251] the author describes the steps involved in a typical metagenomic project.

Metagenomic studies have now shown:

- "Fewer than 0.1% of the microorganisms in soil are readily cultured using current techniques. And, most impressively, the other 99.9% of soil microflora is emerging as a world of stunning, novel genetic diversity. New groups of bacteria have been identified in soil that appear to diverge so deeply from the cultured bacteria that they could represent new phyla, or even new kingdoms of life."[259]
- "We analyzed over 5 Tb of metagenomic sequence data from 3,042 geographically diverse samples to assess the global distribution, phylogenetic diversity, and host specificity of viruses. We discovered over 125,000 partial DNA viral genomes, including the largest phage yet identified, and increased the number

of known viral genes by 16-fold. Half of the predicted partial viral genomes were clustered into genetically distinct groups, most of which included genes unrelated to those in known viruses."[252]

- It is now known that prokaryotes comprise at least half the biomass of the non-viral biosphere and nearly all its physiological biodiversity.[253]

For scientists, there is also a Genomes Online Database that provides access to information regarding genome and metagenome sequencing projects and their associated metadata.[254] Bioinformatic analyses make it possible to mine huge metagenomic datasets and discover general patterns that govern microbial ecosystems.

### 5.3.3 MACROSCALE VERSUS MICROSCALE

This section is taken from "Advances in biodiversity: metagenomics and the unveiling of biological dark matter."[255]

Metagenomic discoveries are showing that the full biosphere is dramatically more complex than previously understood, and that a conception of nature and biological processes based only on multicellular eukaryotes (MCEs) is completely inadequate.

Many core biological concepts are deficient in explaining this expanded world and changing them will be extremely difficult. Quoting the above paper, "Despite MCEs being merely that 'few percent of the whole,' nearly all of classical biology, from Aristotle onwards, has been based on the composition and characteristics of MCEs. To put it bluntly, classical biology has been the study of MCEs by MCEs for MCEs."

**The Effects of Size on Biological Form and Function**

Depending solely on size, organisms exhibit differing ratios of inertial to viscous forces that affect their movement in a medium. The measurement of this is called the *Reynolds number*. For example, a large whale swimming at 10 m/s has a Reynolds number of 300,000,000, while a bacterium moving at 0.01 mm/s has a Reynolds number of 0.00001.

At sufficiently small sizes, mechanical interaction with the environment becomes difficult and then virtually impossible. This means that MCEs primarily interact mechanically with the environment, whereas prokaryotes primarily interact physiologically. As a result, the majority of MCE biodiversity is mechanical or morphological, whereas for prokaryotes, it is physiological.

### Classical (MCE) Biology versus Microorganism (Prokaryotic) Biology

With the advent of metagenomics and the discovery of the rest of the biosphere, the properties and behaviors of these life forms can now be assessed.

Quoting from Robins et al. again, "Most profound is the demonstration that many fundamental notions in classical biology in fact only apply to the MCE realm, viz:

a) Individual organisms are objectively real, fundamental units of the biosphere.
b) Within cells, the content of the genome is extremely stable, protected, and highly regulated.
c) Barring mutation, genetic novelty is acquired only during reproduction, largely as the result of recombinations generated during sexual reproduction.
d) All life can be organized into similarly defined species.
e) With perfect knowledge, the biosphere could be arranged into one true, unified tree of life."[264]

The remainder of this section contains my summary of the paper.

In MCEs, mitosis division produces the growth of *somatic cells* by producing daughter cells with genetic content identical to each other and to the parental cell. Meiosis recombination allows reproduction and genetic novelty of *germ-line cells* through the merging of two different gametes into a zygote. "Individuals" are physically connected and genetically identical somatic cells. These individuals are mortal, whereas germ-line cells are theoretically immortal.

Prokaryotes only divide by mitosis, with no distinction between growth (somatic cells) and reproduction (germ-line cells). Therefore, the concept of individuals cannot occur.

Within MCE cells, genetic information is stored in a very stable, heavily regulated, and strongly protected genome that is essential for maintaining a multicellular, differentiated form, with "genomic instability" in classical biology regarded as a condition associated with pathology. MCE genome variations of as little as 0.75% have been shown to have deleterious results.

This enforced stability of genomic content is not a requirement of life. I will call the prokaryote genome closer to the Wild, Wild West. It has been shown that a typical individual bacterial cell carries as little as 6% of the genes common across the same species. A concept has been developed of the prokaryote *core-genome*, the set of genes found in all members of a particular "species," and the *flex-genome*, the set of genes found in some but not all members of the "species." Together, these make up the species' *pan-genome*. To put it in context, humans are more closely related to mice (30% overlap) than are two different strains of *E. coli* (20% overlap).

Horizontal gene transfer can occur between prokaryote members of the same "species" and between those separated by considerable taxonomic differences. This transfer can be so widespread that "floating" genes are more like attributes of the environment in which they are actively transferred than attributes of any individual organism, strain, or species that carries them.

In classical biology, organisms acquire new hereditary material when it is transmitted during meiosis from parent to progeny during the formation of the zygote. The zygote is a genetically novel cell that forms the clonal basis for the new somatic cells created through mitosis that make up the individual. The study of these processes is called *transmission genetics*.

Prokaryotes do not generate genetic variability through transmission genetics (mitosis) but, as discussed earlier, through *acquisition genetics* – the acquisition of genes directly from the environment via mechanisms not involving reproduction. This eliminates the feasibility of a whole-genome phylogenetic tree for any prokaryote or its pan-genome.

Species concepts applied to MCEs are all lineage-based (the idea of shared evolutionary history and flow of the genetic material through populations over time), resulting in species groups whose members exhibit great similarity of phenotype and ecological role.

None of these species concepts as applied to prokaryotes satisfy any of those conditions. Within microorganisms, most new gene families arise via inter-species horizontal gene transfer and not by intra-species mitosis. A prokaryotic species is not the endpoint of an evolutionarily isolated lineage, and the concept of species cannot be forced to fit onto microorganisms.

Much of classical biology is dedicated to the study of characteristics and behavior of aggregations of somatic cells, i.e., individual organisms. When classical biologists do address germ-line cells, it is usually in terms of gamete production and fertilization from the perspective of the soma.

Prokaryotes, with their physiological relationship to the environment, their non-reproductive gene acquisition, their lack of enforced stability of genomic content, and their lack of differentiated somatic tissue, are the opposite extreme from MCE organismal individuality.

I introduced the holobiont earlier. Now I will use it to challenge even the classical concept of an MCE individual. Every MCE individual carries an associated microbiome that plays vital roles in the normal physiology and function of the host. If the associated microbiome affects the fitness of the MCE host, then even among MCEs, the primary unit of function and survival is the composite of an MCE organism and its associated microbiome – the holobiont. Individual organisms are no longer fundamental units in nature but a reductionist abstraction.

The authors reference the tree(s) of life. Widespread horizontal gene flow among prokaryotes falsifies the principle that the evolutionary history of all organisms and their genes can be reflected unambiguously by a single, tree-like pattern.

MCE ecosystem diversity metrics are defined in terms of "species diversity" over some spatio-temporal range and consist of observations of an individual of a species at a point in space and time.

Not only do prokaryotes not support the concept of a species, but prokaryote populations also operate on completely different spatio-temporal scales. Time-series measurements that adequately characterize an MCE ecosystem community would be off by several orders of magnitude when characterizing the nature of a microbial ecosystem. From Robins et al.:

> If one were to go into any MCE ecosystem, pick a species at random, kill off 99.9 % of its population, and then measure how long it would take the species to recover, the result might be a year or more for a mouse, and a century or more (if then) for elephants. For some prokaryotes, the time to recover from a 99.9 % population cull could be 24 h or less.

The problem of an appropriate measurement scale also applies to space. MCE biodiversity is often assessed by sampling the environment on some grid. Again, from Robins et al.:

> But what would be the appropriate sampling grid for assessing, say, prokaryotic biodiversity in soil? Scaled by body size, assessing soil communities with samples taken five meters apart would be equivalent to assessing mouse biodiversity with samples taken forty miles apart or elephant biodiversity with samples three thousand miles apart.

## 5.3.4 SELF-PROLIFERATION VERSUS HORIZONTAL GENE TRANSFER

Unlike eukaryotes and their direct hereditary lineage, the genomes of prokaryotes are modified through fission and from gene loss/addition through horizontal gene transfer (HGT) via mobile genetic elements (aka, conjugative plasmids) that are available to all accommodating prokaryotes found in spatially local communal pools. These readily available genes can be termed a prokaryote's supergenome.[256]

## 5.3.5 A THEORY OF LIFE

From a different perspective, not only does much of evolutionary theory suffer from these biases but so do most attempts to develop a common theory of life. Because complex multicellular eukaryotes are the only organisms accessible to unaided observation, theorizing about the nature of life has been primarily based upon them.

It can be argued that Archaea and Bacteria (prokaryotes) would be more appropriate subjects for developing a unifying theory of life, absent of extraterrestrial origins.[257]

- Prokaryotes emerged approximately three billion years before the first complex multicellular organisms that appeared around 650 million years ago.
- Multicellular eukaryotes evolved from prokaryotes, representing a special case of the latter.
- Prokaryotes are more metabolically diverse and environmentally tolerant than multicellular eukaryotes.
- The genetic range of prokaryotes is large but poorly understood. In combining a universal dominance scaling law with a lognormal model of biodiversity, a paper[258] predicts that Earth is home to upward of one trillion microbial species, while we have documented only .001 percent of them.

### 5.3.6 Significance to the Real Matrix Argument

My entire argument for the existence of the Real Matrix is anthropocentric. I only care about it because we humans live in it, are made of it, are ignorant of it, and are deceived by it. I bring up these hidden biases because microorganisms are part of the Real Matrix regardless of the degree or nature of their impact on humans. Integrating them into our understanding of biology will directly increase our understanding of the functioning of the Real Matrix, but do not ask me how just yet.

## 5.4 The Real Matrix Sandbox

I did not start this book because of the observable outcome. I started it because of my epiphany concerning the outcome that is hidden and not fully appreciated. I will go back to the beginning – to this definition of genetic code from Section 4.4.9:

"A mapping of genetic information encoded by one type of biological macromolecule, the nucleic acids, into another family, the amino acids, which constitute the building blocks of proteins. The scheme is simple enough to state: a dictionary of 64 possible code-words (codons), is associated with 20 amino acids plus a stop signal."[259]

For MCEs (including humans), all of this is what is inherited (or transferred) and builds the organism. So, how does a specific organism's genome come into being?

Only by *surviving*.

And how does a specific organism's genome remain in the ecosystem?

Only by *being passed to other organisms* (contemporaries or descendants).

Therefore, the only true outcome of evolution is surviving genomes and epigenomes passing to other organisms, or *genotype fitness*. Abiogenesis and evolution are the alpha and omega processes, while the continuous outcome is the Real Matrix. More on that in Section 7.

# 6 REDUX

*We may be in the universe as dogs and cats are in our libraries, seeing the books and hearing the conversation, but having no inkling of the meaning of it all.*
William James

*When we speak of Nature, it is wrong to forget that we are ourselves a part of Nature.*
Henri Matisse

I have shown that all life is the result of the non-directed mechanics of abiogenesis and evolution. Now let us look at the Real Matrix implications.

In the movie, everything concerning the Matrix served the purpose of the machines. What were the two things that the machines needed to build into the Matrix for it to serve their purposes? *Perception* and *motivation*. Perception was a given since being jacked in meant that you were now experiencing (perceiving) the virtual reality of the Matrix as a real experience.

The motivation was more subtle. The earlier versions of the movie Matrix failed (according to Agent Smith) because they were too perfect – a nirvana of existence – and humans were not motivated to strive or live. The Matrix had to be modified to be made more like the former real-world existence, which meant that the reality had to have hardships and challenges, along with the successes and beauty. They needed to build in a *motivation* that kept those who were in the Matrix striving for existence to provide the sentient machines with their power.

So, in this section, I am exploring the equivalent within the Real Matrix, covering perception first, followed by teleology that bridges perception and motivation, and finally, allostasis that drives all motivation.

Some notes:

- I am going to define my terms very clearly, stick to science, and intentionally stay away from philosophical needle-threading and angel-counting. Some things I will explicitly avoid in this section include free will, consciousness, determinism, intelligence, purpose, moral responsibility, the concept of self (Buddhist and otherwise), any philosopher/philosophy, ontology (the study of being), qualia (individual instances of subjective, conscious experience), psychophysics (the study of the relation between stimulus and sensation), mind vs. brain, perception-altering drugs, Carlos Castaneda, etc. Even with these constraints, we will still go to interesting places.
- I originally included sections on optical illusions and magic tricks to demonstrate human perception gaps, but I soon found that it was all just there as window dressing and did not contribute to my purpose, so I removed them. If you do enjoy window dressing, then "Optical Illusions & Visual Phenomena" is a fun read to explore.[260]
- Most, if not all, of this section is from a human perspective that can be extended to the animal kingdom and even to the other kingdoms.

## 6.1 Perception

*It is a false assertion that the sense of man is the measure of things. On the contrary, all perceptions as well of the sense as of the mind are according to the measure of the individual and not according to the measure of the universe.*
Francis Bacon

*The world is a construct of our sensations, perceptions, memories.*
Erwin Schrödinger

*As a man is, so he sees. As the eye is formed, such are its powers.*
William Blake
*The world is, of course, nothing but our conception of it.*

Anton Chekhov

*Reality is merely an illusion, albeit a very persistent one.*
Albert Einstein

*Reality exists in the human mind, and nowhere else.*
George Orwell

*All life is only a set of pictures in the brain, among which there is no difference betwixt those born of real things and those born of inward dreamings, and no cause to value the one above the other.*
H.P. Lovecraft

Let me take you down the rabbit hole now and demonstrate more explicitly how wrong we are to think that our perception is objective and accurate and that our motivation is self-generated. Since our perception and motivation have emerged in, and exist in, non-directional abiogenetic and evolutionary processes, the only conclusion must be that they serve another purpose – that of the Real Matrix.

## 6.1.1 EMPIRICAL THEORY OF PERCEPTION

Philosophers, neuroscientists, psychologists, and I have all been wrestling with trying to understand perception. This has led to many, many theories over millennia (and thousands of papers) with no end in sight. In addition to the complexity of the subject, I believe this inconclusiveness is also due to Gödel's Incompleteness Theorems (introduced back in Section 2.6.2) because we are using our perception (system) to try to understand our perception (same system). It is our interface to everything, built up by and within the Real Matrix. Based on the Incompleteness Theorems, we will *never* get there, perhaps approaching it asymptotically, but I will not let that stop me from discussing it. I will not cover the entire field – just what I think is relevant.

**Perception** is the organization, identification, representation, and interpretation of sensory information (within a *receptive field*) to represent and understand the information. Perception can be split into two processes:

- Transforming the sensory input to higher-level information.
- Processing the sensory input and information against selective mechanisms and preexisting experience and expectations.

The mental result or product of perception is called a *percept*.

I am not going to discuss the over 20 other theories but, instead, cover the *wholly empirical theory of perception*. It skips over the complex biology, anatomy, and philosophy, and goes directly to how perception emerged, which is all I care about. The theory states that perception is determined solely by associations between the sensory patterns that organisms have experienced and the relative success of behavior in response to those patterns. More broadly, the success of behavior in response to sensory impressions tends to increase the prevalence of neural structures that support some ways of interpreting sensory input and decrease the prevalence of those that support other ways. This behavioral/evolutionary process determines the qualities of perception in all sensory modalities. Using terms introduced earlier:

> Percepts vary with the phenotype fitness of past actions in response to sensory stimuli and not directly with the measured properties of the proximal stimulus.

This theory fits hand-in-glove with evolution and the Real Matrix:

Perception emerged from whatever was successful at to maximizing fitness in each generation, not something that tries to
maximize the accuracy of some representation of reality.

Read that again, and this time, pay better attention because it is
the most mind-blowing statement of the book! Evolution and the Real
Matrix are measured exclusively by fitness. There is nothing else.

Some articles discuss this from a vision perspective.[261,262,263] I am
not going to try here, but this theory can be consistently walked
back through the biotic and abiotic history of life.

To support this theory, go back to the Sensory Systems discussions
in Section 4.5 and the long list of non-human sensory capabilities and
specialized equipment sensors. If our capabilities (and those of other
organisms) evolved to maximize the accuracy of our representation
of reality, then we would all certainly be better at it. Each species has
an extremely limited range of sensory and perception capabilities
when compared to the entire spectrum of biological and equipment
sensory ranges. Through our group fitness, the *irregular non-directional pattern* has resulted in the senses that we do and do not have.

## 6.1.2 PERCEPTION WITHOUT AWARENESS

Most of the articles I found on this topic emphasized subliminal
messaging in advertising since that is more sensational. You can
find those easily enough. My focus is on the general scientific theory
stating that perception can occur without conscious awareness and
has a significant impact on subsequent behavior and thought.

If there are many proximal stimuli that we do not sense, what
about the inverse? Are there stimuli that we perceive and yet are
not aware of? The idea that perception can occur without conscious
awareness – and have a significant impact on later behavior and
thought – strikes many as counterintuitive. There are many experimental findings demonstrating that stimuli are perceived even
when observers are unaware of the stimuli.[264] Interesting that when

a visual stimulus is perceived without awareness, it can influence which stimuli are subsequently perceived with awareness and how subsequent visual stimuli are consciously experienced.

The challenge that I cannot overcome is that all the studies focus on measurement – the what – and not one on the evolutionary roots – the where from. This is because the "what" is easy to measure but difficult to capture, resulting in doubts in experimental outcomes. I am much more interested in the "where from" because it could shine a light on *fitness* and all that it implies.

## 6.2 EVERYDAY TELEOLOGY

*I tend to believe that religious dogma is a consequence of evolution.*
E. O. Wilson

*Optimism is the opium of the people.*
Milan Kundera

I introduced and addressed teleology way back in Section 2.5 but from a scientific and journalistic perspective found in the written word. If you recall, my own definition was, *the explanation of a phenomenon by intent.*

As I have mentioned several times, I found that unsupported teleological vocabulary and descriptions of biological behavior runs rampant in much of the scientific literature I reviewed. About three months into writing this book, I had another epiphany – *a fundamental teleological worldview is built into the Real Matrix.* Most of the rest of this discussion will be centered on human behavior, but in the end, it extends to all living organisms.

I am going to move past the teleological arguments concerning the existence of supernatural beings, intelligent design, and any language that explicitly or implicitly suggests that there is any intent within biochemical reactions (or evolution). Religious and mystical beliefs are obviously permeated with teleology, but I do not want to deal with all the noise and baggage (and yelling and screaming). Instead, I am going to repurpose the term to apply to when we act as if inanimate or non-sentient things function with some degree of intent. I think that this behavior is so innate and ubiquitous that it has been overlooked by researchers in a systematic way. At least, I can say I have looked and have not found anything yet, so this is all from me.

## 6.2.1 TELEOLOGICAL BELIEFS AND BEHAVIORS

Let me start by giving you an incomplete list of human beliefs and behaviors that have this form of teleology at their foundation that I know everyone is guilty of, including me. I include some personal stories. Please relate by considering your own.

- I sometimes play solitaire, and I do have feelings about the deck as I deal it to myself or about the cards as I turn them over. When playing Rummy 500 with my wife, she makes noises when I pick up or lay down a bunch of cards that means I am getting more points against her. I do not feel the noises are directed at me but at the cards themselves.
- Belief in fate:
  o I was meant to miss that shot, lose that job, drop that glass, trip on that rock, get nearsighted, etc.
- Anger/swearing at inanimate things or events:
  o I have gotten angry at the screw, screwdriver, and wood when I have stripped the head from a screw I was trying to insert or remove.
  o Swearing at and even dropping a hammer when I bang my finger with it.
- The underlying teleology of the behaviors:
  o Knocking on wood
  o Crossing fingers

- Cursing at someone in their presence:
  - o Saying "fuck you" to someone in their presence is calling on some other power to do bad things to them now or in the future.
- Cursing about someone when they are not around:
  - o Saying "fuck you" to someone absent is still calling on some other power to do bad things to them now or in the future.
  - o Saying/thinking "I wish bad things would happen to someone" is the same.
- Personifying stuffed animals and dolls and other inanimate things:
  - o As a young child, I carried a blanket. That blanket gave me comfort. It had some presence.
  - o As a teenager, I carried a silver dollar given to me by my dad. As to why, I cannot articulate. It was a powerful, yet undefinable moment, when I threw the coin in a quarry pond in a fit of rage over a lost relationship.
- Treating any consumption – candy, alcohol, comfort foods – as something with intent.
  - o It is there to make me feel better.
- Addictions – cigarettes, alcohol, drugs, caffeine, chocolate can take on their own persona.
  - o That next cigarette wants to help calm you down (I do not smoke).
  - o That drink is there to help me escape a little (I do drink).
  - o That iced mocha will bring me joy (oh, yes), even while I am typing these words.
- Photos/videos elicit emotions that make you think the person or experience is somehow connected to you:
  - o Depicting beautiful people and their experiences that you cannot have but will fantasize about, including fashion magazines, movies, and pornography.
  - o A photo/billboard of a person looking at the camera makes me feel that I am the subject of their gaze.

- o Depicting friends/relatives living or deceased that you somehow communicate or somehow connect with.
- o If a framed photo of a loved one falls and breaks, there is extra negative emotion attached.
- o This is a tough one for me – I had someone in my past tear up all the pictures in my baby book. What did they feel when performing this act? Why did it make me feel like someone had gutted me like a fish?
- Having a bad day:
  - o Unrelated things intentionally going bad for you.
- You know the cable for charging an Android phone or Kindle Fire? The one that there is a right way and a wrong way to insert it? Well, I mentally keep track of how often I insert it correctly or incorrectly the first time, and I am convinced that it comes up wrong at least 80% of the time and not the expected 50%! Deep down, beyond my rational commonsense, I think there is something – what that something is I seem to not be able to articulate – that makes the results turn out that way.
- Even with the advent of Google Maps, I can still get lost trying to find a place. When I get upset, I am really getting upset at some external power (maybe Google Maps, maybe its CEO, maybe some other force) that influenced my getting lost.

Note: Something worth exploring is, "Why am I more prone to these teleological beliefs when I am stressed or sleep-deprived?" I do not really get drunk much, but I suspect that these beliefs would also become more dominant for the inebriated. Why else serve alcohol at a casino except to increase the perceived impact of teleology?

Adding nonhuman behavior, while watching our new puppy play with a string, rope, ball, or even empty plastic bottle, I could see where she considers inanimate objects to have intention – that they are acting on their own. I realized that this teleological perception is performed by other animals, especially, but not solely, during play.

## 6.2.2 SUPERSTITION

*The root of all superstition is that men observe when a thing hits, but not when it misses.*
Francis Bacon

*Man is certainly stark mad; he cannot make a worm, and yet he will be making gods by dozens.*
Michel de Montaigne

The teleology of superstition could easily be its own book, but not by me! I will not dawdle much here because I think it is just too obvious once you think about it. Here are some examples from sports:[265]

- Michael Jordan wore his University of North Carolina shorts under his uniform in every game, believing they brought him luck.
- Björn Borg would always prepare for Wimbledon by growing a beard and wearing the same Fila shirt. His lucky beard has become one of most popular superstitions in sports history and has been adopted by many in the NFL and NHL.
- Serena Williams brought her shower sandals to the court, tied her shoelaces a specific way, bounced the ball five times before her first serve and twice before her second, and wore the same pair of socks during a tournament run.
- The former New York Mets reliever Turk Wendell always leapt over the baselines when walking to the mound, chewed black licorice while pitching, and brushed his teeth between innings. He also wore a necklace decorated with the sharp teeth of wild animals he had hunted and killed.
- In NASCAR racing, peanut shells are considered bad luck, and according to racing lore, peanut shells are always found in the smoldering remnants of a badly wrecked car.
- Apparently, the mere mention of the word "no-hitter" in

baseball is more than enough to immediately stop it in its tracks.

- The Blackhawks' great Stan Mikita's pre-game ritual was to flick a lit cigarette over his left shoulder before taking the ice each night.

I am not suggesting that these superstitions are unhelpful. In fact, I am sure that they provide some beneficial mental and performance results. The believer just thinks that the cause of the positive benefits comes from some named or unnamed external power.

## 6.2.3 EVERYDAY PSYCHOKINESIS

Psychokinesis is an alleged psychic ability that allows a person to influence a physical system without physical interaction. There is no scientific evidence that psychokinesis is a real phenomenon, and the topic is generally regarded as pseudoscience.

Now, let me flip that on its head and expand the definition to include not only the *ability* to influence a physical system without physical interaction, but also the *will* to influence a physical system without physical interaction. This is a type of teleology insofar as it includes the assumption of some form of communication (the act of willing, and the hope that it will be heard) between a person and the non-cognitive present or future event.

This is not at all like the cognitive bias termed *illusion of control*, which is the tendency for people to overestimate their ability to control events. What I am referring to is *willing* for true psychokinesis, which is not possible, but attempted, nevertheless.

*Everyone* believes that they possess this form of psychokinesis in a subtle but pervasive way. If confronted, people would consider the belief quite silly but would continue to act in that manner, given what I will call *inciting events*. Let me give some gut emotional examples that should ring true with everyone:

- I drop a piece of buttered bread. As it travels to the floor, I mentally *will* it not to land butter-side down. If it does, I think, *Of course it did, it was fated to.* If it does not, I think that I influenced it.
- Every shot thrown in a basketball game has players and fans that *will* the ball to go in or out.
- I bump a vase that is now out of my reach, and I *will* it not to fall and break.
- My car is out of control and heading for a tree, and I *will* it to miss.
- I gain some weight, and while putting on my pants, I *will* the pants to fit.
- I am awaiting a diagnosis/review/result, and I *will* it to be favorable.
- I play the lottery, and I *will* the numbers I pick to be the winning ones.
- I am running low on gas, and I *will* the car to make it to the next gas station.
- As a door is closing and I realize that I forgot my keys on the other side, I *will* the door not to close before I can get to it.
- I will include prayer in general. That would account for the "Please, God!" associated with many of these events.

## 6.2.4 Ancient Greek Civilization

I recently listened to an interesting TED Talk entitled "What ancient civilizations teach us about reality" by Greg Anderson.[266] I did not agree with much of his presentation and will ignore those pieces here, but he did make an insightful point that made me research further. It was that in the "real world" experienced by ancient Greeks, Egyptians, Chinese, Peruvians, Mexicans, Indians, Balinese, and Hawaiian civilizations, gods controlled all the conditions of existence. Those civilizations were founded on myths and illusions that affected everyday living. When I read more about them and their worldviews, I realize that this teleology gave purpose and direction to its individuals.

The speaker then made the point that, due to the scientific revolution, today, society views reality as a purely material order. I would call that a false premise. Why then religion? Why then what I covered in previous sections? It is true that scientific discoveries have objectively demonstrated this teleology to be false (wherever falsifiable), but I do not think that anyone truly lives as if reality were 100% material order because teleology's evolutionary roots remain built into our DNA. After all, they are beneficial to the Real Matrix.

Modern society has not come as far in its worldview from ancient civilizations as one might think.

## 6.2.5 COSMIC PURPOSE

Even without religious beliefs, there are other insidious influences built into our Real Matrix.

I grew up in a family of eight in a small house. When I was 10-12 years old, I thought I was some sort of secret agent living undercover – the details of my identity and purpose were never clear. One of my secret skills that I do remember was the ability to change my clothes in my room with the door open before anyone could come in to see me in an undressed state. I was always successful, which proved the existence of my power. Don't ask...

Less successfully, I know that if I won the lottery, I would do right by the money I received. I have created multiple variations of fantasies that play out – step 1, step 2, step 3 – in that event (that I am too embarrassed to share). Then, at certain times (when the amount is extremely high, upon entering or leaving the US, or some other special occasion), I will make the purchase and check the results. I am, of course, always disappointed. Yes, I know the odds, but there is something about how I would use the money for good that somehow makes me think my odds are improved – the involvement of some unnamed and unconceptualized higher force. Again, don't ask...

Deep down, I have always thought I was special, much more than just what my mom would say to me, and that I would achieve great things solely through my individual agency. The only way for this to be true would be if there existed some higher intelligent power that gave me that specialness, that cosmic purpose. On the flipside, believing that success only comes from one's individual agency means that failure does as well!

I expect that everyone has these inner monologues that carry them through life, and that this teleological worldview is inherent in the human condition that emerged under evolution to make us more positive and optimistically maximize fitness. Everyone lives under the *optimism bias* – the belief that our chances of experiencing negative events are lower and our chances of experiencing positive events are higher than objectively expected. I believe this is the direct result of the effects of the Real Matrix.

## 6.3 Ubiquitous Allostasis

*Evolutionarily speaking, there is seldom any mystery in why we seek the goals we seek — why, for example, people would rather make love with an attractive partner than get a slap on the belly with a wet fish.*
Steven Pinker

I ended up spending many more pages on this topic than I expected – a lot more since I had never heard of allostasis before starting this book. You will find many ways that I have extended allostasis. My radical conclusion is that allostasis is the sole cause of all behavior, emerging through evolution within the Real Matrix.

Most of this section will center on humans, primarily because it will draw from my thoughts and experiences.

## 6.3.1 EXPANDED DEFINITION

Do you remember my earlier scientific definition of allostasis?

> Allostasis is the process of compensatory responses to events to attain some desired balance within some physiological system through behavioral actions. In effect, it is behavior initiated in the brain to serve physiology.

Now, I will significantly expand that definition to something more comprehensive.

> Allostasis is the process of compensatory, **anticipatory,** and **self-correcting mental or physical choices in response to perceived** events to **attempt to** attain **hormonal balances** within **some conceptual allostatic system or set of systems** that includes **choice optimization given resource and time scarcity** through behavioral actions. In effect, it is behavior initiated in the brain to serve **the brain**.

I changed many things:

- I added *anticipatory* to compensatory response because allostasis processes happen in anticipation of some future event to attain some future balance, whether that event or balance is one second or one year away. This introduces a time component into the allostatic systems that I do not see covered explicitly in the literature.
- I also added *self-correcting* because these choices can be constantly changing in response to system feedback determined by changes in perception and hormonal balances.
- I added *mental or physical* to choices because most allostatic systems exist solely in the mind and not external to the body.
- Since the responses are happening in the brain, I changed

*responses to choices in response to.* The term *response* avoids the implication of it being a brain activity. What is happening is that a decision to act in response to some event (a *choice* being made) takes place in the brain to attain some balance.

- I added *perceived* to events because without it, there is a hidden implication that the events are observed without bias. As you know by now, we perceive a reality, but perceptions go much further. We not only perceive reality but also *perceive* others' thoughts and motivations.

- I added *attempt to* in front of attain. We made these decisions in the hope that they will attain the target hormonal balance. There is no guarantee. I expect that most active allostatic systems fall short of that ideal hormonal balance.

- Instead of *some desired balance*, I changed it to *hormonal balances* for two reasons. First, we may feel that we are motivated by desire, but our allostatic behavior is driven by the brain's subconscious objective of increasing or decreasing specific hormones. Second, with the interplay of all the different types of allostatic systems I will introduce later, there are many hormonal balances that are being pursued by these choices.

  o Here are some "reward" hormones that the brain generates to motivate beneficial (to the Real Matrix) behavior:[267]

    § **Serotonin** – regulates the mood, prevents depression, and makes you feel happy. It can be released by getting exposed to sunlight, eating foods rich in carbohydrates, thinking happy thoughts, and aerobic exercise.

    § **Endorphins** – can make you feel good, reduce your anxiety and your sensitivity to pain. Endorphins are released by intense (anaerobic) exercise.

    § **Dopamine** – helps you to feel mentally alert. The lack of it might cause lack of attention, lack of concentration, and bad moods. Dopamine levels can increase as your brain predicts a reward, including from sex, drugs, gambling, and music.[268]

- § **Phenylethylamine** – results in the feelings we get in the early stages of a relationship.
- § **Ghrelin** – reduces stress and can help you become more relaxed. Ghrelin is released when we become hungry.
- § **Oxytocin** – has a role in sexual stimulation, orgasm, social recognition, monogamous pair bonding, trust and attachment between individuals, increased empathy/trust, anxiety, in-group bias, situational lack of honesty, autism, and maternal behaviors.
- § **Testosterone** – a stress hormone but, in high levels, can increase stamina.
- § **Prolactin** – improves your mood and immune system.
- § **Norepinephrine** – increases arousal and alertness, promotes vigilance, enhances formation and retrieval of memory, and focuses attention.
- § **Vasopressin** – affects social behavior, sexual motivation and pair bonding, and maternal responses to stress.
- § Note: Masturbation causes your body to release dopamine, endorphins, oxytocin, testosterone, and prolactin.[269]
- § Note: Testosterone and estrogen control lust; dopamine, norepinephrine, and serotonin create attraction; and oxytocin and vasopressin mediate attachment.[270]

- o Here are some "punishment" hormones to motivate a change in behavior:[271]
  - § **Cortisol** – the body manufactures cortisol in emergencies to help us make quick responses. It releases into the blood to send greater amounts of glucose to the muscles. The symptoms of having high levels of cortisol during a prolonged period are lack of sense of humor, irritability, feelings of anger, permanent tiredness, headaches, palpitations, hypertension, lack of appetite, digestive problems, and muscular pains or cramps.
  - § **Glucagon** – the body manufactures glucagon to allow the

liver to release glucose when our body has low levels of this substance and needs a greater amount to function properly.

§ **Prolactin** – periods of high stress can cause hyperprolactinemia, which is an increase in prolactin in the blood that immediately causes an inhibition of the production of hypothalamic hormone, which is responsible for synthesizing estrogens that can cause a lack of ovulation, a decrease in estrogen, and lack of menstruation.

§ **Sex hormones** – stress can result in the decrease of estrogen, progesterone, and testosterone.

- I dropped *physiological* so that the target system can now be something outside the body. This increases the potential allostatic systems a million-fold. More on that under Extrospective Allostasis 6.3.3.2.

- I changed *system* to *allostatic system* to represent the entire allostasis model within the target system.

- Then, I added *or set of systems*. This is another expansion of complexity. When we perform allostasis within one system, many other interdependent systems can be affected, their impact considered, and their combined balance cumulative.

- I added *conceptual* to the system or systems because, although the actions and results may exist in reality, the concept of the allostatic systems is created and exists only within the brain. For example, my making the bed to result in the bed being made is a process that exists in my mind before I act, but the actions and the results are in reality.

- I added *choice optimization given resource and time scarcity* because this is our existence, and it is usually overlooked in the literature. By *choice optimization* (my term), I mean that an organism is continuously trying to choose a course of action that is intended to maximize the chance of an optimal hormonal balance. Every organism is faced with resource and time constraints when making these decisions.

o Resources are finite, particularly the available consumable resources at the level of an organism, and the organism must use those resources *over time* to attain some optimal balance. Although finite, once you add the time dimension (below), resources can then be measured on the rate of both production and consumption over time.

o There are several types of time scarcity – 1) an organism can only do one thing at a time, 2) it takes time to both create and consume resources, and 3) an organism's life is finite with unknown duration.

- I changed physiology to *the brain* because perception and subsequent hormonal changes all take place there.

A point I need to reinforce is that these allostatic systems are driven by biology well below cognitive levels – the acting of the Real Matrix.

## 6.3.2 TIME AND RESOURCE CONSTRAINT

*All we have to decide is what to do with the time that is given us.*
J. R. R. Tolkien

Everyone talks about the constraint of resources (energy and matter), but I have not found anything on the constraint of time. There are constraints related to time that exist for an organism:

- The limitations of the given moment – an organism can only do one thing at a time.
- The limitations of a duration – actions take time to perform.
- The inevitability, but indeterminacy, of senescence and death – an organism's life is finite, with unknown future quality and duration.
- Resource production and consumption take place over time.

Using a relatable example, in the wonderful movie *Groundhog Day*, the main character had the advantage of all these constraints being removed or modified. Although during each day, Phil could only do one thing at a time, reliving each day gave him the opportunity to do multiple things "at the same time," just on a different day, with no passage of time. Sometimes, it did not matter how long an action took to perform – learning a language, French poetry, or the piano. Sometimes it did matter – Phil had to start over at the beginning of each day in his task of wooing Rita because she started each day fresh. Also, as Phil stated, he was an immortal. He could not die, and the same day was extending into eternity, but he did have the constraint that everyone else started over the next day at 6 a.m. Finally, he robbed the bank every morning so that he could have unlimited funds for the rest of the day.

Unfortunately, to quote from E.T. *the Extra-Terrestrial*, "This is 'reality,' Greg". We must live in a reality that operates under these time-related constraints.

What does this mean for allostatic systems? Every moment, a choice must be made by an organism on how to optimize the desired hormonal balance, given these constraints – I can only do one thing at a time, everything takes time to perform, someday I am going to die, and I must wait for resources to accumulate or be used up.

## 6.3.3 Types of Allostatic Systems

I will now distinguish between types of allostasis. These are my own concepts and labels. The list goes on and on.

### 6.3.3.1 Introspective First-Party Allostasis

Introspective allostasis occurs when the allostatic system acted upon is the physiology of the organism. *Introspective first-party allostatic systems* are what you read about in all the literature, based on my original definition back in Section 4.6.1.2. I use introspective to mean inward-looking – sensing, responding to, and affecting the physiological systems of the body. Examples include:

- I am thirsty; I drink.
- I am tired; I rest.
- I am hot; I open a window or turn on the air conditioning.
- I am cold; I put on more clothing or turn up the heat.
- I am sleepy; I go to bed.
- I am hungry; I eat.
- I am wet; I dry myself with a towel.
- I stink; I bathe.
- The light is bright; I shade my eyes.

### 6.3.3.2 EXTROSPECTIVE FIRST-PARTY ALLOSTASIS

Extrospective allostasis occurs when the allostatic system acted upon is within the perceptive field but external to the organism. Here is my first expansion of the traditional definition. *Extrospective first-party allostatic systems* are those that are performed by the organism but exist outside the physiological systems of the organism. Extrospective first-party allostatic activities include:

- I want a clean kitchen; I clean the kitchen.
- I want a watered lawn/garden; I water the lawn/garden.
- I want the water from the garden hose to flow to a specific place; I adjust my thumb position and pressure on the end of the hose, my arm height, and the hose angle for the water to go to the desired spot.
- I want to eat homegrown vegetables; I plant vegetables and care for the garden.
- I want a painted room; I go to the store and pick/buy the paint and equipment, bring it home, find the time, prepare the room, paint the room, fix mistakes, and clean up afterward.
- I want dinner; I determine what I want to make, check the

supplies, go to the store for anything missing, make dinner, and eat dinner.
- I want clean clothes; I do the laundry.
- I want to be elsewhere; I drive the car.
- I want my wife happy; I do things that I think will make her happy now or in the future.
- I want my wife happy with me; I do things that I think will make her happy with me now or in the future.

### 6.3.3.3 MENTAL/PHYSICAL ALLOSTASIS

Mental allostasis occurs when the allostatic system exists entirely in the mind, and physical allostasis occurs when the allostatic system exists partially or mostly externally to the organism.

Introspective and mental allostatic systems are similar in that they both look inward to things happening inside a body. I label a system as introspective when it is driving physiological changes, like quenching thirst. A mental allostatic system is primarily driving thoughts occurring in the mind. Most allostatic systems are a blend of mental and physical choices, but some are primarily physical, while others are primarily mental.

Some of the many examples where the allostatic actions and results could exist solely in the mind include:

- Imagining some good or bad event
- Remembering some happy or traumatic event
- Dreaming
- Watching the news, show, or movie
- Reading a book
- Practicing meditation
- Listening to music (those positive hormones have saved my life countless times and ways)
- I almost overlooked the most famous one of all – those occurring while hooked up to the Matrix in the movie!

Some good representative allostatic systems that are mostly mental but still have a physical component (that could also be addictive behaviors) include:

- Turning on your phone and viewing/responding to social media or news
- Turning on the TV and watching the news or sports
- Obtaining and consuming drugs or alcohol
- Playing video games
- Turning on a computer and watching pornography

I would say that masturbation is split right down the middle between mental and physical.

### 6.3.3.4 PRIMARY/SECONDARY ALLOSTASIS

Interdependent allostasis occurs when multiple related allostatic systems are acted upon or affected. These interdependent allostatic systems can be *primary* (the overarching allostatic system that requires subordinate systems to be acted upon to be completed) or *secondary* (the allostatic system acted upon is part of a group of other subordinate systems that must be performed to complete a primary system), and the secondary tasks can be a combination of *parallel* (the related/unrelated allostatic systems are running at the same time) and *sequential*. Here, sequential means that an allostatic system (the predecessor) must be completed before another (the successor) can begin. An allostatic system (the successor) cannot begin before another (the predecessor) has ended. For example, let us say that I want to drink a cold glass of water without ice – this is my primary extrospective allostatic system. In the USA, I would take a glass, walk up to the refrigerator door, insert the glass in the dispenser, let it fill up with cold water, and drink. Well, I regularly visit Bangalore, India (long story). To execute the same extrospective first-party primary allostatic system of drinking a cold glass of water,

I must perform all the following *extrospective first-party* **secondary** *sequential allostatic systems*:

- The city turns on a tap every other day that stays on from around 10 PM to 10 AM and fills our in-ground tank. There is an automatic valve that shuts off when the tank is full. So, I keep track of whether it is a water day or not and the water level of the tank. There is a heavy metal door on the top that I pull up to check.
- If, due to usage, the water level is low, I must wait until another water day to perform the next task (allostatic system).
- That water tank is underground, so there is no water pressure to get water out of our taps. Because of that, we have two elevated sets of tanks. Depending on several factors (e.g., whether it is a water day, what I guess is the level of water in the elevated above-ground tanks, whether it is a day that I will water the yard or do a lot of laundry, etc.), I will turn on a pump and turn a valve that directs the underground water to either the back two elevated tanks or the roof tank. I must stay nearby and listen because these tanks do not have shutoff valves. The only way I am signaled that the tanks are full is when they overfill, and the water pours down the sides onto the ground. I have, on occasion, not been very alert, and the water will overflow for a while.
- Whether or not the tanks are full, the water can now get pushed through the taps due to the pressure from gravity. Outside, I use it to water the garden; inside, I use it for the sinks, showers, the washing machine, cooking, and drinking. I have screwed up the other way and the overhead tanks have inconveniently emptied.
- To get cooking and drinking water, the next step is to get a pot and put it under a wall-mounted electrical water filter called an Aquaguard. I turn it on, and it will begin to fill up the pot with filtered water. I must watch this too. It takes about five

minutes to complete. I have lost track of it more frequently than I would like to admit, and it has overflowed onto the floor. If it is for cooking, then I set that pot aside and the process is complete.

- For drinking water, the next step is to put the filled pot on the gas stovetop and heat it to a boil. That takes about 30 minutes. Just yesterday, I lost track, and it boiled off for another 30 minutes or so.
- Now, the pot must cool. Ideally, I do the boiling at night, so that it is ready when I need it and it has not heated the house too much (high of about 97°F/36°C in the summer months).
- Once cooled, I pour it in batches into a Brita jug for a second filtration.
- From the Brita jug, I fill a tall glass bottle and put it in the refrigerator.
- I then forget about it. Once I think about that cold glass of water, it is usually ready, and I can go pour and drink myself a glass!

I can come up with another example, this time of *extrospective second-party secondary parallel allostatic systems*. At times, I manage IT projects with a bunch of team members. One of my most important responsibilities is effective delegation. In one or more meetings, I give directions to my bosses, peers, and subordinates to perform different activities. For example:

- To bosses – make a design decision, obtain a new resource, schedule an executive review meeting.
- To peers – determine the design methodology to be followed, find out who needs to approve a quality document, schedule a coordination meeting between their team and mine.
- To subordinates – perform requirements gathering, complete a presentation for a proposed design, participate in training.

I must determine what are the necessary tasks, how to provide sufficient instructions, how to motivate them to perform the tasks, how to monitor and guide ongoing activities, how to benefit from the results, etc. The better I am at my delegation responsibility, the greater the chance of project success. Many of these tasks are being performed in parallel independently, even though the overall goal is project success. These tasks are all *secondary parallel extrospective allostatic systems*.

### 6.3.3.5 ANCILLARY ALLOSTASIS

Ancillary allostasis means that the allostatic systems are implicitly affected by other systems. This is a special type of interdependency that is more subtle. Here, your allostatic actions have one objective in mind that contributes to many other systems. For example, I have an allostatic system I will call "exercise so that I can feel in better shape." It has many ancillary systems that add to my motivation. With the better-shaped body, I can more likely:

- Look better in clothes to impress clients.
- Impress my wife, and she will be more attracted to me.
- Have more confidence around male and female friends.
- Go for a run and pass more runners than pass me.
- Compete in a race and do okay.
- Play basketball with my sons and show them my stuff.
- Face an emergency requiring physical strength and be more likely to manage it.
- Play tennis and win more often than lose.
- Live a more active and longer life.

### 6.3.3.6 COMMUNITY ALLOSTASIS

First-party allostasis is when the allostatic system is being acted upon by the organism, whereas second-party allostasis is defined by the allostatic system being acted upon by an organism that is one degree of separation from the initiating organism.

Community allostasis occurs when the allostatic system is being acted upon by an organism that is more than one degree of separation from the initiating organism. In other words, community (or societal) allostatic systems are those that started with an organism but do not have a direct connection to it. I will pick an extreme example related to the history of the place I live now to make a point.

Part of Mahatma Gandhi's approach to societal change was to lead by example. He believed that India could develop self-sufficiency, and so he started what was called the Khadi (clothing) movement to promote the spinning of khadi for self-employment. He led by example by trying to make his clothes and have his followers do the same. His example led to many people making their clothing. Others performing this activity on their own was a type of *extrospective community allostatic system*.

### 6.3.3.7 INTERTWINED ALLOSTASIS

Intertwined allostasis occurs when two or more allostatic systems affect each other in some way. For a long list of reasons, every allostatic system is intertwined with one or more other allostatic systems. This relationship could be potentially beneficial or detrimental to the first allostatic system. Some simple examples include:

- Our coach and teammates all want to win the game – beneficial. The opponent team's coach and members want our team to lose – detrimental.
- The company and you want you to be hired – beneficial. The company HR department wants to pay you the minimum it would take for you to join, while you want the maximum that represents what you think is your value to the company – detrimental.
- You and your date go dancing because you both enjoy it

– beneficial. She's up all night for some fun; you're up all night to get lucky – detrimental.

### 6.3.3.8 Nascent/Mature Allostasis

- Nascent – many of an allostatic system's characteristics are still unknown and experimental, with low confidence of predictable outcomes, and the system may or may not become allostatic.
- Mature – an allostatic system's characteristics are well known and validated, with a high level of predictable outcomes.

Maybe the most accurate measurement of maturity is how many mature allostatic systems someone understands and could act on. A sign of creativeness and flexibility would be the degree to which someone embarks on nascent allostatic systems.

From an individual's perspective, there is an infinite number of nascent allostatic systems – systems that you may begin where you do not know the choices to make to attain the desired balance. Many times during my day, I may begin doing something I am inexperienced at, where I do not know whether the results will be favorable or not, or even correlated to my efforts. For example, since the Covid-19 pandemic, I have been investing time in starting a vegetable garden. I do not have much experience other than spading my mom's garden growing up and it shows. I find that I am better at growing weeds and fungus-attacked tomatoes than anything edible, but I do a little more reading, tear things out, and start over again, hoping for better results (more reward hormonal balance).

### 6.3.3.9 Successful/Failed Allostasis

Some allostatic systems are successful; others fail. We learn from both and keep going. For example, over many years I have suffered from muscle twitches. In response to the twitching, I read, I spoke to doctors, I researched, I got massages, and I took hot baths. Up until recently, nothing worked – a failed allostatic system. Then, someone told me to drink more water. Success! Now, my successful allostatic system is that if I am experiencing any muscle twitches, I drink a big glass of water and the twitching stops.

## 6.3.3.10 COMPENSATORY ALLOSTASIS

Compensatory allostasis occurs when the allostatic system is a substitute for a similar one that is not feasible or may have been unsuccessful. You cannot have most things, so when your allostatic systems do not or will not bring you reward hormones, then you need fallback systems that reliably do. Here are some examples:

- You screwed up at work, so you come home and take it out on the dog.
- You just fought with your spouse, so you play a video game.
- You got rejected by a pretty girl, so you watch pornography.
- You cannot finish all your assignments, so you cruise YouTube for a while.
- You must do chores that you are not looking forward to, so you listen to music on headphones while performing them.

## 6.3.3.11 VICARIOUS ALLOSTASIS

This is when the mostly introspective allostatic system being acted upon is derived from a system being acted upon by another externally. Since childhood, I have wanted to (mostly secretly) be Superman. I am just a regular guy with testosterone. Instead, I watch action movies to imagine that I am such a superhero. That is an introspective allostatic system living inside my brain that brings me comfort in the form of reward hormones.

## 6.3.3.12 Repetitive Allostasis

Repetitive allostatic systems are those that have the same objective and are done over and over. They probably make up the majority of those acted upon. Let me list some, from those that are more similar in repetition, to those that are more different:

- Brushing teeth twice a day, every day
- Making the bed every morning
- Driving to work Monday through Friday
- Doing laundry a few times a week
- Making dinner every night
- Giving a presentation at work several times a week
- Having sex (hopefully)

## 6.3.3.13 Trade-Off Allostasis

Trade-off allostasis occurs when more than one allostatic system is acted upon in parallel, which may result in a more or less optimal result. Trade-off allostatic systems are the rule, not the exception. These are systems that are started while others have not yet finished, getting back to our driving reality that one cannot do two things at once and that life is finite. This choice may result in more allostatic systems being completed with reward hormonal results, but it also may result in one or more of the systems producing less reward, neutral, or punishment hormonal results. These systems can fall into any of the categories I have identified. For clarity, let me give you an extremely basic example set of trade-off allostatic systems:

- Cleaning dishes in the sink, while
- Boiling milk on the stove that was home-delivered and trying to keep an eye on it so that it does not boil over, while
- Having my laptop open at page 149 of this book where I have paused writing, while

- Filling one of the above-ground water tanks and listening for it to overflow, while
- Drinking my morning mocha, while
- Thinking through ideas to add to the "Allostasis" section of the book, while
- Trying to plan when I will exercise today, which is dependent on when my spouse wakes up.

If I were to do these systems sequentially rather than in parallel, I would probably do each of them better, but doing them in parallel helps me to maximize my reward hormonal balance in the least amount of time, unless I screw up and the milk boils over across the stove, counter, and floor, and I have to spend extra time cleaning it up while punishment hormones are coursing through my system!

### 6.3.3.14 CONTRIBUTORY ALLOSTASIS

This is someone affecting someone else's allostatic system in a positive or negative way. Since we are social animals, these are as common as any other allostatic system.

- **Positive** – I do a lot of delegating in my position as a program manager. One of the tools that I use to motivate my staff in performing those delegated tasks is to praise their efforts and accomplishments very selectively. Those tasks are forms of allostatic systems, and my interjected praise is contributing to their motivation (read: positive hormones). That, in turn, contributes to my allostatic system that is to have them complete their tasks in a way that best adds to the overall allostatic system that is the program I am managing. I would call that a positive contributory allostatic system.
- **Negative** – this is when someone is motivated to affect someone else's allostatic system in a negative way – criticism, throw a wrench in the works, argue, fight, etc.

## 6.3.3.15 PROCEDURAL ALLOSTASIS

Procedural memory facilitates the performance of certain tasks without the need for conscious control or attention. It is created by repeating a task until the relevant neural systems work together to automatically produce the task. I classify these tasks performed by procedural memory as procedural allostatic systems. They are more efficient than non-procedural allostatic systems because they free up consciousness to focus on other activities.

## 6.3.3.16 ACTIVE/INACTIVE ALLOSTASIS

Allostatic systems can be active or inactive. We have only been talking about active systems so far, but there are allostatic systems that exist in one's mind that are not currently active. A few examples include:

- I am at home, but when I go out for drinks and order my first drink at a bar, I tell the bartender to keep the change from each $20 bill (do not worry, two is my maximum drink limit), so that I get good service.
- I am at home, but when I go out to a movie, I always get peanut M&Ms so that I can enjoy them during the movie.
- I am at home, but when I travel internationally, I always take six mg of melatonin an hour before bedtime for a few days to help me adjust to the time zone.

## 6.3.3.17 ALLOSTATIC SETS

Allostatic sets are any combination of allostatic systems viewed as leading to a cumulative reward/punishment hormonal balance. We probably have thousands of active allostatic systems operating at the same time. Using our experience and predictive capabilities, we must constantly make choices with the objective of maximizing reward hormones and minimizing punishment ones.

## 6.3.3.18 "The Meaning of Life" Allostasis

"The Meaning of Life" allostasis is the allostatic set that is defined by all an organism's choices within its life duration. Each of us are our own *primary first-party allostatic set*. This is the mother of all allostatic sets. All our choices are intended to lead to a favorable hormonal balance, now and in the future, from birth to death. All the other allostatic systems I mentioned above are secondary to this primary system.

## 6.3.4 Allostatic System Results

Remember that my expanded definition of allostasis includes that the purpose is "to attempt to attain some hormonal balance." That suggests an entire spectrum of results that, again, is missing from the literature I have found. The general possibilities include the active allostatic system(s):

- moving the organism toward a reward hormone balance.
- moving the organism toward a punishment hormone balance.
- not moving the organism in any hormonal direction, maintaining the current balance.
- creating both reward and punishment hormones in the organism.

I will not cover all the possible intricacies that I can think up, but you can see that there is a mountain of complexity in outcomes and how an organism would respond to these results.

Another large complexity is how we make choices from an allostatic perspective. I have not found the research, but it must be some sort of predictive-outcome decision-making process. Examples of such decisions include choosing:

- to start or stop an allostatic system.
- between allostatic systems to start or stop.

- to begin or end an allostatic system concurrently with other active systems.
- to vary some steps within an active or future allostatic system based on real-time and subsequent feedback.

On the topic of feedback, we just brought home a Labrador puppy (a brand-new series of interdependent and initially not well understood allostatic systems). For the first three days, it was like setting off multiple thermonuclear devices within my existing well-coordinated morning allostatic systems. At the beginning of our fourth full day, the intensive, real-time feedback has allowed me to make better decisions that are resulting in better results! I am typing this at 8:30 a.m. after the successful completion of my new morning ritual, and she is happily napping in her crate.

# 7 THE REAL MATRIX

*Maybe each human being lives in a unique world, a private world different from those inhabited and experienced by all other humans. . . If reality differs from person to person, can we speak of reality singular, or shouldn't we really be talking about plural realities?*
Philip K. Dick

*The Sanskrit word 'māyā' refers to all things that can be measured. Human understanding of the world is limited, hence measurable, hence māyā. To believe this māyā is truth is delusion. Beyond māyā, beyond human values and human judgements, beyond the current understanding of the world, is a limitless reality...*
Devdutt Pattanaik

*The world is all a carcass and vanity, The shadow of a shadow, a play. And in one word, just nothing.*
Michel de Montaigne

Do you remember and understand the premise of the movie? It is pretty cool. The truth of our reality is not necessarily so cool. Welcome to our Real Matrix.

## 7.1 MAPPING THE TERMINOLOGY

I will take everything we have learned and construct a model of the Real Matrix. First, I will walk you through some of the key terminology used in *The Matrix* and show how it may be similar or different from our Real Matrix. A lot of this will be repetitive within each term, but it bears repeating for clarity purposes.

## 7.1.1 THE SENTIENT MACHINES

- Key Similarities
  - o The movie Matrix and our Real Matrix were both somehow constructed. In the movie, the sentient machines (the instructors) instructed the Architect (the constructor) to build the Matrix. In our Real Matrix, the nucleic acids that constitute our genome and the regulation of gene expression act as "instructors" and the proteins made by them as "constructors."
- Key Differences
  - o The sentient machines have a conscious purpose for building the movie Matrix (survival). They made decisions with intent. The constructors in our Real Matrix have no purpose, no teleology. Instructors, constructors, and our very fabric exist solely because of successful replication of subsequent variant entities, in whatever way that occurred (i.e., as measured by fitness).

## 7.1.2 THE MATRIX

- Key Similarities
  - o Both have gone through iterations – the movie Matrix, eight; the Real Matrix, 10trillion? For computer scientists, this is clearly an NP-complete problem.[272,273]
  - o Both fool us into thinking we are separate participants from reality, whether intentionally (in the movie, by hooking us up to the Matrix environment) or unintentionally (in reality, by constructing our perceptions and directing our motivations).
  - o Both try to distract us with their constructed realities to

get us to do what they want (or need) us to do. The movie Matrix mimics life so that we go ignorantly along generating power for the sentient machines in their power plants. In the Real Matrix, our perceived reality emerges through successive generations, and that perception only survives because it motivates us to successfully replicate our genes.

- Key Differences
  - o The movie Matrix is outside of our bodies. The Real Matrix is not only our body but is the entire biomass. Each organism maintains its own small, but interrelated, version of the Real Matrix.
  - o A failure of an iteration of the movie Matrix was based on an intellectual evaluation of its performance by the sentient machines. A failure of an organism's *iteration* means that its genes have somehow been removed from the gene pool. The same goes for a species or anything above that.
  - o The movie Matrix was reprogrammed by the Architect to fix unintended outcomes. There may have been some copy/paste of code, but that was not mandatory. It could have been reprogrammed from scratch. The "code" of the Real Matrix consists of existing genetic code that was successfully copied forward, and changes in that code only happened through random errors.
  - o There is one Matrix virtual-reality program in the movie shared only by connected humans (excluding the "Construct"), and each human acts within and can affect this common Matrix. The Real Matrix is truly an intertwined set of matrices of realities across all organisms that has codependently emerged. Each of the trillions of organisms acts within their perceived Matrix.
  - o In the movie, all connected humans share one experience. In the Real Matrix, each organism experiences its own reality through its unique perception, and each probably has an increasingly similar experience because of an increasingly

similar genome as they move from/to a common Kingdom, Phylum, Class, Order, Family, Genus, or Species.

## 7.1.3 HUMANS

- Key Similarities
  - o Humans are still humans.
- Key Differences
  - o In the movie Matrix, humans are "jacked in" to a separate virtual reality software program called The Matrix. In the Real Matrix, there is no "jacking in." Humans do not exist separately from the Real Matrix.
  - o When connected to the movie Matrix, the only sensing function in use is a human's mental perception. In the Real Matrix, we use the entire set of sensing functions (see Section 7.4.1: Sensing System Comparison).
  - o The Real Matrix is biomass. That biomass includes our higher reasoning functions. What we think is a product of the Real Matrix. It is the Real Matrix that "thinks about" the Real Matrix. (Remember the early discussion about Gödel's Incompleteness Theorems? Here we are, thinking about a system while inside and under the rules of the system.)

## 7.1.4 POWER PLANTS

- Key Similarities
  - o Humans provide the power that the sentient machines in the movie and the Real Matrix genome need to exist.
  - o If humans die, that power source is lost, thereby reducing the viability of the existence of the instructors (machines or genome).
- Key Differences
  - o In the movie, the power generated by humans connected to the power plants is a waste byproduct (electricity) that is

used by the machines who exist outside of the Matrix. In the Real Matrix, the low-entropy energy comes from an external source (primarily the sun) that is utilized by the genome to instruct and construct the Real Matrix.

## 7.1.5 REALITY

- Key Similarities
  - o The reality of humans (and all living things), both in the movie Matrix and our Real Matrix, is no more than a perception of underlying reality through sensory systems.
- Key Differences
  - o The movie Matrix was just built to fool humans (no Matrix for dogs!), while the Real Matrix is constructed by the entire biomass genome, and each "organism" perceives its individual, interrelated version of the Real Matrix.
  - o There is one perception-based Matrix in the movie (one program), while the Real Matrix is an integrated set of trillions of different perceptions.

## 7.1.6 THE ARCHITECT

- Key Similarities
  - o Both the movie Matrix and our Real Matrix have been built by something.
- Key Differences
  - o In the movie, the single virtual reality called the Matrix and its iterations were constructed by the Architect. In our Real Matrix, our reality and ourselves have been built by the biomolecules making up our genome acting under abiogenesis/ biological/evolution mechanics. Our RNA acts as the "architect" in that it reads the DNA blueprint and builds the proteins.
  - o The Architect exists inside the Source but outside the Matrix. Our constructors are part of our Real Matrix, part

of us. In the movie context, it would be like saying that the Architect existed as part of – not separate from – each iteration of the Matrix, and that the Architect was building itself along with the Matrix.

o The movie Architect is a program of the machine that creates and maintains the Matrix to meet its needs, while the constructors of the Real Matrix are the chemicals that make up the genes that control life – no intelligence, no intent, no purpose.

## 7.1.7 THE SOURCE

- Key Similarities
  o There is an underlying architecture upon which the movie Matrix and the Real Matrix have been built and executed.
- Key Differences
  o In the movie, the Source is the central computing core for the machine mainframe, while in the Real Matrix, the equivalent function is performed by our DNA that acts as the instructional blueprint.

## 7.1.8 THE HEADJACK

- Key Similarities
  o Bluepills are not aware of the existence or nature of their connection to the movie Matrix or Real Matrix.
- Key Differences
  o There is no headjack in the Real Matrix since the Real Matrix is inside all life.
  o Complementarily, since there is no headjack, there is no way to disconnect from the Real Matrix.

### 7.1.9 BLUEPILLS

- Key Similarities
  - o Bluepills are connected to the Matrix in the movie and reality.
- Key Differences
  - o There are no non-Bluepills in reality and no off-ramp since the Real Matrix is physically part of us (see Section 10: The Purple Pill for another option).

### 7.1.10 AVATARS

- Key Similarities
  - o The movie Matrix and the Real Matrix both have created avatars for living organisms that define how they experience their perceived realities.
- Key Differences
  - o In the movie Matrix, the avatars are outside of us, inside the virtual reality program. In the Real Matrix, the avatars are built into the fabric of our being.
  - o In the movie Matrix, only humans have avatars. In the Real Matrix, in a sense, every living organism has an avatar that interacts with other living organism avatars.

### 7.1.11 AGENTS

- Key Similarities
  - o Restating my earlier non-falsifiable opinion, I believe that the Real Matrix contains agents in the same way that the movie Matrix does.
- Key Differences
  - o We can see and understand the agents in the movie, while the agents that exist in the Real Matrix are embedded and hidden from our perception to allow them to function

effectively against any who might reveal the truth.

o The Real Matrix agents are built into the Real Matrix and are not separate, distinguishable entities.

## 7.1.12 THE RESISTANCE

- Key Similarities
  o None that I can think of.
- Key Differences
  o There is no organized resistance against the Real Matrix or its agents, but perhaps the purplepills (see Section 10) can provide a path forward.

## 7.1.13 THE NEBUCHADNEZZAR

- Key Similarities
  o None.
- Key Differences
  o There is no world accessible to humans outside of the Real Matrix.

## 7.1.14 THE RED PILL

- Key Similarities
  o None.
- Key Differences
  o There is no means of escape from the Real Matrix.

## 7.1.15 THE BLUE PILL

- Key Similarities
  o None I can think of.
- Key Differences
  o See Section 10: The Purple Pill.

## 7.1.16 REDPILLS

- Key Similarities
  - o None.
- Key Differences
  - o No one can exist outside of the Real Matrix.

## 7.1.17 TELEPHONE LINE

- Key Similarities
  - o· None.
- Key Differences
  - o There is no escape from the Real Matrix.

## 7.1.18 NEO

- Key Similarities
  - o None.
- Key Differences
  - o There can be redpills, but I cannot see how there could exist the equivalent of Neo, since there is no escape from the Real Matrix.

## 7.1.19 BINARY CODE

- Key Similarities
  - o There is binary code in the movie Matrix and genetic code in the Real Matrix.
- Key Differences
  - o Because the Real Matrix is not a computer program, its binary code cannot be read from a computer terminal or one's mind. It must be studied, genome by genome, across organisms.

## 7.2 Parallels and Differences

After I had written 99% of this book, I decided just for kicks to go back and re-watch the movie. While viewing, I was surprised by the amount of dialogue that tracked my premise of the Real Matrix. I decided to insert some of the movie dialogue from the script[20] here and show how it either parallels or differs from the Real Matrix.

| From the movie script of The Matrix | In our Real Matrix |
|---|---|
| NEO<br>You ever have the feeling that you're not sure if you're awake or still dreaming? | Our reality is such a perception as in the movie. |
| TRINITY<br>It's the question that drives us, the question that brought you here. You know the question just as I did.<br>NEO<br>What is the Matrix? | It is a question that few people ask, but it is what drove me to write this book. I hope that you now understand the question, its importance, and my answer. |
| MORPHEUS<br>Do you believe in fate, Neo?<br>NEO<br>No.<br>MORPHEUS<br>Why not?<br>NEO<br>Because I don't like the idea that I'm not in control of my life.<br>MORPHEUS<br>I know exactly what you mean. | We are wired to believe that we are in control of our lives (whatever that means), but we are, in truth, built by, made up of, and controlled by the Real Matrix. |

| From the movie script of The Matrix | In our Real Matrix |
|---|---|
| MORPHEUS<br>Let me tell you why you are here. You have come because you know something. What you know you can't explain but you feel it. You've felt it your whole life, felt that something is wrong with the world. You don't know what, but it's there like a splinter in your mind, driving you mad. It is this feeling that brought you to me. Do you know what I'm talking about?<br>NEO<br>The Matrix? | This is not far from the truth for me when I began to understand fundamental genetics and biology and then continued my reading. |
| MORPHEUS<br>The Matrix is everywhere, it's all around us, here even in this room. You can see it out your window or on your television. You feel it when you go to work, or go to church or pay your taxes. It is the world that has been pulled over your eyes to blind you from the truth.<br>NEO<br>What truth?<br>MORPHEUS<br>That you are a slave, Neo. Like everyone else, you were born into bondage, kept inside a prison that you cannot smell, taste, or touch. A prison for your mind. | This is the truth. |
| MORPHEUS<br>Unfortunately, no one can be told what the Matrix is. You have to see it for yourself.<br>*Morpheus opens his hands. In the right is a red pill. In the left, a blue pill.*<br>This is your last chance. After this, there is no going back. You take the blue pill and the story ends. You wake in your bed and you believe whatever you want to believe.<br>*The pills in his open hands are reflected in the glasses.*<br>You take the red pill and you stay in Wonderland and I show you how deep the rabbit-hole goes. | In the Real Matrix, there is no red pill since there is no escape. There is a blue pill, which is the equivalent of you closing this book and not thinking about it again. |

| From the movie script of The Matrix | In our Real Matrix |
|---|---|
| MORPHEUS<br>What if you were unable to wake from that dream, Neo? How would you know the difference between the dreamworld and the real world? | We can never wake from this dream, which would mean leaving the Real Matrix. |
| NEO<br>This -- This isn't real?<br>MORPHEUS<br>What is real? How do you define real? If you're talking about what you feel, taste, smell, or see, then real is simply electrical signals interpreted by your brain. | Absolute truth! |
| MORPHEUS<br>You have been living inside a dreamworld, Neo. As in Baudrillard's vision, your whole life has been spent inside the map, not the territory. | Yes, we experience only the proximal objects and never the distal objects. |
| MORPHEUS<br>The Matrix is a computer-generated dreamworld built to keep us under control in order to change a human being into this.<br>*He holds up a coppertop battery.*<br>NEO<br>No! I don't believe it! It's not possible!<br>MORPHEUS<br>I didn't say that it would be easy, Neo. I just said that it would be the truth.<br>NEO<br>Stop! Let me out! I want out! | The Real Matrix is a gene-generated dreamworld, built to keep us under control to support the replication of these genes.<br>And there is no exit ramp. |
| MORPHEUS<br>I feel that I owe you an apology. There is a rule that we do not free a mind once it reaches a certain age. It is dangerous. They have trouble letting go. Their mind turns against them. I've seen it happen. I'm sorry. I broke the rule because I had to. | Is it too late for me, for you, for mankind? |

| From the movie script of The Matrix | In our Real Matrix |
|---|---|
| MORPHEUS<br>When the Matrix was first built there was a man born inside that had the ability to change what he wanted, to remake the Matrix as he saw fit. It was this man that freed the first of us and taught us the truth; as long as the Matrix exists, the human race will never be free. | This original "The One" is glossed over in the movie. Again, I do not know how such a being would exist or function in our Real Matrix.<br>Oh, and we can never be free. Now what? |
| MORPHEUS<br>I'm trying to free your mind, Neo, but all I can do is show you the door. You're the one that has to step through. | True words in our Real Matrix, but I cannot predict the results. |
| NEO<br>I thought it wasn't real.<br>MORPHEUS<br>Your mind makes it real. | Our real in the Real Matrix is our perception of proximal objects. Anything further is just semantics. |
| MORPHEUS<br>The Matrix is a system, Neo, and that system is our enemy. | Yes, the Real Matrix is a system, but no, it is not our enemy. The concept of enemy requires that it have cognition and intent, but the Real Matrix has neither. |

## 7.3 ENTRY TO YOUR REAL MATRIX

*Man is the product of causes which had no prevision of the end they were achieving; that his origin, his growth, his hopes and fears, his loves and his beliefs, are but the outcome of accidental collocations of atoms.*
Bertrand Russell, A *Free Man's Worship*

All life today, meaning the characteristics of our Real Matrix, is a result of billions of years of abiogenesis and evolution. But, what about *your life*, specifically? Where do you fit in as an individual, and what are its implications? Again, I am staying comfortably in the confines of science to share another shattering epiphany I had while writing this book.

You emerged within the prison of the Real Matrix when your father's sperm fertilized your mother's egg. That sperm and that egg were the results of that multi-billion-year process. You as that fertilized egg are one of trillions of results within the ever-emerging Real Matrix along that process. You *are* the Real Matrix, although an exceedingly small part of it.

That is the full extent of the significance of your existence. Your much higher sense of your own personal significance is solely a result of the increased fitness (measured by passing genes and traits to future generations) over billions of years that resulted from it. Any apparent significance to fertilization and birth were placed there by the non-directional, non-intentional Real Matrix.

So, if you choose to pay attention to the man behind the curtain, you as a fertilized egg were created by, within, and as part of the Real Matrix.

The statement you will find in some philosophies is that "You did not choose to be born." More accurately, "You did not choose to emerge within the prison of your personal Real Matrix." And, of course, no one else chose that prison. This point will be especially important when I get to the upcoming discussion on philosophies.

## 7.4 THE REAL MATRIX MODEL

*The reality we can put in words is never reality itself.*
Werner Heisenberg

*For me, it is far better to grasp the Universe as it really is than to persist in delusion, however satisfying and reassuring.*
Carl Sagan

## 7.4.1 Sensing Systems Comparison

I will begin with a table that shows the sensing system you would be taught in my biology class if I ever taught biology (summarized from Section 4.5: Sensory Systems).

### Sensing System – The Real World

| | Distal Object | Energy | Sensory Receptor | Sensory Stimulus | Sensory Transduction | Proximal Stimulus | Perception | Sensory Information |
|---|---|---|---|---|---|---|---|---|
| **Real World** | Reality | Reality | *Sensor/ Receptor Proteins* | *Received Stimulus* | *Sensor to Neural Proteins* | *Neuro- transmitters* | *The Brain* | *The Brain* |

Italics = within a living Organism

*Table 4 – The Real-World Sensing System*

Now, based on my understanding of the movie *The Matrix*, people jacked in would experience the following:

### Sensing System – The Movie Matrix

| | Distal Object | Energy | Sensory Receptor | Sensory Stimulus | Sensory Transduction | Proximal Stimulus | Perception | Sensory Information |
|---|---|---|---|---|---|---|---|---|
| **The Movie Matrix** | None | The Matrix | | | None | | The Matrix | *The Brain* |

Italics = within a living Organism

*Table 5 – The Matrix Sensing System*

A few things stand out:

- There is no *Reality* involved in the movie Matrix's sensing system.
- Even *perception* is handled in the movie Matrix. It is after that moment that human brains kick in to accept the *sensory information* they are receiving.

- The brain is obviously a necessary component of the movie's sensing system, but Reality is not!

I do want to point out what I believe is a flaw in this great movie. Remember the scene in the movie where Neo has just been pulled from the power plant and is hooked up to the electrodes? The dialogue goes like this:

DOZER: He still needs a lot of work.

DOZER *and Morpheus are operating on Neo.*

NEO: What are you doing?

MORPHEUS: Your muscles have atrophied. We're rebuilding them.

*Fluorescent light sticks burn unnaturally bright.*

NEO: Why do my eyes hurt?

MORPHEUS: You've never used them before.

*Morpheus closes Neo's eyes and Neo lays back.*

Not only had Neo never used his eyes, but he also never used *any* of his senses. So, not only would his muscles have atrophied but so would all of the human sensory systems listed in Section 4.5.2: Biological Sensory Systems. Therefore, they would have had to rebuild his muscles in addition to somehow rebuilding his senses.

One could debate that while the movie Matrix controlled human perception, it could have also influenced or controlled human motivation, e.g., should you turn right or left? Hard to draw a line there, but remember, it was only a movie.

I will now compare the two:

### Sensing Systems – The Real World vs. The Matrix

| | Distal Object | Energy | Sensory Receptor | Sensory Stimulus | Sensory Transduction | Proximal Stimulus | Perception | Sensory Information |
|---|---|---|---|---|---|---|---|---|
| Real World | Reality | Reality | Sensor/ Receptor Proteins | Received Stimulus | Sensor to Neural Proteins | Neuro-transmitters | The Brain | The Brain |
| The Movie Matrix | None | The Matrix | | | None | | The Matrix | The Brain |

Italics = within a living Organism

Table 6 – The Real World vs. Matrix Sensing Systems

When one looks at the *Real World* row, one automatically takes comfort in all those blue cells because they represent us and show us in control. In the *Movie Matrix* row, only the *Brain* cell representing perception is us, which leaves one feeling very uncomfortable – it is wrong, against nature, fooling/controlling us, etc.

Now, let us look at the same columns, representing the Real Matrix I have been talking about.

### Sensing System – The Real Matrix

| | Distal Object | Energy | Sensory Receptor | Sensory Stimulus | Sensory Transduction | Proximal Stimulus | Perception | Sensory Information |
|---|---|---|---|---|---|---|---|---|
| The Real Matrix | Reality | Reality | Sensor/ Receptor Proteins | Received Stimulus | Sensor to Neural Proteins | Neuro-transmitters | The Brain | The Brain |

Italics = within the Real Matrix

Table 7 – The Real Matrix Sensing System

All those red cells represent the Real Matrix, including our brain. Only Reality is outside of it. You will get a clearer view when I combine all three.

### Sensing Systems – The Real World, The Matrix, The Real Matrix

| | Distal Object | Energy | Sensory Receptor | Sensory Stimulus | Sensory Transduction | Proximal Stimulus | Perception | Sensory Information |
|---|---|---|---|---|---|---|---|---|
| **Real World** | Reality | Reality | Sensor/ Receptor Proteins | *Received Stimulus* | *Sensor to Neural Proteins* | *Neuro-transmitters* | *The Brain* | *The Brain* |
| **The Movie Matrix** | None | The Matrix | | | None | | The Matrix | *The Brain* |
| **The Real Matrix** | Reality | Reality | Sensor/ Receptor Proteins | *Received Stimulus* | *Sensor to Neural Proteins* | *Neuro-transmitters* | *The Brain* | *The Brain* |

Italics = within the Real Matrix

*Table 8 – All Sensing Systems*

Now, look at the *Real Matrix* row. All those red cells (sensory system components) emerged through and are part of the Real Matrix. From this perspective, it is clear here that the Real Matrix is the equivalent of all biology.

## 7.4.2 A New Picture (Someday)

I saved the creation of this section to the very end of my writing effort. The challenge I gave myself was, "How do I create a complete and explanatory picture of our Real Matrix that could stand on its own if it is the only thing you see without the benefit of reading the book or even a caption?" I wanted the picture to show what I first introduced in Section 1.2:

- Our Real Matrix is each living organism's (including each human's) individual, unique, and interrelated perception of, and response to, Reality that resides internally in the organism.
- This perception gives the false appearance of being Reality, when it is only the interpretation of the signals received and transmitted by each organism's sensory receptors.

- The Real Matrix emerged and continues in a non-directional way through the processes of abiogenesis (emergence of life) and evolution.
- The Real Matrix is both the reality that life perceives and life itself.
- Inanimate objects are inside reality but outside the Real Matrix.
- The Real Matrix is both a biological process for all organisms and the result of that process.
- The structure, content, perceptions, and motivations of all life emerge because of this process.
- The resultant biomass emerges through the process of genome/phenome fitness.

After making maybe 10 attempts, I discovered that I do not know how to draw that picture. I would rather not provide something than fall short and confuse everyone, and I was hoping to someday finish this book. After you read Section 10, maybe you will be inspired to help me.

# 8 How to Live Life

*To understand the actual world as it is, not as we should wish it to be, is the beginning of wisdom.*
Bertrand Russell

*True wisdom comes to each of us when we realize how little we understand about life, ourselves, and the world around us.*
Socrates

*Do what you can with what you have where you are.*
Teddy Roosevelt

*Be happy while you're living, for you're a long time dead.*
Scottish Proverb

French philosopher and historian Pierre Hadot posited that philosophy should be therapeutic, characterized by exercises intended to transform the perception and being of those who practice it. My motivation for including so many quotes in this section (and the entire book) has been to help enable such a process and personal journey.

How can existing philosophies be applied or even extended to account for the Real Matrix? How should we humans approach life now, given our understanding of the shackles of our filtered reality?

Decades before I had the idea of this book, I stumbled across three philosophies that are worth looking at and perhaps extending – Zen Buddhism, Stoicism, and Existentialism – that I will briefly describe and entice you to dig further. You may have your own supporting philosophies that I would be happy to understand.

To continue following my rule, I am not going to use precious real estate to go into the history of any of these philosophies, nor the lives of their proponents, nor provide in-depth guidebooks. If any of this speaks to you, hundreds of books and websites cover those topics. These philosophies often carry extra and unnecessary baggage, including metaphysics and the supernatural. I am going to discard this extra stuff and go right to the essence.

## 8.1 ZEN BUDDHISM

### 8.1.1 FUNDAMENTALS

Buddhism is an Indian religion founded on the teachings of a spiritual teacher Siddhārtha Gautama (named the Buddha, meaning the Enlightened One), who lived 2,500 years ago. Buddhism is built on the *Four Noble Truths* and the *Noble Eightfold Path* found within the fourth Noble Truth:

- **#1 Suffering** – any clinging is suffering. The five categories of suffering in Buddhism are:
  o Birth
  o Aging
  o Sickness
  o Dissociation from loved ones
  o Not getting what one wants
- **#2 Origin of suffering** – any craving/desire is the origin of suffering. The origins of suffering categories are:
  o Sensual desires
  o Desire to become or attain
  o Desire to get rid of
- **#3 Cessation of suffering** – the rejection, relinquishing, leaving, and renouncing of craving
- **#4 Way leading to the cessation of suffering** – this is the *Noble Eightfold Path*:

o **#1 Right view or understanding** – the understanding of the four Noble Truths.

o **#2 Right intention or thought** – thoughts of selfless renunciation or detachment, thoughts of love and thoughts of non-violence, which are extended to all beings.

o **#3 Right speech** – abstaining from telling lies, from slander and talk that may bring about hatred, enmity, disunity, and disharmony, from harsh, rude, impolite, malicious, and abusive language, and from idle, useless, and foolish babble and gossip.

o **#4 Right action** – abstaining from destroying life, from stealing, from dishonest dealings, from illegitimate sexual intercourse, and helping others to lead a peaceful and honorable life in the right way.

o **#5 Right livelihood** – gaining one's livelihood by benefiting others and by not selling weapons, poisons, or intoxicants.

o **#6 Right effort** – maintaining an energetic will to prevent and get rid of evil and unwholesome states of mind, and to cause to arise and maintain good and wholesome states of mind.

o **#7 Right mindfulness** – being aware, mindful, and attentive to the activities of the body and mind.

o **#8 Right concentration** – practicing correct meditation.

## 8.1.2 THE TWO TRUTHS

This concept was taken from *The Stanford Encyclopedia of Philosophy*.[274] If you really want to get into it, please read the entire entry. I am going to reuse the two hooks for my own coats.

It is said that Siddhārtha Gautama became a buddha because he understood the meaning of the two truths – conventional/mundane truth (saṁvṛti-satya) and ultimate truth (paramārtha-satya) – and that the reality of all the objects of knowledge is comprised of these two truths. Since that time, multiple Indian schools of philosophy (and their philosophers) have emerged and have their own interpretations of what constitutes the two truths. Since all of them have their own interpretations, I thought, *why not, I could have my own.*

I completely agree with how cocky this looks, but perhaps if the Buddha had been alive today, had access to our science, had read this book, and we had sat down for a chat, he would have come up with a different definition of the two truths (realities). Go back to Section 4.5.1: Sensing System Components to find my simple distinction between the two truths (i.e., realities):

- **Truth #1 – Conventional Reality** = Perception, experienced
- **Truth #2 – Ultimate Reality** = Distal Object, unattainable

### 8.1.3 ZEN BUDDHIST QUOTES

In my opinion, this is the most important quote from the Buddha:

> *Do not believe in anything simply because you have heard it; Do not believe in traditions, because they been handed down for many generations; Do not believe in anything, because it is spoken and rumored by many; Do not believe in anything simply because it is found written in your religious books. But after observation and analysis, when you find that anything agrees with reason and is conducive to the good and benefit of one and all, then accept it and live up to it.*
> The Buddha, from the *Kalama Sutta*

In addition, for your dining pleasure, here is my own selection from the Dhammapada – a collection of sayings of the Buddha in verse form and one of the best-known Buddhist scriptures.[275] Please take your time and come back to it when you have the need.

- *Meditate. Live purely. Be quiet. Do your work with mastery.*
- *We are what we think. All that we are arises with our thoughts.*

*With our thoughts, we make the world.*

- *All that we are is the result of what we have thought. The mind is everything. What we think, we become.*
- *You too shall pass away. Knowing this, how can you quarrel?*
- *Understand that the body is merely the foam of a wave.*
- *Wanting nothing with all your heart. Stop the stream.*
- *The end of desire is the end of sorrow.*
- *All forms are unreal.*
- *Travel on alone, rather than with a fool for company.*
- *Do not speak harshly to anyone; those who are spoken to will answer you in the same way.*
- *Do not carry with you your mistakes. Do not carry your cares.*
- *It is better to do nothing than to do wrong. For whatever you do, you do to yourself.*
- *Everything arises and passes away.*
- *Do not look for bad company or live with men who do not care. Find friends who love the truth.*
- *Why do what you will regret? Why bring tears upon yourself? Do only what you do not regret and fill yourself with joy.*
- *The fool who knows he is a fool is that much wiser.*
- *Believe nothing, no matter where you read it, or who said it, no matter if I have said it, unless it agrees with your own reason and your own commonsense.*
- *Peace comes from within. Do not seek it without.*
- *How easy it is to see your brother's faults, how hard to face your own.*
- *Never be angry.*
- *With gentleness, overcome anger. With generosity, overcome meanness. With truth, overcome deceit.*
- *The winner sows hatred because the loser suffers. Let go of winning and losing and find joy.*
- *Live in joy, in love, even among those who hate.*
- *No one purifies another. You are the source of all purity and impurity.*

- *To straighten the crooked, you must do a harder thing – straighten yourself.*
- *Never speak harsh words, for they will rebound upon you.*
- *See yourself in others. Then whom can you hurt? What harm can you do?*
- *It is better to conquer yourself than to win a thousand battles.*

And then a few more that I have picked up over the years, more Zen than Buddhism:

*When hungry, eat your rice; when tired, close your eyes. Fools may laugh at me, but wise men will know what I mean.*
Lin-chi

*Barn's burnt down. Now I can see the Moon.*
Zen saying

*Unformed people delight in the gaudy and in novelty. Cooked people delight in the ordinary.*
Zen saying

*Attention! Attention! Attention!*
Zen saying

*Zen is not some kind of excitement, but concentration on our usual everyday routine.*
Shunryu Suzuki

*Every man is rich or poor according to the proportion between his desires and his enjoyments.*
Samuel Johnson

## 8.1.4 How Buddhism Helps Me

There is a lot of material here, and much more available online and in hundreds of books on Buddhism. In my readings and contemplations, I have a few takeaways that help me in my everyday life:

- **Attachments** – in my early readings, I concluded that following the Buddhist philosophy meant giving up all attachments, since they result in suffering. I have since fundamentally changed my understanding (correctly or not) and believe that attachments are just fine – we need and can enjoy the pleasure and motivations that come with them. What is *not* healthy is any attachment to our attachments. I can desire wealth, health, accomplishments, etc. I may even attain some of these desires. But all life is temporary and mostly out of our control. These desires may never be attained or attained and lost. Bad things may and will happen. What one must do is let go and move on when attachments are not attained or attained and lost.
- **Attention to the moment** – I know people who meditate every day. The best book that has worked for me is *Breathe Sweeps Mind*.[276] I highly recommend it to anyone with that discipline. My own practice has been inconsistent. What I have been able to accomplish in going about my day are brief moments where I focus solely on right now and leave memories and objectives/anticipations to another time. It is not something one can do all day because there are always obligations that require looking backward and forward. However, while drinking my iced mocha, going on a walk, between meetings, having a focused conversation, playing with our new puppy, exercising, and many other situations, I can try to calm my mind and just focus on the here and now.
- **Lovingkindness** – this is a specific Buddhist term that just means, in your actions with others, try to be loving and kind. We are all in this together on this spinning planet heading for

mutual oblivion. My acts of lovingkindness are not purely about the other; they are also self-serving. Being loving and kind to others requires me to pause and be in the moment and makes me feel so much better during and afterward. It is a form of detachment from self that I find very calming and rewarding.

## 8.2 STOICISM

*The part of life we really live is small. For all the rest of existence is not life, but merely time.*
Seneca

*Man alone is born crying, lives complaining, and dies disappointed.*
Samuel Johnson

### 8.2.1 FUNDAMENTALS

Stoicism, a school of Hellenistic philosophy, was founded about 2,300 years ago by Zeno of Citium. According to its teachings, the path to happiness is found in accepting the moment as it presents itself by not allowing desires to control oneself, using one's mind to understand the world, and working together and treating others fairly and justly.

About a decade ago, I found and downloaded *Meditations* by Marcus Aurelius (a leading stoic) from *The Internet Classics Archive*.[277] I was happy to find his writings from this editable source because much of the text was padding, and I wanted to have the ability to pare it down to its essence. I first highlighted what I thought were his key points, and then I created a new document that organized those points into related areas. I took the original 45,000 words, padded with references to gods and contemporaries, and boiled it down to 3,000 (see Appendix B). You could read the source, but it is much easier to absorb it without the clutter. There is a lot of content, but I have found that dwelling on one quote at a time brings me great life insights. Again, please take your time and come back to it regularly.

Note: Some of the realizations that have come to me during writing this book have sometimes been very depressing. I took advantage of this section by rereading it, and it has helped me significantly.

## 8.2.2 STOIC QUOTES

*Until we have begun to go without them, we fail to realize how unnecessary many things are. We've been using them not because we needed them but because we had them.*
Seneca

*It is not the man who has too little that is poor, but the one who hankers after more.*
Seneca

*What really frightens and dismays us is not external events themselves, but the way in which we think about them. It is not things that disturb us, but our interpretation of their significance.*
Epictetus

*It is more necessary for the soul to be cured than the body; for it is better to die than to live badly.*
Epictetus

*And whenever you encounter anything that is difficult or pleasurable, or highly or lowly regarded, remember that the contest is now: You are at the Olympic Games, you cannot wait any longer, and that your progress is wrecked or preserved by a single day and a single event.*
Epictetus

*Neither can the wave that has passed by be recalled, nor the hour which has passed return again.*
Ovid

*Stoicism is Buddhism without the dogma.*
Bill Madden

*Every instant of our lives is essentially irreplaceable; you must know this in order to concentrate on life.*
André Gide

*Not being able to govern events, I govern myself.*
Michel de Montaigne

*Everyone on Earth is afraid of losing his/her life, and only a few are afraid of losing their time.*
Sunday Adelaja

*There's nothing certain in man's life except this: That he must lose it.*
Aeschylus

*Listen closely... the eternal hush of silence goes on and on throughout all this, and has been going on, and will go on and on. This is because the world is nothing but a dream and is just thought of and the everlasting eternity pays no attention to it.*
Jack Kerouac

*Look to this day!*
*For it is life, the very life of life.*
*In its brief course*
*Lie all the verities and realities of your existence:*
*The bliss of growth;*
*The glory of action;*

*The splendor of achievement;*
*For yesterday is but a dream,*
*And tomorrow is only a vision;*
*But today, well lived, makes every yesterday*
*a dream of happiness,*
*And every tomorrow a vision of hope.*
Attributed to Kalidasa, a Sanskrit dramatist

*Our revels now are ended. These our actors,*
*As I foretold you, were all spirits and*
*Are melted into air, into thin air:*
*And, like the baseless fabric of this vision,*
*The cloud-capp'd towers, the gorgeous palaces,*
*The solemn temples, the great globe itself,*
*Yea, all which it inherit, shall dissolve*
*And, like this insubstantial pageant faded,*
*Leave not a rack behind. We are such stuff*
*As dreams are made on, and our little life*
*Is rounded with a sleep.*
The Tempest, Act 4 Scene 1

## 8.2.3 How Stoicism Helps Me

Stoicism agrees with the Buddhist teaching about attachment, attention to the moment, and lovingkindness. Furthermore, Stoicism is explicit on a few more things that I find helpful:

- **You are not important** – everyone reaches the same end. Poof! I am dead. No matter how long, life is brief when compared to what came before and what will come after. I try not to get hung up on my own importance. I am nothing.
- **And neither is anyone else** – no one is more important than I am in my lack of importance. I try not to get hung up on others' actions or opinions. I am a little bit of an anarchist at heart and

have little patience for leaders.

- **Only self-discipline matters** – while observing others closely, the only thing I try to concern myself with is my own thoughts and actions.

## 8.3 EXISTENTIALISM

### 8.3.1 FUNDAMENTALS

This is a tough one, but let me try. There are many philosophers who can be considered part of the existentialism camp, and they all have their own ways of articulating their related worldviews. I am going to completely gloss over these complexities and settle on the simplest common position. Existentialists believe that life does not have an objective nor any certainty but that the individual is free and creates value by affirming it and living it, not by talking about it. Everything else is a consequence of this position. This lack of objective and certainty is probably why existentialism is so difficult to articulate, even by members of its camp, which I think has led directly to its lost impact on philosophy.

### 8.3.2 THE MYTH OF SISYPHUS

Life in *The Myth of Sisyphus* by Albert Camus is demonstrated as *absurd* – what we want (whether it be meaning, order, or reasons) and what we find (formless chaos), followed by death. According to Camus, this lack of intrinsic meaning requires the readers to make one of three choices:

1. Take the blue pill – surrender to religion, superstition, teleology, or just the mind-numbing day-to-day grind, while ignoring our true reality. Do not get me wrong – I am not knocking

this choice (conscious or not). Most of the world's population follows this path, with or without the benefit of reading this book, and that is fine. It can provide comfort, morality, empathy, etc. However, it can also have deleterious results.

2. Take the purple pill (Chapter 10) and follow the path of *existential nihilism* – life is without objective meaning, purpose, or intrinsic value, which necessarily leads one to commit suicide.

3. Take the purple pill and live in this world devoid of any intrinsic meaning or purpose. Living with the absurd is a matter of acceptance and maintaining awareness of it. There are three characteristics of this life, for however long it lasts:
   a. *Revolt* – there is no answer nor reconciliation to this absurdity.
   b. *Freedom* – we are free to think and behave as we choose.
   c. *Passion* – we must pursue a life of rich and diverse experiences.

Camus never explicitly identifies those who had not and never will read his book or become aware of its implications. That would be about 99.9999% of the general population. As I mentioned much earlier, I call this population the "Nopills" – those never given that opportunity to accept or reject.

When writing this, Camus had no understanding of the existence nor implications of the Real Matrix, but I do not see any change in his fundamental conclusions. He proposed that life is absurd when it is *truly absurd*. We must accept that before and above all else.

## 8.3.3 EXISTENTIALIST QUOTES

*Life has no meaning a priori... It is up to you to give it a meaning, and value is nothing but the meaning that you choose.*
Jean-Paul Sartre

*This heart within me I can feel, and I judge that it exists. This world I can touch, and I likewise judge that it exists. There ends all my knowledge, and the rest is construction. (...) Forever I shall be a stranger to myself.*
Albert Camus, The Myth of Sisyphus

*Real generosity toward the future lies in giving all to the present.*
Albert Camus

*Life is meaningless, but worth living, provided you recognize its meaningless.*
Albert Camus

*Should I kill myself, or have a cup of coffee?*
Albert Camus

*Since we're all going to die, it's obvious that when and how don't matter.*
Albert Camus

*The literal meaning of life is whatever you're doing that prevents you from killing yourself.*
Albert Camus

*Sometimes, carrying on, just carrying on, is the superhuman achievement.*
Albert Camus

*The very meaningless of life forces man to make his own meaning.*
Stanley Kubrick

*He was free, free in every way, free to behave like a fool or a machine, free to accept, free to refuse, free to equivocate; to marry, to give up the game, to drag this death weight about with*

*him for years to come. He could do what he liked, no one had the right to advise him, there would be for him no Good or Evil unless he thought them into being.*
Jean-Paul Sartre

*The cradle rocks above an abyss, and common sense tells us that our existence is but a brief crack of light between two eternities of darkness.*
Vladimir Nabokov

## 8.3.4 How Existentialism Helps Me

Existentialism agrees with the Buddhist teaching about attachment and attention to the moment (but maybe not explicitly on lovingk-indness!). It also agrees with Stoicism on no one being important and focusing on our own thoughts and actions. Its novel contributions to how I live my life include:

- **Life is absurd** – this is the foundation of Existentialism that drives everything else. This is why it speaks so well to my con-cept of the Real Matrix. Contemplating this conclusion makes it easier for me to forgive myself and others in our struggles in this absurdity by recognizing there is no escape from it.
- **We find our own meaning** – I used to think that this existential concept of "finding our own meaning" was important and spe-cial. It made me feel superior in that recognition and pursuit. I have since put together more of the pieces and now realize the power of "The literal meaning of life is whatever you're doing that prevents you from killing yourself." Not only does life have no meaning, but the meaning we may find or pursue in life has no meaning. Just carry on.

## 8.4 Common and Consistent

These three philosophies arose in quite different contexts but have a few unifying themes. I believe that they are common because they best represent a healthy and stripped-down approach to living.

- Life is to be lived within the space between birth and death.
- You oversee your own life.
- You are in control of your thoughts.
- It is not important what others think.
- No one is more important than anyone else. Actually, no one is important at all.
- Do the best you can for yourself, be good to others, and damn the rest.
- Don't worry; be happy.
- We, and everyone you know, are all forever gone and forgotten in the end.

Now, in the context of the Real Matrix, I would add a few more:

- Keep in mind that you have been built by, and are part of, the Real Matrix, with no escape. You are a creation of the Real Matrix and insignificant beyond its mechanics.
- All you can know is what you sense and then perceive, which is not Reality.
- Your perception and subsequent worldview are defined by the Real Matrix.
- Try to remove everyday teleology and religion from your thoughts. Things happen with no intent.
- Understand and acknowledge how you are driven by layers and layers of allostasis, and work to build even more complex layers to expand your reach.

- Life is not only absurd, but it is *absurd* because of our existence within our Real Matrix.

## 8.5 WE ARE ALL FOOLED, FOOLED, FOOLED

### 8.5.1 "THE MEANING OF LIFE" ALLOSTASIS

Let us get real now. Remember what I wrote back in Section 6.3.3.17?

> *Each of us are our own primary first-party allostatic set. This is the mother of all allostatic sets. All our choices are intended to lead to a favorable hormonal balance, now or in the future, from birth to death. All the other allostatic systems I mentioned above are secondary to this primary system.*

We all pretend otherwise, but *everything, everything, everything* we (and all living organisms) do is grounded in this fundamental concept. As in our Real Matrix, there is *no escape* from this allostatic system. In the end, we are driven by our innate need to maximize our positive hormones and minimize our negative one, striking some balance between the short and long term, based on our flawed assumption that we understand reality.

### 8.5.2 OUR REALITY IS ABSOLUTELY NOT REALITY

If I work hard at it, I can intellectually accept that the reality we think is out there is not true Reality. *Reality does not exist for the benefit of our senses nor the signals we might measure and perceive.* But stop and consider that all human behavior and the behavior of all living organisms is based on the premise that what we perceive is in fact the same thing as reality. This is how we are built within the Real Matrix, and there is no physical or intellectual escape. And life on Earth is not special. All life forms that may exist in the universe face the same limitations. There is no *escape*.

Before I dump a bunch more quotes on you, let me leave you with this humorous one:

*I'm not crazy about reality, but it's still the only place to get a decent meal.*
Groucho Marx

## 8.5.3 Expand What I Mean by "We"

No one can prove nor disprove the following statements, meaning that they are non-falsifiable, at least until we can collect a few samples!

Let me expand my use of "we" to include all life forms in the universe. Based on my own logic:

1. All extraterrestrial life, regardless of its composition, must have emerged through its own abiogenetic mechanics and evolution.
2. All extraterrestrial life must therefore exist within its own inescapable Real Matrix.
3. Just as the fundamental nature of our Real Matrix is beyond our complete understanding, the nature of the intelligence of any advanced extraterrestrial will also be beyond our comprehension.

These positions are a little squishy since I avoid defining "life" and "intelligence."

# 9 WHY TO LIVE LIFE

I am not a philosopher. I am not your guru. I cannot guide you. That burden is yours. I do not have my own personal final answer to being lodged in the Real Matrix but will continue my studies of Buddhism, Stoicism, and Existentialism, make life choices that align with them, and muddle along.

I can leave you with two things – 1) even more quotes to ruminate on and 2) the subsequent section that introduces a possible path for struggling forward together. Here are the quotes. As with all the earlier ones, please take your time contemplating and applying them.

*Happiness is the meaning and the purpose of life, the whole aim and end of human existence.*
  Aristotle

*You will never be happy if you continue to search for what happiness consists of. You will never live if you are looking for the meaning of life.*
Albert Camus

*Man cannot endure his own littleness unless he can translate it into meaningfulness on the largest possible level.*
Ernest Becker

*If we possess a "why" of life, we can put up with almost any how.*
Friedrich Nietzsche, *Twilight of the Idols*

*What I look forward to is continued immaturity followed by death.*
Dave Berry

*All the labor of all the ages, all the devotion, all the inspiration, and all the noonday brightness of human genius are destined to extinction. So now, my friends, if that is true, and it is true, what is the point?*
Bertrand Russell

*Doubt is not a pleasant condition, but certainty is absurd.*
Voltaire

*Life has to be given a meaning because of the obvious fact that it has no meaning.*
Henry Miller

*Humans are born to die, anything in between is just pure nonsense.*
Anupam S. Shlok

*There is not one big cosmic meaning for all; there is only the meaning we each give to our life, an individual meaning, an individual plot, like an individual novel, a book for each person.*
Anaïs Nin

*Ultimately, man should not ask what the meaning of his life is, but rather must recognize that it is he who is asked. In a word, each man is questioned by life; and he can only answer to life by answering for his own life; to life he can only respond by being responsible.*
Viktor Frankl

*The chances of finding out what's really going on in the universe are so remote, the only thing to do is hang the sense of it and keep yourself occupied.*
Douglas Adams

*I distrust 'reality' and its moron mother, the universe, while you fasten your innocence to fallible devices which pretend at happy endings.*
Ray Bradbury

*We are here, and it is now. Further than that, all human knowledge is moonshine.*
H.L. Mencken, *A Mencken Chrestomathy*

*A man walking across a field encountered a tiger. He fled, the tiger chasing after him. Coming to a cliff, he caught hold of a wild vine and swung himself over the edge. The tiger sniffed at him from above. Terrified, the man looked down to where, far below, another tiger had come, waiting to eat him. Two mice, a white one and a black one, begin gnawing on the vine. The man saw a luscious strawberry near him. Grasping the vine with one hand, he plucked the strawberry with the other. How sweet it tasted!*
Zen parable

*You remember when I said how I was gonna explain about life, buddy? Well the thing about life is, it gets weird. People are always talking ya about truth. Everybody always knows what the truth is, like it was toilet paper or somethin', and they got a supply in the closet. But what you learn, as you get older, is there ain't no truth. All there is is bullshit, pardon my vulgarity here. Layers of it. One layer of bullshit on top of another. And what you do in life like when you get older is, you pick the layer of bullshit that you prefer and that's your bullshit, so to speak.*
Bernie LaPlante in *Hero*

# 10 THE PURPLE PILL

*The time will come when diligent research over long periods will bring to light things which now lie hidden. A single lifetime, even though entirely devoted to the sky, would not be enough for the investigation of so vast a subject... And so this knowledge will be unfolded only through long successive ages. There will come a time when our descendants will be amazed that we did not know things that are so plain to them... Many discoveries are reserved for ages still to come, when memory of us will have been effaced.*
Seneca, Natural Questions

*Whether you can or cannot observe a thing depends on the theory which you use. It is the theory which decides what can be observed.*
Albert Einstein

*Ignorance more frequently begets confidence than does knowledge: it is those who know little, not those who know much, who so positively assert that this or that problem will never be solved by science.*
Charles Darwin, *The Descent of Man*

*The most merciful thing in the world, I think, is the inability of the human mind to correlate all its contents... someday the piecing together of dissociated knowledge will open up such terrifying vistas of reality, and of our frightful position therein, that we shall either go mad from the revelation or flee from the light into the peace and safety of a new Dark Age.*
H.P. Lovecraft

*United with his fellow-men by the strongest of all ties, the tie of a common doom, the free man finds that a new vision is with him always, shedding over every daily task the light of love.*
Bertrand Russell, A Free Man's Worship

## 10.1.1 THE PURPLE PILL

In *The Matrix*, those ignorantly living within its virtual reality were called Bluepills, including those who never realized it and those who chose to forget. Once informed of the existence of the Matrix and its implications, taking the blue pill was a choice of rejection that sent you back to oblivion. Anything to do with the blue pill was a dead end – the complete acceptance of the false reality of the Matrix.

The movie's Redpills were much more interesting because they had several characteristics:

- They were outside the Matrix and had an awareness of it as a separate virtual reality.
- Those who were born within the Matrix could return to it (get jacked in) and leave it (through the telephone line); those who were born outside of it could never experience it.
- With the Redpills' awareness came free choice; they could act any way they wanted in their perceived reality, inside or outside.

I can offer you the blue pill – forget about this book, do not try to incorporate its findings or conjectures into your worldview, and lead your life as before – but I cannot offer you the red pill because there is no leaving or escaping the Real Matrix.

What I would like to offer you is the *purple pill* as a call to arms. Taking it means that you accept what you have learned here and will try to integrate it into your life choices. Just like in taking the red pill, I cannot dictate what choices you will make – only that you will forevermore be making those choices in awareness and context of existing within our Real Matrix.

## 10.1.2 In a World of Bluepills and Nopills

You will find it in Plato's "Allegory of the Cave" (when the free person returns to the cave) and lightly covered in some of the writings of atheist philosophers such as Bertrand Russell, but, in addition to choosing how to live life, a Purplepill must choose how to live that life in a world filled with Bluepills and Nopills.

## 10.1.3 The Purplepills Society

All who accept the conclusions of this book can call themselves *Purplepills*! Maybe we can start our own little society. In support of this, I have set up and will support a Purplepills' environment at Purplepillssociety.org.

# 11 Epilogue

> A *stupid man's report of what a clever man says can never be accurate, because he unconsciously translates what he hears into something he can understand.*
> Bertrand Russell

## 11.1 Surprises

I did not expect this, but I have traveled further personally in writing this book than you may have in reading it. I thought that I would be more educated but was surprised when I was also changed. I did not know 95% of the content in the Science, Abiogenesis, and Evolution sections before I started writing, but I expected that. I had no idea what I would be covering in the Redux and How/Why to Live Life sections until I was done with at least two-thirds of the rest of the book. Writing these sections is what unexpectedly affected my worldview.

To quote Michel de Montaigne in *On Giving the Lie*:

> I *have no more made my book than my book has made me: 'tis a book consubstantial with its author, of a peculiar design.*

I do not want to discuss those personal changes – that would make me appear as that false guru. I stated earlier that I have little patience for leaders. That impatience also applies to me whenever I take a leadership role. The path is for you alone to discover.

## 11.2 Positives and Negatives

My lack of a science education had both a positive and negative impact on writing this book. Some of the negatives have been:

- It has taken me three years to get to a final draft of this book, mostly because I had so much science to learn.
- I could not grasp the technical content, nor probably the importance, of many scientific articles and books, so their potential contribution was lost.

The positives included:

- My thorough education and experience in economics, systems analysis, and business transformation consulting helped me to break down and present my questions and answers in what I think was a clear and understandable way.
- To quote Shunryu Suzuki, "In the beginner's mind there are many possibilities, but in the expert's mind there are few." I think my status as a novice allowed me to investigate areas with a fresh and open mind.

## 11.3 Future Editions

There were six editions of *On the Origin of Species*. Instead of future editions of this book, if the Purplepills Society is successful, then I could edit an annual anthology based on member contributions.

## 11.4 Did I Succeed?

Way back in Section 2.6.3, I wondered if, given all the threats, I would be successful in my quest to completely understand and effectively explain the Real Matrix. I wrote those words before I had really begun the book. I was hoping for the best. Did I succeed in my quest?

Well, as I probably knew deep inside at the time, I was destined to fail. I have been able to chip around the edges, but the essence of the Real Matrix is beyond any human's ability to truly comprehend at a fundamental level. We are trapped and controlled by the Real Matrix, and there is no red pill available to allow us to step outside and look back in. Even an Einstein-level intellect could never succeed since that person would also be trapped with no escape. And let me reemphasize that no escape means *no escape* for any living organism. We are made up of the Real Matrix – it is nothing that can be tossed off.

## 11.5 A Freaky Idea

While writing that last paragraph, a freaky idea (my final epiphany) came to mind. Theoretically, there may be a path to completely understanding the Real Matrix, but you are not going to like it. Remember in the movie that sentient machines built the Matrix to fool humans. What if we could build sentient machines that could exist outside the Real Matrix and look back in! These machines could continually expand their sensing capabilities to match all living things and other machines and perhaps find ways to expand even further. I did not have this in mind when I wrote Section 4.5.7, Specialized Equipment Sensors, but that list of 400 would be the beginning of that journey. How their motivations might evolve is for "Terminator" fans to theorize.

The part you are not going to like is that there would be no way for those machines to come back and explain what they learned to their (human) creators, since humans would still be trapped in their own sensing and motivation capabilities within their Real Matrix. The robots would only be able to explain it to each other! From our perspective, this would be much worse than *The Matrix* or even *Terminator.* I will not be around to experience this but maybe my grandchildren's grandchildren will be. I am giving an early warning on this outcome.

# 12 GLOSSARY

**THE BIOCHEMISTRY (supporting Section 4.3)**

**Biological Supermolecules (Biomolecules) (supporting Section 4.3.3)**

**Nucleic acids** (*polynucleotides*) – informational biomolecules. DNA contains the genetic components and instructions in a cell, while RNA primarily makes proteins. They consist of nucleotide polymers: adenosine (A), guanine (G), cytosine (C), thymine (T) (DNA-only), and uracil (U) (RNA-only) joined by covalent bonds. Nucleotide monomers are formed of a nitrogen base bonded to a 5-carbon sugar, with attached phosphate groups to form the backbone of the DNA chain. The famous double-strand helix structure is held together by hydrogen (noncovalent) interactions between the nucleotides in the chain.

**Amino acids** – organic compounds that are the building blocks of proteins. There are 20 standard amino acids of which almost all proteins are made. Each amino acid has the same fundamental structure, consisting of a central carbon atom bonded to an amino group, a carboxyl group, and a hydrogen atom. Every amino acid also has another atom or group of atoms bonded to the central atom known as the R group (its *side chain*). The properties of this side chain determine the 3D structure and biological activity of the proteins containing the amino acids. Only water is more abundant in organisms.

**Proteins/peptides** (*polyamides*) – informational biomolecules that contain polymers of amino acids joined by covalent bonds and provide enzymes, structure, receptors, transport, and more to cells. *Proteins* are polypeptides containing more than approximately 50 amino acids. Polymerization occurs at ribosomes. Every protein has a specific sequence of amino acids, and that sequence makes the protein take different shapes and have different functions. These functions are due to their ability to bind to other molecules. Each protein has a chemical reactivity that depends not only on which side chains are exposed but also on its three-dimensional structure. There are over 60,000 known proteins. Types of proteins (i.e., types of work) include:[278]

- **Structural** –these are strong, fibrous proteins. *Keratin* forms the structure of skin, nails, hair, and teeth. *Collagen* serves as a connective structure for tendons, bones, muscles, cartilage, and skin. *Elastin* coils provide the elasticity of structures such as skin, blood vessels, heart, lungs, intestines, tendons, and ligaments.
- **Storage** – *hemoglobin* stores oxygen in red blood cells. *Ferritin* stores iron, which helps make red blood cells.
- **Hormonal** – these proteins carry signals through the *endocrine* (directed into the bloodstream) and *exocrine* (directed to tissues that line the outer surfaces of organs and blood vessels) systems. For example, *insulin* is transported through the bloodstream to remove sugar when blood sugar levels are elevated.
- **Enzyme** – these proteins are biological catalysts needed for chemical reactions. They provide an environment within which a given reaction is energetically more favorable. One type of enzyme reduces carbohydrates and starches to *glucose*, and another reduces proteins to amino acids. *Enzyme catalysis* is the term used to describe this activity.
- **Receptors** – these bind to signaling molecules and initiate a physiological response. Different receptors are specific for different molecules. We will discuss receptors in much more

detail under the Cell Signaling, Sensory Systems, and Response Systems sections.

- **Immunoglobulins** – these proteins act as antibodies, released in response to *antigen* (any substance that can stimulate an immune response) recognition. Each immunoglobulin protects against a different antigen type.

**Carbohydrates** (*saccharides*) – provide short-term energy storage to cells and structure to plant cell walls. They include *monosaccharides* (glucose, fructose, and galactose), *disaccharides* (maltose, lactose, and sucrose), and *polysaccharides* (starch in plants and glycogen in animals).

**Lipids** (fatty acids) – provide long-term energy storage and support cell signaling. They also provide physical structure and insulation in animals. They include fats, oils, waxes, triglycerides, phospholipids, and steroid derivatives such as cholesterol. They are not polymers. Lipids are usually characterized by a water-loving (hydrophilic) "head" connected to a nonpolar water-fearing (hydrophobic) "tail."[279]

- In animals, when there is an oversupply of dietary carbohydrate, the excess carbohydrate is converted to triglycerides (fat).
- *Beta oxidation* is the metabolic process by which fatty acids are broken down to generate acetate, which is ultimately converted into ATP, $CO_2$, and $H_2O$ using the citric acid cycle and the electron transport chain.

**Ligand** – the substance bound by a protein. Nonpolar ligands diffuse across the cell membrane and bind to internal receptors, while polar ligands interact with membrane receptor proteins. The ability of a protein to bind selectively and with high affinity to a ligand depends on the formation of a set of noncovalent interactions plus favorable hydrophobic interaction. The region of a protein that associates with a ligand is its *binding site*.

## Biological Pathways[35]

### Metabolic

- Carbohydrate
- Energy
- Lipid
- Nucleotide
- Amino acid
- Cofactors and vitamins

### Genetic information processing

- Transcription
- Translation
- Folding, sorting, degradation
- Replication and repair

### Environmental information processing

- Membrane transport
- Signal transduction
- Signaling molecules and interaction

### Cellular processes

- Transport and catabolism
- Cell growth and death
- Cellular community
- Cell motility

**Organismal systems**

- Immune system
- Endocrine system
- Circulatory system
- Digestive system
- Excretory system
- Nervous system
- Sensory system
- Development and regeneration
- Aging
- Environmental adaptation

**Metabolic Pathways**[280]

**Catabolic reactions** – break down large organic molecules into smaller molecules, releasing the energy contained in the chemical bonds. ATP *hydrolysis* is the catabolic reaction process by which chemical energy that has been stored in high-energy bonds in adenosine triphosphate (ATP) is released by splitting these bonds, producing adenosine diphosphate (ADP), an inorganic phosphate ion, and free energy.

**Anabolic reactions** (biosynthesis reactions) – involve the joining of smaller molecules into larger ones. These reactions require energy to perform, which is generated by catabolic reactions. *Polymerization* is an anabolic pathway that builds biomolecules like nucleic acids, proteins, and polysaccharides. These processes produce growth and differentiation of cells, increase in body size, and revitalization of organs.

**Oxidation-reduction reactions** – transfer electrons across molecules by *oxidizing* one molecule (removing an electron), *reducing* another (adding an electron), and collecting the released energy to convert a phosphate and ADP into ATP.

## THE BIOLOGY (supporting Section 4.4)

### Biological Processes

**Homeostasis** – regulation of the internal environment to maintain a constant state; for example, sweating to reduce internal temperature.

**Metabolism** – transformation of energy by converting chemicals and energy into cellular components (anabolism) and decomposing organic matter (catabolism). Living things require energy to maintain internal organization (homeostasis) and to produce the other phenomena associated with life.

**Growth** – maintenance of a higher rate of anabolism than catabolism. A growing organism increases in size in all its parts, rather than simply accumulating matter.

**Adaptation** – the ability to change over time in response to the environment. This ability is fundamental to the process of evolution and is determined by the organism's heredity, diet, and external factors.

**Response to stimuli** – a response can take many forms, from the contraction of a unicellular organism, to external chemicals, to complex reactions involving all the senses of multicellular organisms. A response is often expressed by motion; for example, the leaves of a plant turning toward the sun (phototropism), and chemotaxis (movement in response to a chemical stimulus).

**Reproduction** – the ability to produce new individual organisms, either asexually from a single parent organism or sexually from two parent organisms.

**Interaction between organisms** – the processes by which an organism has an observable effect on another organism of the same or different species.

### Biomolecular Aggregates (supporting Section 4.4.3)

**Amphiphile** – a chemical compound possessing both hydrophilic (water-loving, polar) and hydrophobic (not attracted to water, non-polar) properties.

- **Hydrophile** – a molecule that is attracted to polar solvents, like water, and tends to dissolve in them.
- **Hydrophobe** – a molecule that is repelled from a mass of water and tends to be nonpolar and to join with other neutral molecules and nonpolar solvents. Because water molecules are polar, hydrophobes do not dissolve well among them. Hydrophobic molecules in water often cluster together, forming micelles.

**Micelle** – an aggregate of amphiphilic biomolecules dispersed in a liquid colloid. Micelles form spontaneously in water. A typical micelle in an aqueous solution forms an aggregate with the hydrophilic (attracted to water) "head" regions that are in contact with a surrounding solvent, sequestering the hydrophobic (not attracted to water) single-tail regions in the micelle center. This type of micelle is known as a normal-phase micelle (oil-in-water micelle). Inverse micelles have the head groups at the center with the tails extending out (water-in-oil micelle).

- **Colloid** – a mixture in which one substance of dispersed insoluble or soluble particles is suspended throughout another substance. For example, milk is a colloidal mixture of butterfats suspended in water.

**Biological micelle**[281] – in a biological system, the micelle molecules tend to arrange themselves in such a manner that the inner core of these structures are hydrophobic, and the outer layers are hydrophilic. This is a monolayer; everything following relates to a bilayer.

**Vesicle** – a structure consisting of liquid or cytoplasm enclosed by a lipid bilayer. A vesicle is a complex, organic micelle. The structure can be found inside or outside a cell. A cell is also a vesicle.

**Lipid** – mentioned earlier as a type of biomolecule, lipids are soluble in nonpolar solvents. Non-polar solvents are typically hydrocarbons that do not easily dissolve in water. The amphiphilic nature of some lipids allows them to form structures, such as vesicles. Functions of lipids include:[282]

- Acting as an energy source
- Protects and structures organs
- Insulation
- Generating heat
- Giving cell membranes structure
- Allows signaling proteins to lock into it
- Allows the cell membrane to remain hydrophobic

**Lipid Bilayer** – a thin polar membrane made of two layers of lipid molecules; a class of lipids called *phospholipids*. These membranes are flat sheets that form a continuous barrier around all cells. When phospholipids are placed in water, the molecules spontaneously arrange such that the tails are shielded from the water, resulting in the formation of membrane structures, such as bilayers, vesicles, and micelles.

**Liposome**[289] – liposomes are composed of a bilayer of *amphipathic* (having both hydrophilic and hydrophobic parts) molecules. The molecules are arranged in two concentric circles, such that the hydrophilic heads of the outer layer are exposed to the outer environment, and the hydrophilic heads of the inner layer make the inner hydrophilic core. The hydrophobic tails are tucked between the two layers.

**Protocell** – a protocell is more of a concept than a real thing, as are many of our transitional entities. It is a transitional vesicle between a micelle and a biological cell that performs some, but not all, of the functions of a cell. In our abiogenesis discussion, I referred to my *entity* as a *protocell*. The minimum functions that would have needed to co-emerge to form a protocell include:[283]

- Spatially and temporally stable, yet selectively permeable, compartments (emerging as a cell membrane).
- Energy harvesting from primary sources to chemical bonds to chemical energy (emerging as respiration).
- Making its own building blocks through autocatalysis networks/assemblies (emerging as metabolism).
- Passing similar contents to descendant protocells (emerging as templated replication).

**Cell** – a cell is the basic structural, functional, and biological unit of all known organisms and is the smallest unit of life. It is a self-contained, self-assembling, self-adjusting, self-maintaining, and self-perpetuating system of biomolecules that extracts free energy and raw materials from its environment. It is enclosed by a membrane, which forms a selective barrier that allows nutrients to enter and biomolecules and waste products to leave. The cell maintains itself in homeostasis in disequilibrium with its environment. Each human organism is composed of 30 to 40 trillion cells. The nutrients required by a cell in a large amount (*macronutrients*) are:[284]

- *Carbon* – component of carbohydrates, proteins, nucleic acids, lipids, and many other compounds; accounts for about 50% of the composition of the cell.
- *Nitrogen* – component of proteins, nucleic acids, and other cell constituents; represents 12% of the composition of the cell.
- *Hydrogen* and *Oxygen* – part of many organic compounds and the building blocks of water ($H_2O$).
- *Phosphorus* – required by all organisms for the synthesis of nucleotides and phospholipids.
- *Sulfur* – a component of some amino acids and present in several vitamins and coenzymes.
- *Potassium*, *Magnesium*, *Calcium*, and *Sodium* – enable the structure and function of the prokaryotic cell.

Micronutrients include *iron, boron, chromium, manganese*, and more.[292]

**Organism** – an organism is an individual entity that embodies the properties of life. It is a synonym for "life form." Organisms are classified by taxonomy into groups such as multicellular animals, plants, and fungi; or unicellular microorganisms, such as protists, bacteria, and archaea. All types of organisms are capable of reproduction, growth and development, maintenance, and response to stimuli.

- In multicellular organisms, cells specialize into different types that are adapted to specific functions.
- Multicellularity has emerged independently at least 25 times.[285,286]

**Holobiont** – a group consisting of a host organism and any other organisms living in or around it (called bionts), which together form a discrete symbiotic integrated unit. These associated microbiomes have great effects on the function and fitness of any host organism, including anatomy, development, physiology, genetics, and immunity.[287] This is not to be confused with a super-organism, which is a group of synergistically interacting organisms of the *same* species.[251,288]

• Symbionts can be acquired horizontally by the host or trans-mitted vertically through reproductive cells and larvae.[289]
• The microbiota found in humans (consisting of all bacteria, archaea, fungi, protozoa, algae, and viruses) may contain up to 100 times as many genes (the microbiome) as the human genome itself. This does not include the micro-animals that also co-exist on and inside us. This begs the question of what it is to be human since we are all holobionts.

## Cell Types (supporting Section 4.4.4)

**Prokaryote** – an organism that lacks a membrane-bound nucleus, mitochondria, or any other membrane-bound organelle. Prokaryotes are asexual, reproducing without fusion of *gametes* (see next).

**Eukaryote** – an organism whose cells have a nucleus enclosed within membranes. Eukaryotes have their own (third) domain, Eukaryota. The three different types of eukaryote cells are:

• **Somatic cell** – a *diploid* (paired chromosomes) cell that forms the body of an organism – 99.999% of the cells in an organism are somatic cells.
• **Gamete** – a *haploid* cell that carries half of the genetic material necessary to form a complete organism. A gamete is an egg cell (female gamete) or a sperm (male gamete). Gametes are formed by the process of meiosis.
• **Zygote** – a type of somatic, diploid cell. A zygote is the result

of the union of two gametes. It remains a zygote until it begins to divide, at which point, the zygote becomes an embryo. A zygote produces somatic cells by mitosis.

**Some Key Cell Components (supporting Section 4.4.5 )**

**Biological Membrane** – an enclosing or separating membrane that acts as a selectively permeable barrier within living things.

- **Cell membrane** – a biological membrane that separates the cell interior from its exterior and controls the movement of substances in and out of cells and organelles. It is selectively permeable to ions and organic molecules. Cell membranes have numerous roles, including compartmentalization, energy transduction (respiration), nutrient and ion transport, signal transduction, and enzyme-catalyzed metabolic reactions, including the growth of the membranes themselves. The two types of *membrane transport* are:
  o **Passive transport** – primarily the movement of molecules and simpler biomolecules, such as oxygen, monosaccharides, water, carbon dioxide, lipids, and small proteins across a cell membrane without need of energy input, driven by the tendency of the system to grow in entropy. The kinds of passive transport include simple diffusion, facilitated transport that uses integral, carrier, and channel proteins, filtration, and osmosis.
  o **Active transport** – the movement of larger biomolecules, such as proteins and complex carbohydrates, against the concentration gradient across a cell membrane, from a region of lower to higher concentration. Active transport requires cellular energy to achieve this movement and is also enabled by special carrier proteins. There are two types: *primary active transport* that uses ATP or NADPH and *secondary active transport* that uses an electrochemical

gradient created by pumping ions in and out of the cell.

- **Cell wall** – a structural layer surrounding some types of cells, just outside the cell membrane. It can be tough, flexible, and sometimes rigid. It provides the cell with structural support, protection, and a pressure vessel, and acts as a filtering mechanism. Cell walls are present in most prokaryotes, algae, fungi, and eukaryotes, including plants, but are absent in animals.

**Cytoplasm** – all of the material within a cell is enclosed in the cytoplasm, except for the cell nucleus. The main components of the cytoplasm are:

- **Cytosol** – the portion of the cytoplasm not contained within membrane-bound organelles. Dissolved in the cytosol are many proteins and the RNA molecules that encode them, the monomer amino acids and nucleotides used to assemble them, *metabolites* (intermediate end products of metabolism), and coenzymes (nonproteins that work with enzymes, i.e., vitamins).
- **Cytoskeleton** – a network of interlinking protein filaments with diverse functions that extend from the cell nucleus to the cell membrane.
- **Cytoplasmic inclusions** – small particles of insoluble substances suspended in the cytosol.

**Ribosome** – acts as an assembly line where messenger RNA (mRNA) from the nucleus is used to synthesize proteins from amino acids. Ribosomes consist of the small subunits, which read the mRNA codons, and the large subunits, which join amino acids to form proteins. There are *membrane-bound ribosomes* and *free ribosomes*. The membrane-bound ribosomes synthesize proteins destined for export, lysosomes, and insertion into the nuclear or plasma membranes. The free ribosomes synthesize proteins that will remain and function within the cytosol.

- *Ribosome biogenesis* is the process of making ribosomes. In prokaryotes, this process takes place in the cytoplasm, and in eukaryotes, it takes place in the cytoplasm and nucleolus (a small part of the nucleus). The ribosomal proteins are encoded by ribosomal genes. This process may have predated cells, and genes and cells may have evolved to enhance the reproductive capacity of ribosomes.
- *Ribozymes* are RNA enzymes that can catalyze specific biochemical reactions, including RNA splicing in gene expression, like the action of protein enzymes. They are part of the large subunit of ribosomal RNA that link amino acids during protein synthesis. They also participate in RNA splicing, viral replication, and transfer RNA (tRNA) biosynthesis. Their discovery about 40 years ago led to the development of the "RNA world hypothesis" for the origin of life since RNA can be both genetic material (like DNA) and a biological catalyst (like protein enzymes).

**Endoplasmic reticulum** – helps with the biosynthesis, folding, modification, and transport of transmembrane proteins and lipids. It synthesizes proteins through *membrane-bound ribosomes* that are attached to the membrane walls of the *rough endoplasmic reticulum*. Depending on where it is found, the *smooth endoplasmic reticulum* synthesizes lipids, removes toxins, and stores calcium.

### Prokaryote-only
- The cytoplasmic region of a prokaryote has no organelles and contains the genome, ribosomes, and different inclusions.
- Its DNA is a singular circular chromosome. The nuclear region in the cytoplasm is called the *nucleoid*.
- *Flagella* and *pili* extend from the cell's surface. They are made of proteins that enable movement and communication between cells.

**Eukaryote-only**

- **Organelle** – a specialized subunit within a cell that has a specific function. Organelles are either separately enclosed within a lipid bilayer (also called membrane-bound organelles) or are spatially distinct functional units without a surrounding lipid bilayer (non-membrane bound organelles). There are dozens of types of organelles within cells. Some of the key ones that I will reference later include:

  o **Nucleus** – a double-membrane-bound organelle that contains all the cell's genome, except for a small fraction of mitochondrial DNA. It is the largest organelle in animal cells. The material inside the nucleus and contained within the nuclear membrane is termed the *nucleoplasm*. The *nucleolus* is the largest structure in the nucleus of eukaryotic cells and is the site of ribosome biogenesis (see below). Ribosomal RNA produced in the nucleolus passes into the cytoplasm through the nuclear pores.

  o **Mitochondrion** (plural, mitochondria) – a double-membrane-bound organelle that converts oxygen and nutrients (glucose, amino acids, and fatty acids) into ATP and waste (i.e., carbon dioxide), a process called *aerobic respiration*. The reactions involved in respiration are catabolic. The number of mitochondria present in a cell can range from one to thousands of organelles. The mitochondrion has an independent genome (DNA, RNA, and ribosomes) that shows considerable similarity to bacterial genomes.

  o **Chloroplast** – an organelle that conducts *photosynthesis*, where the photosynthetic pigment chlorophyll captures energy from the photons in sunlight and converts this excitation into ATP and reduced nicotinamide adenine dinucleotide phosphate (NADPH). Photosynthetic plant cells contain both chloroplasts and mitochondria. Chloroplasts, like mitochondria, contain their own DNA, RNA, and ribosomes.

- o **Hydrogenosome**[290] – an organelle that produces ATP and hydrogen from the oxidation of pyruvate or malate; found in various anaerobic unicellular eukaryotes.
- o **Golgi apparatus** – processes and packages the biomolecules, such as proteins and lipids, that are synthesized within the rough endoplasmic reticulum. These proteins are inserted into membrane vesicles that then fuse with the Golgi complex. As a protein passes through the Golgi complex, enzymes modify it to "address" it to its specific destination as it leaves the Golgi complex in a transport vesicle budding from the opposite side.
- o **Lysosome** – acts as the waste disposal system of the cell by receiving obsolete or un-used materials in the cytoplasm and degrading them to their simple components (amino acids, monosaccharides, fatty acids, etc.) that are then released to be recycled into new cellular components or further catabolized. Plants have *vacuoles* that carry out similar degradative reactions.
- o **Peroxisome** – removes toxic peroxides. *Glyoxysomes* are peroxisomes found in plant cells that convert stored fats into carbohydrates during seed germination.
- o **Vacuole** – sequester waste products and store water in plant cells.
- o **Cilium** (plural is cilia) – is an organelle in the shape of a slender protuberance that projects from the cell body. The *primary (non-motile) cilia* coordinate many cellular signaling pathways. *Motile cilia* are found on the surface of cells and beat rhythmically.
- o **Plasmid** – a small, extrachromosomal DNA molecule within a cell that is physically separated from chromosomal DNA and can replicate independently. They are units of DNA capable of replicating autonomously within a suitable host. Plasmids, like viruses, are not classified as life.

**The Cell-Division Cycle (supporting Section 4.4.6)**

**Interphase** (both eukaryotes and prokaryotes) – when the cell obtains nutrients and metabolizes them, grows, reads its DNA, and conducts other continuous cell functions.

- **Gap 1 phase** – the cell grows and functions normally. During this time, protein synthesis occurs, and the cell grows.
- **Synthesis phase** – the cell synthesizes its DNA, and the chromosome number is doubled.
- **Gap 2 phase** – the cell resumes its growth in preparation for division. The mitochondria (in animals) or the chloroplasts (in plants) divide, and the cell continues to grow.

**Mitosis** (eukaryotes) – when replicated chromosomes are separated into two new nuclei, it produces identical cells. Mitosis is used by single-celled organisms to reproduce; it is also used for the organic growth of tissues, fibers, and membranes.

- **Preprophase** (plant cells) – the nucleus migrates into the center of the cell.
- **Prophase** – chromosomes become tightly condensed and mitotic spindle formation is initiated.
- **Prometaphase** – the nuclear envelope disintegrates into small membrane vesicles. As this happens, microtubules invade the nuclear space.
- **Metaphase** – the chromosomes get pulled toward opposite ends of the cell.
- **Anaphase** – two identical daughter chromosomes are formed, which are pulled to opposite ends of the cell. The cell then elongates.
- **Telophase** – the cell elongates even more, a new nuclear envelope forms around each set of separated daughter chromosomes, and the nucleolus reappears. Both sets of chromosomes

begin to "relax" or decondense. Each daughter nucleus has an identical set of chromosomes.

**Cytokinesis** (eukaryotes) – the physical division of the parent cell into the two daughter cells, each containing their own copy of the daughter chromosomes.

**Meiosis** (eukaryotes) – produces gametes (i.e., the sex cells – egg and sperm). It consists of the same phases as mitosis, but it goes through them twice (meiosis I and meiosis II). The gametes combine to create new, genetically different offspring. Meiosis results in four genetically different daughter haploid (chromosome number is halved from the parent cell) sex cells. In mitosis, DNA replicates once and divides once; in meiosis, DNA replicates once but divides twice.

- **Sexual reproduction** – the process in which new organisms are created by combining the genetic information from two individuals of different sexes. The genetic information is carried on chromosomes within the nucleus of gametes. The two gametes (egg and sperm) join in a fusion process (fertilization) to create a zygote, which is the precursor to an embryo offspring, taking half of its DNA from each of its parents.

**Fission** (prokaryotes and mitochondria/chloroplasts) – replication when a nucleus is absent. The DNA molecule first replicates, then attaches each copy to a different part of the cell membrane. When the cell begins to pull apart, the replicated and original chromosomes are separated. The consequence of this asexual method of reproduction is that all the cells are genetically identical (barring random mutations).

**Two Types of Organisms (supporting Section 4.4.7)**

**Autotroph (producer)** – an organism that produces complex organic compounds from simple substances present in its surroundings (e.g., carbon dioxide or minerals).

- **Photoautotroph** – uses energy from light (photosynthesis). We call them plants.
- **Chemoautotroph** – uses inorganic chemical reactions (chemosynthesis). They are mainly found on ocean floors where underwater volcanos can provide heat as an energy source.

**Heterotroph (consumer)** – an organism that does not produce its own food. Instead, they take nutrition from other sources of organic carbon, mainly plant or animal matter. Heterotrophs include all animals and fungi, some bacteria and *protists* (a group of mostly unicellular eukaryotic organisms), and parasitic plants.

## Energy Storage and Usage (supporting Section 4.4.8)

### The Storage Processes

- **Autotrophic – photosynthesis** – a process used by photoautotrophs to convert light energy into carbohydrates (glucose). Photosynthesis takes place within the chloroplast in two distinct stages. In the *light reactions*, photons are absorbed by chlorophyll pigments that then drive the synthesis of ATP and NADPH, along with the formation of O2 (as a waste product) from H2O. The *dark reactions* begin by incorporating CO2 from the air into organic molecules already present in the chloroplast. It then reduces the fixed carbon to carbohydrates by the addition of energized electrons from NADPH and the chemical energy stored in ATP.
- **Heterotrophic – ingestion, digestion, absorption, transport** – *ingestion* is the consumption of a substance by an organism.

*Digestion* (mechanical/chemical) is the breakdown of large insoluble food molecules into small water-soluble food molecules (i.e., polysaccharides and disaccharides into monosaccharides). *Absorption* is the uptake of nutrients from the digestive system by osmosis, active transport, and diffusion. Finally, (intracellular) *Primary Active Transport* uses ATP to transport packets of components to intracellular locations by attaching them to molecular motors that haul them along microtubules and actin filaments.

o Prokaryotic cells do not have this transport mechanism because there are no membranous organelles and compartments to traffic between.

o This process breaks down complex organic compounds (e.g., carbohydrates, fats, and proteins) into simpler compounds (e.g., carbohydrates into glucose, fats into fatty acids and glycerol, and proteins into amino acids).

## The Storage Molecules

- **Monosaccharides** (simple carbohydrates) – **glucose** is the most important source of energy in all organisms. Glucose is partially stored as a polymer - in plants, mainly as starch and amylopectin, and in animals, as glycogen. Glucose circulates in the blood of animals as blood sugar. **Fructose** is found in many plants, where it is often bonded to glucose to form sucrose. **Galactose** is composed of the same elements as glucose, just rearranged. It usually converts to glucose, or can combine with glucose to form lactose, to lipids to make glycolipids (for example, molecules that constitute blood groups A, B, and AB), or to proteins to make glycoproteins (e.g., in cell membranes).
- **Polysaccharides** (complex carbohydrates) – **starch** consists of numerous glucose units and is produced by most green plants as energy storage. **Glycogen** is the main energy storage form of glucose in animals, fungi, and bacteria.

- **Lipids** – in most organisms, excess carbohydrates can be catabolized to form acetyl-CoA, which is input to the fatty acid synthesis pathway for long-term energy storage. The hydrophobic character of lipids makes them a more compact form of energy storage than hydrophilic carbohydrates.
- **Coenzymes** (metabolic intermediates to carry chemical groups between different reactions) – for example, **adenosine triphosphate (ATP)** – the chemical fuel of the cell that powers most of a cell's metabolic activities. The significance of ATP is in its ability to store and transfer potential energy. It is the intermediate link between energy-releasing to energy-requiring cell processes. ATP contains three high-energy phosphate groups. Energy is released (as a catabolic pathway) when these phosphate groups break off. When ATP loses one phosphate group (using a water molecule), it becomes *adenosine **di**phosphate* (ADP). When ATP loses two phosphate groups it becomes *adenosine **mono**phosphate* (AMP). The released phosphate binds with a *protein pump (phosphorylation)* that moves sodium and potassium ions across a cell membrane. The reverse (anabolic pathways) happens when a phosphate group and free energy (energy that is available to do work) are used to regenerate ADP from AMP and ATP from ADP.
- **Another Coenzyme – nicotinamide adenine dinucleotide phosphate hydrogen (NADPH)** – a source of energized electrons released by photosynthesis (anabolic reaction).

**The Usage Processes (cellular respiration and fermentation)**

- **Oxygen-Independent – glycolysis** – occurs in the cytosol of all healthy cells. It is the process of breaking down a glucose molecule into two pyruvate molecules while storing energy released during this process as four ATP and two NADH molecules. The pyruvate then moves across the mitochondrion membrane that can be further oxidized to access more energy in later processes. The wide occurrence of glycolysis indicates that it is an ancient metabolic pathway.

- **Aerobic – krebs (citric acid) cycle** – converts pyruvate and NADH (the output of glycolysis) to four molecules of carbon dioxide, six molecules of NADH, and two molecules of ATP and FADH2 inside mitochondria.

- **Aerobic – oxidative phosphorylation** (aka, the Electron Transport Chain) – still inside mitochondria (or chloroplasts during photosynthesis); reduces NADH to NAD and accepts the electrons from the molecules. The flow of these electrons across the mitochondria or chloroplast inner membrane through electron carriers is called *chemiosmosis*. This contributes most of the ATP produced, compared to glycolysis and the Krebs cycle. As the electrons are transferred to each carrier within the chain, free energy is released and is used to form water and ATP (34 ATP are made from one molecule of glucose).

- **Anaerobic – organic source (fermentation)**[291] – in the cytoplasm; converts pyruvate that was the output of glycolysis to either lactate or ethanol and carbon dioxide. Lactic acid fermentation is used in mammalian red blood cells and in muscles used to the point of fatigue that have an insufficient oxygen supply to allow aerobic respiration to continue.

- **Anaerobic – inorganic source** (e.g., methanogenesis)[299] – occurs in the cytosol and converts inorganic molecules to NADH/NAD. Examples include the group of archaea called methanogens that reduce carbon dioxide to methane to oxidize NADH, and sulfate-reducing bacteria and archaea that reduce sulfate to hydrogen sulfide to regenerate NAD+ from NADH. Other inorganic inputs include iron, manganese, cobalt, uranium, nitrate, fumarate, and sulfur. As discussed earlier, hydrogenosomes produce ATP and hydrogen from the oxidation of pyruvate or malate.

## Genetics (supporting Section 4.4.9)

**Nucleotide** – a nucleotide is the basic structural unit and building block for DNA. A *ribonucleotide* is a nucleotide containing *ribose* as its *pentose* (a type of 5-carbon simple sugar) component. The genetic code with information for the amino acid sequence of the protein is contained in the sequence of three nucleotides (bases) in DNA (made up of deoxyribonucleotides) and RNA (made up of ribonucleotides). This linear sequence of nucleotides is its primary structure. Each three-base sequence of nucleotides is called a *codon*, each of which codes for an amino acid. In other words, nucleic acids are polymeric macromolecules assembled from monomer nucleotides.

- Nucleotides play a central role in metabolism, including providing chemical energy (e.g., in the form of the *nucleoside triphosphate*, ATP), participating in cell signaling, and as part of enzymatic reactions.
- For DNA, the four nucleotides combined in the three-base sequence are adenosine, guanine, cytosine, and thymine – A, G, C, T. 4 x 4 x 4 = 64, so there are 64 codons found in DNA. The same goes for RNA, but thymine is replaced by uracil – A, G, C, U.
- There will not be a test, but for clarity: a nucleotide is a *nucleoside* linked to a phosphate, while a nucleoside is a *nucleobase* linked to a sugar. Adenosine, guanine, cytosine, thymine, and uracil are the nucleobases that then get the sugar and phosphate added on. Adenosine and guanine are called the *purine bases*, while cytosine, thymine, and uracil are the *pyrimidine bases*.

**DNA** (Deoxyribonucleic acid) – one of the two nucleic acids (RNA is the other). It is a linear biopolymer shaped like a double helix. DNA (the *genome*) carries all the information for your physical characteristics (the *phenome*) through its instructions for making proteins.

- DNA replication is performed by enzymes called DNA *poly-merases* that synthesize DNA from *nucleoside triphosphates*, the precursors of DNA. They read the existing DNA strands to create two new strands that match the existing ones. Before this replication can take place, an enzyme called *helicase* unwinds the DNA molecule by breaking the hydrogen bonds between the nucleotide bases to give two single strands of DNA that are used as templates for replication.
  - o DNA polymerase edits DNA during replication by proofreading every newly added base before adding the next one. An incorrect base is removed and replaced by the correct base. If a base remains mismatched, special repair enzymes can often recognize, excise, and replace it with the correct base. Some errors are not corrected until after replication is completed. Mistakes not corrected can result in a mutation. DNA polymerase replication is so accurate that its extreme fidelity results in DNA being replicated with one wrong nucleotide incorporated once per 108–1010 nucleotides polymerized.[292]
- **Base pair** – a DNA unit consisting of two nucleobases bound to each other by hydrogen bonds that form the building blocks of the DNA double helix (its secondary structure) and contribute to the folded structure of both DNA and RNA (their tertiary structure). The complementary nature of this base-paired structure (the *Watson–Crick base pairs* of guanine-cytosine and adenine-thymine, oftentimes in the literature represented as G·C and A·T) provides a redundant copy of the genetic information encoded within DNA. Also, base-pairing provides the mechanism through which DNA polymerase replicates DNA, and RNA polymerase transcribes DNA into RNA.

**Chromatin** – this is a complex of unpaired DNA, RNA, and proteins found in eukaryotic cells. Chromatin package DNA molecules into structural units called *nucleosomes*, which reinforce the DNA during cell division, preventing DNA damage and regulating gene expression and DNA replication. Chromatin represents DNA folded on nucleoproteins called *histones* by a magnitude of 50. Genetic information is thus encoded using data compression and packing.

**Chromosomes** – these are single-stranded base pairings of condensed chromatin. A chromosome consists of a long strand of DNA containing many genes. They contain protein and a piece of DNA that is wound up and bunched together through a twisting process called *supercoiling* into an even more compact structure, condensed at least by two million times onto itself. There are two strings of nucleotides coiled around one another in each chromosome: a double helix. C on one string is always opposite from G on the other string; A is always opposite T. During the cell division processes of mitosis and meiosis, chromosomes replicate to ensure that each new daughter cell receives the correct number of chromosomes.

**Chromatid** – either of the two strands of a replicated chromosome.

**Gene** – a gene is a sequence of nucleotides in DNA or RNA that encodes the synthesis of a gene product, either RNA or protein. More rigorously, a gene can be considered as a union of genomic sequences encoding a coherent set of potentially overlapping functional products.[293]

- **Allele** – one of two or more alternate forms of a gene. If a gene on a chromosome encodes a characteristic, another copy of the gene at the same position (*locus*) also encodes that characteristic – both are alleles. A diploid organism that possesses two identical alleles is *homozygous* for that locus. One that possesses two different alleles is *heterozygous* for the locus.
- **Transposons** – DNA sequences that can change position within a genome, sometimes creating or reversing mutations and altering the cell's genetic identity and genome size.

- o *Retrotransposons* (class I transposable element) copy and paste themselves into different genomic locations by converting RNA back into DNA through the process of reverse transcription using an RNA transposition intermediate. They replicate themselves to become plentiful in eukaryotic genomes, such as maize (49–78%) and humans (42%).
- o DNA *Transposons* (class II transposable element) have a cut-and-paste transposition mechanism that does not involve an RNA intermediate. There is a large variation among species in the level of amplification of their DNA transposon populations.

**RNA** (ribonucleic acid) – the other nucleic acid is like DNA, except that it is usually a single-stranded biopolymer that can fold into the intra-strand double helix in certain applications. RNA is essential in various biological roles in coding, decoding, regulation, and expression of genes, and it helps synthesize, regulate, and process proteins.

- **mRNA** – The *messenger* RNA (mRNA) molecule carries the information, or message, for making a protein from the DNA out of the nucleus into the cytoplasm to the ribosome. The coding sequence of the mRNA determines the amino acid sequence in the protein that is produced.
- A *non-coding* RNA (*ncRNA*) is an RNA molecule that is not translated into a protein. Nearly 97% of the human DNA sequences are non-coding sequences. Most of these are believed to be involved in the gene regulation process. *Introns* are the non-coding sections of DNA and pre-mRNA, while *exons* are the sections that code for proteins. More than 98% of the human DNA sequences are non-coding, but that percentage varies widely across species.[294] Important types of ncRNAs include (among many others):
  - o **tRNA** – the *transfer* RNA (tRNA) molecule is the link between the mRNA and the amino acid sequence of proteins. tRNA

carries an amino acid to the protein synthetic machinery of a cell (ribosome) as directed by the codon in an mRNA. tRNA works from both sides by forming hydrogen bonds with mRNA and covalent bonds with amino acids, enabling the connection.

o **rRNA** – the *ribosomal* RNA (rRNA) forces the tRNA and mRNA to process and translate the latter into proteins. It makes up about 80% of cellular RNA.

**Gene expression** – genes encode proteins, and proteins dictate cell function. Gene expression is the process by which information from a gene is used in the synthesis of *functional gene products* – proteins or *non-coding* RNA (ncRNA). It is the phenotypic manifestation of genes that creates each cell's characteristics. How genotype is translated into phenotype depends on penetrance and expressivity.[295] *Penetrance* refers to whether the gene is expressed or not. *Expressivity* determines how much the trait affects or how many features of the trait appear in organisms that carry that gene. Gene expression consists of two major steps: *transcription* (DNA à RNA) and *translation* (RNA à protein).

- **Transcription** – DNA is the template for making an mRNA chain through the operation of a specific enzyme called DNA-*directed* RNA *polymerase* (RNAP) through transcription. It uses a protein called a *transcription factor* that binds to a DNA transcription unit consisting of at least one gene and regulates gene expression by promoting or suppressing transcription. RNAP not only initiates mRNA transcription but also guides the nucleotides into position, facilitates attachment and elongation, has proofreading and replacement capabilities, and has termination-recognition capability. In eukaryotic cells, once pre-*messenger* RNA (pre-mRNA) has been transcribed from DNA, it is processed to messenger RNA (mRNA). Called RNA *splicing*, it removes its introns and keeps its exons.

- **Translation** – in translation, the mRNA sequence is decoded to produce a specific polypeptide/protein according to the rules specified by the genetic code. Translation occurs after the mRNA has carried the transcribed "message" from the DNA to protein-making factories in the cell called ribosomes. The message (i.e., the sequence of codons) carried by the mRNA is read by a tRNA carrier molecule that assembles the protein, one amino acid at a time. Of the 64 possible codons, 61 represent amino acids, and the remaining three represent stop signals, which trigger the end of protein synthesis. Because there are 20 different amino acids but 64 possible codons, most amino acids are indicated by more than one codon.

- **Coding and noncoding DNA/RNA** – the Central Dogma is executed from genome *coding regions* that only make up a small fraction of the human genome (<2%). The rest are noncoding. Some noncoding DNA is transcribed into functional non-coding RNA molecules. Other functions include the transcriptional and translational regulation of protein-coding sequences. On the other end of the spectrum, the bladderwort plant has only 3% noncoding DNA and 97% of coding DNA.

**Gene regulation** – regulation of gene expression gives control over the timing, location, and amount of a given gene product (protein or ncRNA) present in a cell that determines cellular structure and function. Regulation of gene expression is the basis for cellular differentiation, development, and morphogenesis. In prokaryotes, it is regulated at the level of transcription. In eukaryotes, it is regulated at multiple levels, including transcription/post-transcription, translation/post-translation, and epigenetic. Here is a simple diagram that shows both gene expression and regulation:[296]

**Proteins** – they do the work. As stated earlier, proteins are polymers of long chains of amino acids. The sequence of amino acids determines each protein's structure and function. A protein is a biomolecule that binds to substrates. This way, these substrates are held in the right place so they can undergo a chemical reaction. This reaction is often facilitated by a cofactor (e.g., vitamin), which is also held in place by the protein and serves as the actual catalyst. Examples of protein functions include:

- **Antibodies** – bind to specific foreign particles, such as viruses and bacteria, to help protect the body.
- **Contraction proteins** – cause muscles to compress (such as actin and myosin).
- **Enzymes** – catalysts that carry out almost all the chemical reactions that take place in cells. They also assist with the formation of new molecules by reading the genetic information stored in DNA.
- **Hormones** – a class of signaling molecules produced by glands that are transported to target distant organs to regulate physiology and behavior. They affect these cells by binding to specific receptor proteins that results in a change in cell function. Some hormones are completely active when released into the bloodstream (e.g., insulin and growth hormones), while others are *prohormones* that must be activated in their target cells.
- **Messenger** – transmits signals to coordinate biological processes between different cells, tissues, and organs.
- **Structural component** – provides structure and support for cells. On a larger scale, they also allow the body to move.
- **Transport/storage** – binds and carries atoms and small molecules within cells and throughout the body.
- **Removing toxins** – neutralizing poisonous substances (such as bee venom and snake venom).

**RNA-dependent RNA polymerase** (RdRP) – *RNA-dependent RNA polymerase* (*RdRP*) is an enzyme that primarily catalyzes the transcription and replication of genomes from the RNA template in RNA viruses. RdRPs are also found in cells involved in RNA interference in which RNA molecules inhibit gene expression or translation by neutralizing targeted mRNA molecules.

**Genotype** – the genetic makeup of a cell, including gene expression, which determines its characteristics (phenotype). It is hidden from the observer.

- The genotype is the complete set of alleles that an individual organism possesses.

**Phenotype** – the composite of an organism's observable characteristics. It includes the organism's physical structure, its developmental processes, its biochemical and physiological properties, its behavior, and the products of its behavior. It is the result of the expression of its genotype and the influence of environmental factors. The phenotype of an individual organism changes continuously during its life.

**Hologenome** – the combined genome of all bionts (host and symbiotic microbiota) in the holobiont.


### Neurons (supporting Section 4.4.10)

**Sensory neurons** – nerve cells that are activated by sensory input from the environment.

**Motor neurons** – nerve cells that transmit impulses from the spinal cord to muscles. There are two types of motor neurons: upper motor neurons that travel between the brain and spinal cord and lower motor neurons that travel from the spinal cord to muscles.

**Interneurons** – nerve cells that transfer signals between sensory and motor neurons. Interneurons can also communicate with each other within the brain, forming circuits of varying complexity.

- **Second messengers** – intracellular mediators whose concentration inside the cell changes rapidly on receptor activation.
- Signaling neurons function by activating the next signaling protein in the signal transduction cascade or by modifying the concentration of second messengers. Examples include:[297]
  - o **Relay proteins** – pass the signal on to the next member of the chain.
  - o **Messenger proteins** – carry the signal from one part of the cell to another.
  - o **Amplifier proteins** – either activate many downstream signaling proteins or generate large numbers of second messenger molecules.
  - o **Transducer proteins** – change the signal into a different form.
  - o **Bifurcation proteins** – branch the signal to different signaling pathways.
  - o **Integrator proteins** – receive two or more signals from different pathways and integrate their input into a common signaling pathway.
  - o **Modulator proteins** – regulate the activity of a signaling protein.
- Other proteins involved include:[305]
  - o **Anchoring proteins** – tether members of the signaling pathway to ensure that the signal is being relayed to the right place.
  - o **Adaptor proteins** – link one signaling protein with the next at the correct time, without signaling themselves.
  - o **Scaffold proteins** – bind several signaling proteins and sometimes tether them, forming a much more efficient functional complex.

## Cell Signaling (supporting Section 4.4.11)

**Intracrine** – signals are produced by the target cell that stay within the target cell.

**Autocrine** – signaling targets receptors in the same cell that originated the signal. Sometimes, autocrine cells target nearby cells if they are the same type of cell as the emitting cell. This type of signaling can occur during the development of an organism so that cells take on proper functions.

**Juxtacrine** – signaling targets adjacent cells.

**Paracrine** – signaling targets cells near the signaling cell. Paracrine signals diffuse through extracellular fluid to reach their destination. Neurotransmitters represent an example.

**Endocrine** – signaling involves hormones that target distant cells. These cells produce hormones that travel through the blood to reach all parts of the body.

Internal Receptors

**Nuclear receptors** – nuclear, intranuclear, or nuclear hormone receptors are activated by lipid-soluble molecules, such as estrogen and progesterone, and lipid-soluble signals, including retinoic acid, oxysterols, and thyroid hormone (types of ligands) that alter DNA and RNA expression. This results in an alteration of the production of cellular proteins. Unlike most intercellular messengers, the ligands cross the cellular membrane and directly interact with nuclear receptors inside the cell. Once activated, nuclear receptors directly regulate the transcription of genes that control a wide variety of biological processes, including cell proliferation, development, metabolism, and reproduction.[49]

**Cytoplasmic receptors** – cytoplasmic receptors are found in the cytoplasm or nucleus that binds signaling molecules and triggers changes that influence the behavior of cells. The major groups are the steroid hormone receptors and the thyroid hormone receptors.

## Cell-Surface Receptors

**Enzyme-linked (catalytic) receptors** – enzyme-linked receptors bind with an extracellular ligand and cause enzymatic activity on the intracellular side. The activated enzyme leads to an intracellular cascade of events executing the response. They respond to extracellular signal proteins that promote the growth, proliferation, differentiation, or survival of cells in animal tissues. These signal proteins are often collectively called growth factors. They also mediate direct, rapid effects on the cytoskeleton, controlling the way a cell moves and changes its shape. They include receptors that are essential for the normal functioning of the cardiovascular system.

**G Protein-coupled receptors** – G protein-coupled receptors are the largest family of membrane proteins and mediate most cellular responses to hormones and neurotransmitters. They are responsible for vision, olfaction, and taste. They detect ligand molecules outside the cell and activate internal signal transduction pathways and, ultimately, cellular responses. They bind with an extracellular ligand and activate a membrane protein called a G protein. G proteins act as molecular switches inside cells and are involved in transmitting signals from a variety of stimuli outside a cell to its interior. They mediate most of our physiological responses to hormones, neurotransmitters, ions, photons, and other stimuli.[298]

Interestingly, almost half of the drugs we utilize exert their action by modifying these receptors.[299] These receptors are involved in:

- Photoreceptors
- Gustatory receptors – sweet, bitter, and umami tastes
- Nociception (pain sense)
- Olfactory receptors
- Behavior and mood regulation
- Regulation of immune system activity and inflammation
- Autonomic nervous system transmission
- Cell density sensing
- Homeostatic modulation (e.g., water balance)
- Growth and metastasis of some types of tumors
- The endocrine system

**Ion-channel-linked receptors** – ion-channel-linked receptors are transmembrane proteins that open to allow ions, such as Na+, K+, Ca2+, and/or Cl– to pass through the membrane in response to the binding of a chemical ligand messenger. The ions pass down their electrochemical gradient through ion channels without requiring ATP or metabolic energy. The channels remain open briefly, after which the ligand dissociates from the receptor, making it available to bind with a new ligand. These receptors play an important role in the transmission of neuronal signals at the synapses and neuro-muscular junctions. They mediate mechanosensation, thermosensation, and acid and salt taste.

**Integrins** – upon ligand binding, integrins activate signal transduction pathways that mediate cellular signals, such as regulation of the cell cycle, organization of the intracellular cytoskeleton, and movement of new receptors to the cell membrane.

## Viruses, Viroids, Virusoids, Satellites, and Prions (supporting Section 4.4.12)

**Virus** – a biological entity that only replicates inside the cells of an organism. When infected by a virus, a host cell produces thousands of copies of the original virus. Viruses contain DNA or RNA, giving them the ability to mutate and evolve.

The six basic virus stages:

- **Attachment** is the binding between viral capsid proteins and receptors on the host cellular surface. Attachment to the receptor can induce the viral envelope protein to undergo changes that result in the fusion of viral and cellular membranes, or changes of non-enveloped virus surface proteins that allow the virus to enter.
- **Penetration** occurs when virions enter the host cell through membrane fusion or receptor-mediated *endocytosis* – a process by which cells absorb metabolites, hormones, proteins, or viruses by the inward budding of the plasma membrane.
- **Uncoating** is the process in which the viral capsid is removed. This may be by degradation by viral enzymes or host enzymes or by simple dissociation. The result is the release of the viral genomic nucleic acid.
- **Replication** involves the synthesis of viral mRNA, viral protein synthesis, possible assembly of viral proteins, and viral genome replication. This may be followed by further rounds of mRNA synthesis. The genome replication of most DNA viruses takes place in the cell's nucleus or the cytoplasm for RNA viruses.
- **Assembly** of the virus particles then occurs through structure-mediated self-assembly. The cytopathic effect refers to structural changes in host cells that are caused by a viral invasion.
- **Release** of viruses from the host cell is done by *lysis*, a process

that kills the cell by bursting its membrane and cell wall. The lysis process is sometimes deferred by the *lysogenic cycle*, where the viral genome is incorporated by genetic recombination into a specific place in the host's chromosome. Whenever the host divides, the viral genome is also replicated. The viral genome is mostly silent within the host, sometimes for months or years. At some point, it may give rise to an active virus, which then enters the lysis cycle and kills the host cell.

**Retrovirus** – a double-stranded RNA virus that inserts a copy of its genome into the DNA of a host cell, thus changing the genome of that cell (a Group VI virus). Retroviruses are entirely restricted to vertebrate hosts. Once inside the host cell's cytoplasm, the virus uses its own *reverse transcriptase enzyme* that it brought along to produce DNA from its RNA genome, the reverse of the usual pattern of transcription from DNA to RNA.

The new DNA is then incorporated into the host cell genome. Because reverse transcription lacks the proofreading of DNA replication, the mutation rate of retroviruses is high. The host cell treats the viral DNA (now called a *provirus*) as part of its genome, transcribing and translating the viral genes along with the cell's genes and producing the proteins required to assemble new copies of the virus. If this occurs in a host germ cell, the provirus may be inherited by the host's progeny as an *endogenous retrovirus*. Endogenous retroviruses have contributed to about half of human genomic sequences. *Exogenous retroviruses* are transmitted horizontally among hosts, a type of transposon (see Section 4.4.9). A well-known detrimental retrovirus is the human immunodeficiency virus (HIV).

**Bacteriophage** – a virus that infects and replicates within bacteria and archaea. It is composed of proteins that encapsulate a DNA or RNA genome and replicates within the bacterium following the injection of its genome into its cytoplasm using a lytic or lysogenic cycle. Bacteriophages are among the most common and diverse entities in the biosphere.

**Viroid** – similar to a virus, but is composed solely of a short strand of circular, single-stranded RNA that has no protein coating; the smallest known infectious pathogens.

**Virusoids** – circular single-stranded RNA(s) dependent on viruses for replication and encapsidation.

**Satellite RNAs and satellite viruses** – short RNA molecules that depend on helper viruses for replication, encapsidation, movement, and transmission. They share little or no nucleotide sequence similarity with their helper viruses. In contrast, satellite viruses are satellite RNAs that encode and are encapsidated in capsid proteins.[55]

**Prions** – misfolded proteins that can transmit their abnormal three-dimensional structure onto normal variants of the same protein, conferring infectious properties.

## SENSORY SYSTEMS (supporting Section 4.5)

### Sensing System Components (supporting Section 4.5.1)

**Distal object** – the agent that emits what may eventually be received by receptors. This is what exists (reality) and is independent of observation, something that does not necessarily need to emit nor create a stimulus.

**Energy** – what is being emitted by the distal object and received by sensory receptors.

**Sensory receptor** – a structure that receives and transduces energy. *Reception* is the process of activating a sensory receptor by a stimulus. A receptor's *receptive field* is determined by the distance it can be from the distal object and still receive its energy.

**Sensory (proximal) stimulus** – a signal detected by a sensory receptor. Proximal means nearby, while distal (earlier) means not nearby.

**Sensory transduction** – the process of converting a sensory stimulus into a receptor potential.

**Sensory input** – what comes out of transduction and is available to perception. This is also called conduction or transmission.

**Perception** – the organization, identification, and interpretation of sensory input. This can include processing low-level information to higher-level information and processing based on restorative/ selective mechanisms and concepts/expectations.

**Sensory information/noise** – sensory input that has been processed as either information or noise.

## Biological Sensory Systems (supporting Section 4.5.2)

**Visual system** (sense of sight) – has directly associated specific organs (a *special* sense). *Visual perception* is the ability to interpret the environment using the sensed part of the electromagnetic spectrum reflected or transmitted by the objects in the environment. The stimulus modality for vision is some part of the electromagnetic spectrum.

**Auditory system** (sense of hearing) – includes both the auditory parts of the sensory system and specific sensory organs (a *special* sense). *Auditory perception* is the ability to perceive sound by detecting vibrations, which are changes in the pressure of the surrounding medium through time (i.e., sound waves). The stimulus modality for hearing is sound. Sound may be heard through solid, liquid, or gaseous matter.

**Chemoreception** – the transduction of a chemical substance into a biological signal.

**Olfactory system** (sense of smell) – olfaction occurs when odorant stimuli bind to specific sites on olfactory receptor cells on the membrane of the cilia, causing an action potential that sends this information to the brain. It has directly associated specific organs (a *special* sense).

- In humans, olfactory stimulation is the only sensory information that directly reaches the cerebral cortex, whereas other sensations are relayed through the thalamus.
- **Human social chemosignals** – It has been shown that human social chemosignals are processed as cues for behavioral adaptations.[300] Through the communication of chemosignals:
  o social bonds can be formed and maintained (kin recognition).
  o the health status of the immune system in the population is monitored.
  o relevant changes in motivational (e.g., reproductive behavior) and emotional systems are transmitted.

**Gustatory system** (sense of taste) – is the sensation produced when a substance reacts chemically with taste receptor cells located on taste buds, which then depolarize and release a neurotransmitter for a cell to uptake and transmit the chemical message. It has specific organs (a *special* sense).

**Proprioception** – the sense of self-movement and body position that uses mechanosensory neurons located within muscle spindles, tendons, and joints, which are called *proprioceptors*. The most elementary function of proprioceptive feedback is to stabilize and protect the body. It includes various sub-modalities:[301]

- *Proprioception* (joint position sense) – the sense of joint/limb positioning.
- *Kinaesthesia* (motion sense) – the awareness of motion of the body.
- *Sense of force* – the ability to reproduce (or match) a desired level of force.

**Somatosensory system** ("body" senses) – a complex system of sensory neurons and neural pathways that connect with, or respond to, various receptor cells. These sensory receptors are found in the skin, epithelial tissues, muscles, bones, joints, internal organs, and cardiovascular system.

**Vestibular system** (sense of balance and spatial orientation) – coordinates movement with balance, integrated with proprioception and the visual system. In vertebrates, it is part of the inner ear. With changes in position, and thus changes in inner-ear fluid motion, the shifting of hair cells causes the opening of receptor channels, leading to action potentials propagating to the auditory nerve.

**Equilibrioception** – the perception of balance and spatial orientation. It is the result of the visual system, vestibular system, and proprioception working together.

**Interoception** – the process of receiving, accessing, and appraising internal bodily signals. It encompasses the process of integrating signals relayed from the body into specific brain subregions to maintain homeostatic/allostatic conditions and aid in self-awareness. Interoception is the ability to detect the feelings of internal bodily sensations, including *proprioception* and *visceroception* (the perception of internal body signals).[302] Examples include:

- Hunger, which is governed by parts of the brain that are responsible for homeostasis.
- Respiratory rate controlled by pulmonary stretch receptors.
- Suffocation, a feeling induced by peripheral chemoreceptors when carbon dioxide levels get too high.
- Gas distension, sensed by stretch receptors in the gastrointestinal tract.
- Sensations felt in the throat when swallowing, vomiting, or during acid reflux that result from stimulation of sensory receptors in the esophagus.
- Cardioception, or the perception of the activity of the heart.

**Thermoreception** (sensation and perception of temperature) – measures the temperature differences inferred from heat flux.

**Nociception** – nociception is the sensory nervous system's response to certain harmful or potentially harmful stimuli. The three types of pain receptors are cutaneous (skin), somatic (joints and bones), and visceral (body organs). Intense chemical, mechanical, or thermal stimulation of sensory nerve cells called nociceptors produce a signal that travels via the spinal cord to the brain. Nociception triggers a variety of physiological and behavioral (nocifensive) responses and usually results in a perception of pain. It can cause autonomic responses before or without reaching consciousness to cause pallor, sweating, fast heartbeat, hypertension, lightheadedness, nausea, and fainting. Nociception is integrally connected to proprioception, thermoreception, and chemoreception.

**Electroreception** – detects and perceives electrical fields.

**Magnetoreception** – detects a magnetic field to perceive direction, altitude, or location.

**Chronoception** – refers to how the passage of time is perceived and experienced.

**Active sensory system** – activated by probing the environment with self-generated energy. Using self-generated energy allows more control over signal intensity, direction, timing, and spectral characteristics.

- **Teleceptive active sensory systems** – collect information by directing propagating energy and detecting objects using cues, such as time delay and intensity of return signal. Examples include echolocation of bats and electrosensory detection of electric fish.
- **Contact active sensory systems** – use physical contact between stimuli and organism. Insect antennae and whiskers are examples of contact active sensory systems.

**Spatial orientation and navigation** – in mammalian brains, neurons called *place cells* encode location information. Neurons called *head direction cells* encode the directional heading in the horizontal plane but are not dependent on the Earth's geomagnetic field. Neurons called *grid cells* are involved in determining distance and tracking a route over time. Grid cells discharge at multiple locations within an environment, and these locations form a regular, repeating pattern, or grid, across the entire environment.[303]

**Nutrient sensing** – receptors exist that detect intracellular and extracellular levels of sugars, amino acids, lipids, and surrogate metabolites. The sensing of a nutrient may involve the direct binding of the stimuli (sensed molecule) to the sensor or may occur by an indirect mechanism relying on the detection of a surrogate molecule that reflects nutrient abundance.[304]

**Quorum sensing** – a process in microorganisms to estimate their population densities. Molecular census-taking has been shown to occur in more than 70 types of microorganisms. Many bacterial processes are effective only when carried out by large numbers of bacteria acting in a coordinated fashion through some currently unknown communication system.[305]

**Biological Sensory Components (supporting Section 4.5.3)**

Sensory Receptors

**Mechanoreceptors** – respond to mechanical forces by transducing mechanical force on cells into electrical signals. As the membrane tension increases, the structure of the mechanoreceptor protein flattens and stretches out to occupy a larger area, which, in turn, opens an ion channel to pass the electrical signal.[306] There are many types of mechanoreceptors, including those that respond to light touch, adapt rapidly to changes in texture (vibrations around 50 Hz), detect tension deep in the skin and fascia, detect sustained pressure, detect rapid vibrations (of about 200–300 Hz), sense when a hair changes position (on the body or in the cochlea of the inner ear to enable hearing), or are excited by the stretch of a blood vessel.

- **Proprioceptors** – provide spatial information about limbs and other body parts.
- **Auditory receptors** – attached to hair cells and mechanically respond to the bending of those cells to either amplify or transmit sound information to the auditory nerve. Scientists have recently isolated the primary auditory protein (called TMC1) found in mammals, birds, fish, amphibians, and reptiles.[307]

- **Hydrodynamic reception** – the ability of fish, some aquatic amphibians, platypuses, marine mammals, and semi-aquatic mammals to sense water movements. This is useful for orientation, hunting, predator avoidance, and schooling.
- **Muscle-spindle sensory receptors** – stretch receptors within the body of a muscle that primarily respond to the absolute magnitude and the rate of muscle stretch. This information is processed as proprioception. The response to changes in length can result in activating motor neurons via the stretch reflex to resist muscle stretch. Receptors in joints, tendons, ligaments, and skin also participate.

**Thermoreceptors** – respond to differences in both external and internal temperatures. There are two types that detect temperatures, one for above and one for below body temperature.

**Olfactory receptors** – responsible for the detection of odorants that enable the sense of smell. Activated olfactory receptors trigger nerve impulses that transmit information about the odor to the brain.

- **Baroreceptors** – a type of olfactory receptor that is sensitive to changes in blood pressure.

**Nociceptors (pain) receptors** – process pain and temperature changes when stimulated by lack of O2, chemicals released from damaged cells and inflammatory cells. They are found in internal organs and on the surface of the body.

- Thermal nociceptors are activated by extreme heat or cold.
- Mechanical nociceptors respond to excess pressure or mechanical deformation.
- Chemical nociceptors respond to many types of chemicals. Some nociceptors become responsive to heat and mechanical stimulation only upon prolonged stimulation.

- When found in internal organs, nociceptors are a type of *interoceptor* – an internal receptor that responds to changes inside the body. Other interoceptors include the *aortic body* and the *carotid body*, which detect changes in chemical properties in the blood, such as oxygen concentration and blood pressure.

**Chemoreceptors** – a specialized sensory receptor cell that responds to certain chemical stimuli and transduces that signal into an electrical action potential. It detects changes in levels of O2, CO2, and H+ ions, as well as chemicals that stimulate taste and smell receptors. Chemoreceptors are involved in:

- Olfaction (*olfactory receptors* that detect stimuli as gases – distance chemoreceptors).
- Gustation (*gustatory receptors* that detect stimuli as liquids – direct chemoreceptors).
- Heart rate (*peripheral chemoreceptors* from sensing decreased O2, increased CO2, and changes in pH).
- Breathing (*particular chemoreceptors* that detect the levels of carbon dioxide and oxygen in the blood).

**Photoreceptors** – capable of phototransduction, a process that converts light (electromagnetic radiation) into a membrane potential. All photoreceptors possess photosensitive pigments. In the eye, light is the stimulus, and retinal is the receptor. *Cones* respond significantly to color, *rods* are sensitive to the intensity of light, and intrinsically photosensitive *retinal ganglion cells* play a role in synchronizing circadian rhythms to the current 24-hour light/dark cycle, the regulation of pupil size, and the regulation of the release of the hormone melatonin.

- **Infrared receptors** – respond to infrared radiation.
- **Ultraviolet receptors** – respond to ultraviolet radiation.

- Plants have *chromoproteins* that are comprised of a protein covalently bonded to a light-absorbing pigment called a chromophore.

**Hygroreceptors** – detect changes in the moisture content of the environment and are found in many insects. Often, hygroreceptors and thermoreceptors are one receptor, called *thermohygroreceptors*, and can exhibit additional olfactory sensing.

**Osmoreceptors** – detect changes in osmotic pressure and are usually found in the hypothalamus. They contribute to osmoregulation, controlling fluid balance in the body, and are involved in the detection of thirst.

**Electroreceptors** – stimulated by an electrical field.

**Somatic receptors** – initiate sensations from skin, muscles, and bones. It is known as tactile sense or the sense of touch. *Somatosensation* is a mixed sensory category and includes all sensation received from the skin and mucous membranes, as well from as the limbs and joints. Somatosensation occurs all over the exterior of the body and in some interior locations as well.

**Pattern recognition receptors** – detect conserved molecular structures of pathogens, such as bacteria and viruses, as part of the immune system. They identify two classes of molecules: those associated with microbial pathogens and those associated with components of the host's cells that are released during cell damage or death. They are present at the cell surface to recognize extracellular pathogens, such as bacteria or fungi, in the endosomes where they sense intracellular invaders, such as viruses, and in the cytoplasm.[308]

**Dermal pressure receptors** – detect small changes in the pressure of the water and facilitate the detection of food.

**Vomeronasal receptors** – detect pheromones. A *pheromone* is a chemical released by an animal that affects the behavior or physiology of other animals. They are not consciously perceived in the same way as other odors. Pheromonal signals are sent not to the main olfactory bulb but to a different neural structure that projects directly to the amygdala. There are several different types of pheromones, which are released in urine or as glandular secretions.[309] Pheromones:

- function as an attractant to potential mates.
- function as a repellant to potential competitors of the same sex.
- play a role in mother-infant attachment.
- influence the timing of puberty.
- modify reproductive cycles.
- prevent embryonic implantation.

## Sensory Input

**Visual cortex** – the part of the cerebral cortex which processes visual information. It is in the occipital lobe. Visual nerves run straight from the eye to the primary visual cortex to the visual association cortex.

**Auditory cortex** – the primary auditory cortex is responsible for translating and processing all sounds and tones. The secondary auditory cortex enables sound localization and analysis of complex sounds while also contributing to vocalizations and communication. It also has a role in auditory memory.

**Primary olfactory cortex** – along with the nearby olfactory bulbs, this is a portion of the cerebral cortex involved in olfaction.

**Gustatory cortex** – the brain structure responsible for the perception of taste.

**Primary somatic sensory cortex** with the nearby **somatic sensory association cortex** – using tactile stimuli from the joints, muscles, and skin, it creates sensations of touch, pressure, pain, temperature, and proprioception, which are then localized to specific body regions. This area also assesses the size, shape, and texture of objects.

**Audiovisual system** – auditory information is not spatially represented, unlike visual stimuli, but once one has the spatial mapping from the visual information, multisensory integration brings the information from both the visual and auditory stimuli together to make a more robust mapping. A dynamic neural mechanism exists for matching the auditory and visual inputs from an event.

**Sensorimotor system** – eye-hand coordination is the tactile sensation in the context of the visual system. The visual system is very static, but the tactile sensory collection is dynamic. This sensory collection is included in the mapping of both the tactile and visual sensations.

**RESPONSE SYSTEMS (supporting Section 4.6)**

**Processes (supporting Section 4.6.1)**

**Homeostasis** – the ability of an open system to regulate its internal environment to maintain stable conditions through multiple dynamic equilibrium adjustments controlled by interrelated regulation mechanisms.

**Allostasis** – the process of compensatory responses to events to attain some desired balance within some physiological system through behavioral actions

## Senescence

Nine hallmarks of aging that are common between organisms with emphasis on mammals are:[115]

- **Genomic instability** – the integrity and stability of DNA is continuously challenged by exogenous physical, chemical, and biological agents, as well as by endogenous threats, including DNA replication errors, spontaneous hydrolytic reactions, and reactive oxygen species.
- **Telomere attrition** – some chromosomal regions, such as telomeres, are particularly susceptible to age-related deterioration.
- **Epigenetic alterations** – these involve alterations in DNA methylation patterns. Post-translational modification of histones and chromatin remodeling are age-associated epigenetic marks.
- **Loss of proteostasis** – this involves mechanisms for the stabilization of correctly folded proteins and is altered with aging.
- **Deregulated nutrient sensing** – metabolism and its byproducts damage cells via oxidative stress, ER stress, calcium signaling, and mitochondrial dysfunction. Organisms depend on multiple nutrient-sensing pathways to make sure that the body takes in just the right amount of nutrition. This sensing capability decreases with aging.
- **Mitochondrial dysfunction** – the efficacy of the respiratory chain tends to diminish, thus increasing electron leakage and reducing ATP generation because of aging.
- **Cellular senescence** – cellular senescence contributes to rid

tissues of damaged cells. This requires an efficient cell replacement system. In aged organisms, this system may become inefficient or may exhaust the regenerative capacity of progenitor cells, resulting in the accumulation of dying cells that may aggravate the damage and contribute to aging.

- **Stem cell exhaustion** – deficient proliferation of stem and progenitor cells is detrimental for the maintenance of an organism.
- **Altered intercellular communication** – aging results in the deregulation of endocrine, neuroendocrine, or neuronal intercellular communication.

## Motor Control Systems

**Primary motor cortex** – main contributor to the generation of neural impulses that control the execution of movement.

**Premotor cortex** – responsible for some aspects of motor control.

**Supplementary motor area** – functions include internally generated planning of movement, planning of sequences of movement, and the coordination of the two sides of the body.

**Posterior parietal cortex** – guides planned movements, spatial reasoning, and attention.

**Dorsolateral prefrontal cortex** – important for executive functions, including working memory, cognitive flexibility, and abstract reasoning.

**Basal ganglia** – interconnected subcortical masses of cerebral gray matter that are involved in motor control.

Sensorimotor Control Systems

To generate efficient actions, the motor system must compensate for characteristics inherent in sensorimotor control, including:

- **Nonlinearity** – the number, strength, and temporal properties of the initiated motor neurons demonstrate nonlinearity in muscle velocity, muscle length, tendon properties, and joint angles.
- **Nonstationarity** – the way motor systems respond to motor commands can change during interaction with objects as muscles become fatigued, and as the motor abilities change over time.
- **Delays** – delays are present in all stages of the sensorimotor system, from the delay in receiving sensory information to the delay in our muscles responding to efferent motor commands.
- **Redundancy** – motor systems have redundancy because there is an infinite number of ways that the same task could be achieved, leading to an abundance of possible solutions.
- **Uncertainty** – sources of uncertainty include receptor bandwidth, environment representation, and ambiguity in sensory processing, and in goals, tasks, and consequences.
- **Noise** – noise is present from sensory processing and from variability in estimating the internal states of the body and external states of the world, leading to variability in movement.

## Homeostasis Support Systems in Mammals

**Autonomic nervous system** – regulates bodily functions, such as the heart rate, digestion, respiratory rate, pupillary response, urination, and sexual arousal.

**Parathyroid gland** – produces and secretes parathyroid hormone in response to a low blood calcium.

**Juxtaglomerular apparatus** – responds to a decrease in sodium concentration.

**Hypothalamic-pituitary-adrenal axis** – controls reactions to stress and regulates many body processes, including digestion, the immune system, mood and emotions, sexuality, and energy storage and expenditure.

**Hypothalamic-pituitary-thyroid axis** – responsible for the regulation of metabolism and responds to stress.

**Hypothalamic-pituitary-gonadal axis** – controls development, reproduction, and aging in animals.

**Hypothalamic-neurohypophyseal system** – controls uterine contractions and lactation, stimulates water retention, and raises blood pressure by contracting arterioles.

**Renin-angiotensin system** – a hormone system that regulates blood pressure, fluid, electrolyte balance, and systemic vascular resistance.

## THE THEORY OF EVOLUTION (supporting Section 5)

### Evolution is Change

Some sources of evolutionary change:

**Mutagenesis** – a process by which the genetic information of an organism is changed, resulting in a mutation. A *mutation* is a random, permanent change in the nucleic acid sequence that can be replicated. Mutations may or may not produce discernible changes in the observable characteristics (phenotype) of an organism. Cells have processes to mitigate mutations by repairing DNA damage. The mutations may be beneficial, neutral, or harmful and can be both harmful and beneficial simultaneously (known only after the fact). Mutations are the major source of genetic variation, which fuels evolutionary change. Mutation rates for single nucleotide sites for most organisms are extremely low, roughly $10^{-9}$ to $10^{-8}$ per site per generation, though some viruses have higher rates. Sources of mutation include:

- Errors during DNA replication – substitution, insertion, deletion, or translocation (frameshift of DNA sections)
- Exposure to radiation, chemicals, and other environmental stressors
- Insertion or deletion of segments of DNA due to mobile genetic elements

**Genetic recombination** – the exchange of genetic material during reproduction (meiosis or mitosis) that leads to the production of offspring with traits that differ from those found in either parent.

**Exon shuffling** – a process where two or more exons from different genes are brought together to form a new gene.

**Gene retroposition** – refers to RNA-based gene duplication that usually produces gene copies on chromosomes different from that of the parental gene copy.

**Network evolution** – the origination of a lineage through the partial merging of two ancestor lineages.

- **Horizontal gene transfer**
- **Symbiosis** and **Symbiogenesis**

- **Hybridization** – offspring from parents of two different species

**Infectious heredity** – genome transfer through infections from viruses that are inheritable.

## Epigenetics

- **DNA methylation** – the addition of a methyl group to DNA that often modifies the function of the genes and affects gene expression. It is carried out by a family of enzymes at several different levels in cells. During development and cell differentiation, DNA methylation is dynamic, but some DNA methylation patterns are retained as epigenetic memory.
- **Self-sustaining metabolic loops** – when an mRNA or protein product of a gene stimulates transcription of the gene.
- **Gene silencing** – when small RNA strands interfere with the transcription of DNA or translation of mRNA.
- **Conformation of proteins** – when prions replicate by changing the structure of normal proteins to match their own.
- **Niche construction** – the repeated activities of organisms in their environment that generates a legacy of an effect that modifies and feeds back into the selection regime of subsequent generations. Descendants inherit genes plus environmental characteristics generated by the ecological actions of ancestors.

# 13 Marcus Aurelius' Meditations (Condensed)

*Truth about life*
- Contemplate the formative principles (forms) of things bare of their coverings: the purposes of actions; consider what pain is, what pleasure is, death, and fame; who is to himself the cause of his uneasiness; how no man is hindered by another; everything is opinion.
- How ridiculous and what a stranger he is who is surprised at anything which happens in life.
- How worthless everything is after which men violently strain.

*Perception*
- In everything always observe what the thing is which produces for you an appearance, and resolve it by dividing it into the formal, the material, the purpose, and the time within which it must end.
- Perceive at last that you have in you something better and more divine than the things which cause the various affects that, as it were, pull you by the strings. What is there now in my mind? Is it fear, or suspicion, or desire, or anything of the kind?

*Bad people*
- With respect to those who have offended me by words or done me wrong, to be easily disposed to be pacified and reconciled, as soon as they have shown a readiness to be reconciled.
- The best way of avenging yourself is not to become like the wrongdoer.

- Let the wrong which is done by a man stay there where the wrong was done.

*Self-discipline*
- Refrain from fault-finding.
- Endurance of labor, and to want little, and to work with my own hands, and not to meddle with other people's affairs, and not to be ready to listen to slander.
- Begin the morning by saying to yourself, I shall meet with the busy-body, the ungrateful, the arrogant, the deceitful, the envious, and the unsocial. All these things happen to them by reason of their ignorance of what is good and evil.
- A man then must stand erect, not be kept erect by others.
- The soul does violence to itself when it is overpowered by pleasure or by pain, when it plays a part, does or says anything insincerely and untruly, when it allows any act of its own and any movement to be without an aim, and does anything thoughtlessly without considering what it is; it being right that even the smallest things be done with reference to an end.
- Never value anything as profitable to yourself which shall compel you to break your promise, to lose your self-respect, to hate any man, to suspect, to curse, to act the hypocrite, or to desire anything which needs walls and curtains.
- It is in your power whenever you shall choose to retire into yourself, constantly then give to yourself this retreat and renew yourself; let your principles be brief and fundamental, which, as soon as you shall recur to them, will be sufficient to cleanse the soul completely and to send you back free from all discontent with the things to which you return.
- Does anyone do wrong? It is to himself that he does the wrong.
- Let it make no difference to you whether you are cold or warm, if you are doing your duty; whether you are drowsy or satisfied with sleep; whether ill-spoken of or praised; whether dying or doing something else. For it is one of the acts of life, this act

by which we die: it is sufficient then in this act also to do well what we have in hand.

- Take pleasure in one thing and rest in it.
- When you have been compelled by circumstances to be disturbed in a manner, quickly return to yourself and do not continue out of tune longer than the compulsion lasts, for you will have more mastery over the harmony by continually recurring to it.
- Make yourself neither the tyrant nor the slave of any man.
- How easy it is to repel and to wipe away every impression that is troublesome or unsuitable and to be immediately in all tranquility.
- A man when he has done a good act, does not call out for others to come and see, but he goes on to another act.
- Where a man can live, there he can also live well.
- Let the part of your soul which leads and governs be undisturbed by the movements in the flesh, whether of pleasure or of pain; let it not unite with them, but let it circumscribe itself and limit those affects to their parts. But when these affects rise up to the mind by virtue of that other sympathy that naturally exists in a body which is all one, then you must not strive to resist the sensation, for it is natural. However: let not the ruling part of itself add to the sensation the opinion that it is either good or bad.
- Accustom yourself to attend carefully to what is said by another and as much as it is possible, be in the speaker's mind.
- Only attend to yourself and resolve to be a good man in every act which you do.
- Pain is neither intolerable nor everlasting, if you bear in mind that it has its limits and add nothing to it in imagination. And remember this too: that we do not perceive those many things that are disagreeable to us as the same as pain, such as excessive drowsiness, and the being scorched by heat, and the having no appetite. When then you are discontented about any of

these things, say to yourself that you are yielding to pain.

- You have leisure or ability to check arrogance; you have leisure to be superior to pleasure and pain; you have leisure to be superior to love of fame and not to be vexed at stupid and ungrateful people, nay even to care for them.
- Receive wealth or prosperity without arrogance and be ready to let it go.
- Neither the future nor the past pains you, only the present. But this is reduced to a very little, if you only circumscribe it. Chide your mind, if it is unable to hold out against even this.
- A cucumber is bitter. Throw it away. There are briars in the road. Turn aside from them. This is enough. Do not add.
- Practice yourself even in the things which you despair of accomplishing. For even the left hand, which is ineffectual for all other things for want of practice, holds the bridle more vigorously than the right hand, for it has been practiced in this.

*Simplicity*
- Adorn yourself with simplicity and modesty and with indifference toward the things which lie between virtue and vice.
- For instance, if a man should stand by a limpid pure spring and curse it, the spring never ceases sending up potable water. If he should cast clay into it or filth, it will speedily disperse them and wash them out and will not be at all polluted. How then shall you possess a perpetual fountain and not a mere well? By forming yourself hourly to freedom conjoined with contentment, simplicity, and modesty.
- Be good, modest, true, rational, a man of equanimity, and magnanimous.

*Right action*
- If it is not right, do not do it; if it is not true, do not say it.
- First, do nothing inconsiderately nor without a purpose. Second, make your acts refer to nothing else than to a social end.

- While you live, while it is in your power, be good.

*Our thoughts*
- It is not men's acts which disturb us, for those acts have their foundation in men's ruling principles, but it is our own opinions which disturb us.
- Consider how much more pain is brought on us by the anger and vexation caused by such acts than by the acts themselves at which we are angry and vexed.
- I have often wondered how it is that every man loves himself more than all the rest of men, but yet sets less value on his own opinion of himself than on the opinion of others. If then a god or a wise teacher should present himself to a man and bid him to think of nothing and to design nothing which he would not express as soon as he conceived it, he could not endure it even for a single day. So much more respect have we to what our neighbors shall think of us than to what we shall think of ourselves.
- Wipe out your imaginations by often saying to yourself: now it is in my power to let no badness be in this soul, nor desire, nor any perturbation at all; rather, looking at all things, I see what their nature is, and I use each according to its value.
- The mind that is free from passions is a citadel.
- If you are pained by any external thing, it is not this thing that disturbs you but your own judgment about it. It is in your power to wipe out this judgment now.
- Our perturbations come only from the opinion which is within.
- Now a man should take away not only unnecessary acts, but also, unnecessary thoughts, for thus superfluous acts will not follow after.
- The soul is dyed by the thoughts.
- Those who do not observe the movements of their own minds must of necessity be unhappy.
- Do not waste the remainder of your life in thoughts about others.

*Self-worth*
- Every man is worth just so much as the things are worth about which he busies himself.
- Look within. Within is the fountain of good and it will ever bubble up, if you will ever dig.
- Consider that you also do many things wrong and that you are a man like others. Even if you abstain from certain faults, still you have the disposition to commit them, through either cowardice, or concern about reputation, or some such mean motive.

*Contentment*
- Be content if the smallest thing goes on well and consider such an event to be no small matter.
- Equanimity is the voluntary acceptance of the things which are assigned to you by the common nature.
- He who follows reason in all things is both tranquil and active at the same time, as well as cheerful and collected.

*Viewed by others*
- When you have done a good act and another has received it, why dost you look for a third thing besides these, as fools do, either to have the reputation of having done a good act or to obtain a return?
- He who does not know what the world is, does not know where he is. And he who does not know for what purpose the world exists, does not know who he is nor what the world is. But he who has failed in any one of these things could not even say for what purpose he exists himself. What then dost you think of him who avoids or seeks the praise of those who applaud, of men who know not either where they are or who they are?
- When another blames you or hates you, or when men say about you anything injurious, approach their poor souls, penetrate within, and see what kind of men they are. You will discover

that there is no reason to take any trouble that these men may have this or that opinion about you. However, you must be well disposed towards them, for by nature they are friends.

- A man must learn a great deal to enable him to pass a correct judgment on another man's acts.
- Neither worse than nor better is a thing made by being praised.
- Judge every word and deed which are according to nature to be fit for you; and be not diverted by the blame which follows from any people nor by their words, but if a thing is good to be done or said, do not consider it unworthy of you. For those persons have their peculiar leading principle and follow their peculiar movement with things that do not you regard; rather, go straight on, following your own nature and the common nature; thus the way of both is one.
- How much trouble he avoids who does not look to see what his neighbor says, or does, or thinks, but only to what he does himself.

*Impermanence of life*
- Consider yourself to be dead and to have completed your life up to the present time, and live according to nature the remainder which is allowed you.
- How quickly all things disappear.
- Since it is possible that you may depart from life this very moment, regulate every act and thought accordingly.
- The longest-liver and he who will die soonest lose just the same.
- Short then is the time which every man lives, and small the nook of the Earth where he lives; and short too the longest posthumous fame, and even this only continued by a succession of poor human beings, who will very soon die, and who know not even themselves, much less him who died long ago.
- Do not act as if you were going to live ten thousand years. Death hangs over you.

- In a word, your life is short. You must turn to profit the present by the aid of reason and justice.
- For all things soon pass away and become a mere tale and complete oblivion soon buries them. And I say this of those who have shone in a wondrous way. For the rest, as soon as they have breathed out their breath, they are gone, and no man speaks of them. And, to conclude the matter, what is even an eternal remembrance? A mere nothing.
- You are a little soul bearing about a corpse.
- Pass then through this little space of time conformably to nature, and end your journey in content.
- Do not then consider life a thing of any value. For look to the immensity of time behind you and to the time which is before you, another boundless space. In this infinity, then, what is the difference between him who lives three days and him who lives three generations?
- Often think of the rapidity with which things pass by and disappear, both the things which are and the things which are produced. For substance is like a river in a continual flow, and the activities of things are in constant change, and the causes work in infinite varieties; there is hardly anything which stands still. And consider this which is near to you, this boundless abyss of the past and of the future in which all things disappear. How then is he not a fool who is puffed up with such things or plagued about them and makes himself miserable? For they vex him only for a time, and it is a short time.
- Alexander the Macedonian and his groom by death were brought to the same state.
- In this flowing stream then, on which there is no abiding, what is there of the things that hurry by on which a man would set a high price?
- Death is a cessation of the impressions through the senses, and of the pulling of the strings, which move the appetites,

and of the discursive movements of the thoughts, and of the service to the flesh.

- Be not dissatisfied then that you must live only so many years and not more; for as you are satisfied with the amount of substance which has been assigned to you, so be content with the time.
- What kind of people are those whom men wish to please, and for what objects, and by what kind of acts? How soon will time cover all things, and how many it has covered already.
- Near is your forgetfulness of all things, and near the forgetfulness of you by all.
- Look at the minds of those who seek fame, observe what they are, and what kind of things they avoid, and what kind of things they pursue. And consider that as the heaps of sand piled on one another hide the former sands, so in life the events which go before are soon covered by those which come after.
- The perfection of moral character consists in this, in passing every day as the last.
- In a little time, you will be nobody and nowhere
- Do not despise death but be well content with it since this too is one of those things which nature wills. For such as it is to be young and to grow old, and to increase and to reach maturity, and to have teeth and beard and grey hairs, and to beget, and to be pregnant and to bring forth, and all the other natural operations which the seasons of your life bring, such also is dissolution. This, then, is consistent with the character of a reflecting man, to be neither careless, nor impatient, nor contemptuous with respect to death, but to wait for it as one of the operations of nature.
- Turn your thoughts now to the consideration of your life, your life as a child, as a youth, your manhood, your old age, for in these also every change was a death. Is this anything to fear?
- He who dies at an extreme old age will be brought into the same condition with him who died prematurely.

- Everything is so constituted by nature as to die.
- When a man kisses his child, said Epictetus, he should whisper to himself, "To-morrow perchance you will die."
- Consider that before long you will be nobody and nowhere, nor will any of the things exist which you now see, nor any of those who are now living. For all things are formed by nature to change and be turned and to perish in order that other things in continuous succession may exist.
- All things are changing, and you yourself are in continuous mutation, and in a manner, in continuous destruction.

*Here and now*
- The present is the only thing of which a man can be deprived.
- No man loses any other life than this which he now lives, nor lives any other than this which he now loses.
- Confine yourself to the present.
- If you shall strive to live only what is really your life, that is, the present, then you will be able to pass that portion of life which remains for you up to the time of your death, free from perturbations, nobly, and obedient to your own daemon (to the god that is within you).
- Every man lives the present time only and loses only this.
- Attend to the matter which is before you, whether it is an opinion, or an act, or a word.

*Nature*
- Nothing is evil which is according to nature.
- To be vexed at anything which happens is a separation of ourselves from nature.
- That which is really beautiful has no need of anything.
- Frequently consider the connection of all things in the universe and their relation to one another.
- I am a part of the whole which is governed by nature.

# 14 NOTES

[1] Ridley M. 2006. Genome: the autobiography of a species in 23 chapters. New York (NY): Harper Perennial.

[2] Shubin N. 2008. Your inner fish: a journey into the 3.5-billion-year history of the human body. New York (NY): Vintage Books.

[3] Weiner J. 2014. The beak of the finch: a story of evolution in our time. New York (NY): Vintage Books.

[4] Hofstadter DR. 1999. Gödel, escher, bach: an eternal golden braid. New York (NY): Basic Books.

[5] Darwin C. 1859/2017. On the origin of species. Hampshire (UK): Macmillan Collector's Library.

[6] Hofstadter DR. 2006. I am a strange loop. New York (NY): Basic Books.

[7] The Interacademy Partnership. 2006 June 26. IAP statement on the teaching of evolution. The Interacademy Partnership; [accessed 2020 Apr 10]. https://www.interacademies.org/10878/13901.aspx.

[8] Popper K. 2020 Jan 7. Karl Popper. Wikipedia; [accessed 2020 Jan 12]. https://en.wikipedia.org/wiki/Karl_Popper.

[9] Trifonov E. 2011. Vocabulary of definitions of life suggests a definition. J Biomol Struct Dyn. 29(2): 259-266.

[10] Koskela M, Annila A. 2012. Looking for the last universal common ancestor (LUCA). Genes. 3(1). 81-87.

[11] Scharf C, Virgo N, Cleavesll HJ, Aono M, Aubert-Kato N, Aydinoglu A, Barahona A, Barge LM, Benner SA, Biehl M, et al. 2015. A strategy for origins of life research. Astrobiology. 15(12): 1031-1042.

[12] Preiner M, Asche S, Becker S, Betts HC, Boniface A, Camprubi E, Chandru K, Erastova V, Garg SG, Khawaja N, et al. 2020. The future of origin of life research: bridging decades-old divisions. MPDI. 10(3). https://www.mdpi.com/2075-1729/10/3/20/htm.

[13] Torino D, Martini L, Mansey SS. 2013. Piecing together cell-like systems. Curr Org Chem. 17(16): 1751-1757.

[14] Abel DL. 2011. Examining specific life-origin models for plausibility. In: Abel DL, editor. The first gene. New York (NY): LongView Press. p. 231-286.

[15] Pascal R, Pross A. 2014. The nature and mathematical basis for material stability in the chemical and biological worlds. J Syst Chem. 5(4).

[16] Ruiz-Mirazo K, Pereto J, Moreno A. 2010. Defining life or bringing biology to life. Origins Life Evol B. 40(2): 203-213. https://www.researchgate.net/publication/41563009_Defining_Life_or_Bringing_Biology_to_Life.

[17] Mayr E. 1989. Toward a new philosophy of biology: observations of an evolutionist. Cambridge (MA): Harvard University Press.

[18] Weinberg S. 1995. The quantum theory of fields. Cambridge (UK): Cambridge Universtiy Press.

[19] Raatikainen P. 2015. Gödel's incompleteness theorems. In: Stanford encyclopedia of philosophy. Stanford (CA): Stanford University Press; [updated 2015 Jan 20; accessed 2020 Jan 12]. https://plato.stanford.edu/entries/goedel-incompleteness/.

[20] Wachowski L, Wachowski, A. 1998. The Matrix script. Daily Script. http://www.dailyscript.com/scripts/the_matrix.pdf.

[21] 2019. The Matrix wiki. Fandom; [accessed 2018 Jan 16]. https://matrix.fandom.com/wiki/Main_Page.

[22] Baudrillard J. 1994. Simulacra and simulation, the body, in theory. Ann Arbor (MI): The Univeristy of Michigan Press.

[23] Hanley R. [date unknown]. Simulacra and simulation, Baudrillard and The Matrix. WhatIsTheMatrix; [accessed 2020 July 28]. https://www.bibliotecapleyades.net/ciencia/ciencia_matrix04.htm.

[24] Pross A. 2014. Life's restlessness. Aeon; [accessed 2017 Oct 25]. https://aeon.co/essays/paradoxes-of-stability-how-life-began-and-why-it-can-t-rest.

[25] Moelling K, Broecker F. 2019. Viruses and evolution – viruses first? A personal perspective. Front Microbiol. 10(523).

26 Sun F, Caetano-Anolles G. 2008. Evolutionary patterns in the sequence and structure of transfer RNA: early origins of archaea and viruses. PLoS Comput Biol. 4(3): e1000018.

27 Holmes EC. 2011. What does virus evolution tell us about virus origins? J Virol. 85(11): 5247–5251.

28 Durzyńska J, Goździcka-Józefiak A. 2015. Viruses and cells intertwined since the dawn of evolution. Virol J. 12(169).

29 Forterre P, Gribaldo S. 2007. The origin of modern terrestrial life. HFSP J. 1(3): 156–168.

30 Koskela M, Annila A. 2012. Looking for the last universal common ancestor (LUCA). Genes. 3(1): 81-87.

31 Root-Bernstein M, Root-Bernstein R. 2015. The ribosome as a missing link in the evolution of life. J Theor Biol. 367: 130–158.

32 Berg JM, Tymoczko JL, Stryer L. 2002. Biochemistry. 5th ed. New York (NY): W H Freeman.

33 Tertiary structure definition. Biology Dictionary; [updated 2020 May 5; accessed 2019 Oct 28]. https://biologydictionary.net/tertiary-structure/.

34 Pathway maps. KEGG PATHWAY Database; [2020 March 10; accessed 2020 June 22]. https://www.genome.jp/kegg/pathway.html.

35 WikiPathways. WikiPathway; [2020 June; accessed 2020 June 23]. https://www.wikipathways.org/index.php/WikiPathways.

36 Reactome. Reactome; [2020 June 17; accessed 2020 June 22]. https://reactome.org/.

37 Michael J. 2007. Conceptual assessment in the biological sciences: a National Science Foundation-sponsored workshop. Adv Physiol Educ. 31(4): 389–391.

38 Pace NR. 2009. Problems with "procaryote." J Bacteriol. 191(7): 2008–2010.

39 Robbins RJ, Krishtalka L, Wooley JC. 2016. Advances in biodiversity: metagenomics and the unveiling of biological dark matter. Stand Genomic Sci. 11(69).

40 O'Donnell M, Langston L, Stillman B. 2013. Principles and concepts of DNA replication in bacteria, archaea, and eukarya. Cold

Spring Harb Perspect Biol. 5(7): a010108.

[41] Bashford JD, Jarvis PD. 2008. Spectroscopy of the genetic code. In: Abbott D, Davies PCW, Pati AK, editors. Quantum aspects of life. London (UK): Imperial College Press. p. 147-186.

[42] Macromolecule. Wikipedia; [updated 2019 Nov 3; accessed 2019 Oct 28]. https://en.wikipedia.org/wiki/Macromolecule.

[43] Types of neurons. The University of Queensland, Australia; [updated 2018 Mar 26; accessed 2020 Apr 10]. https://qbi.uq.edu.au/brain/brain-anatomy/types-neurons.

[44] Wheeler-Jones CPD. 2005. Cell signaling in the cardiovascular system: an overview. Heart. 91(10): 1366–1374.

[45] Sever R, Glass CK. 2013. Signaling by nuclear receptors. Cold Spring Harb Perspect Biol. 5(3): a016709.

[46] Cell surface receptors: types & downstream mechanisms. Lecturio Online Medical Library; [updated 2020 Mar 23; accessed 2020 Apr 29]. https://www.lecturio.com/magazine/cell-surface-receptors-types-downstream-mechanisms/.

[47] Virus. Encyclopaedia Britannica; [updated 2020 Apr 15; accessed 2020 July 15]. https://www.britannica.com/science/virus.

[48] Biology for AP® courses: 21.1 viral evolution, morphology, and classification. Openstax; [2020; accessed 2020 July 15]. https://openstax.org/books/biology-ap-courses/pages/21-1-viral-evolution-morphology-and-classification.

[49] Venkataraman S, Prasad BVLS, Selvarajan R. 2018. RNA dependent RNA polymerases: insights from structure, function and evolution. 10(2): 76. https://www.mdpi.com/1999-4915/10/2/76.

[50] Tsagris EM, Martínez de Alba ÁE, Gozmanova M, Kalantidis K. 2008. Viroids. Cell Microbiol. 10(11), 2168–2179.

[51] Hu C, Hsu Y, Lin N. 2009. Satellite RNAs and satellite viruses of plants. Viruses. 1(3): 1325-1350.

[52] Vaseghi SV. 2000. Advanced digital signal processing and noise reduction. 2nd ed. New Jersey: John Wiley & Sons Ltd. p. Chapter 2, Noise and distortion. p. 35–50.

[53] Difference between signal and noise. Difference Between; [2011

Aug 10; accessed 2020 Apr 5]. https://www.differencebetween. com/difference-between-signal-and-vs-noise/.

[54] Simmons WK, Avery JA, Barcalow JC, Bodurka J, Drevets WC, Bellgowan P. 2013. Keeping the body in mind: insula functional organization and functional connectivity integrate interoceptive, exteroceptive, and emotional awareness. Hum Brain Mapp. 34(11): 2944–2958.

[55] Bartee L. 2017. Types of receptors. OpenOregon; [2017; accessed 2020 Mar 17]. https://openoregon.pressbooks.pub/mhccmajorsbio/ chapter/types-of-receptors/.

[56] Ravindran S. 2016. What sensory receptors do outside of sense organs. The Scientist; [accessed 2020 Mar 4]. https://www.the-scientist.com/features/what-sensory-receptors-do-outside-of-sense-organs-32942.

[57] Sensory systems. Biology Online; [2020; accessed 2020 Mar 16]. https://www.biologyonline.com/tutorials/sensory-systems.

[58] Lee MJ, Yaffe MB. 2020. Protein regulation in signal transduction. Cold Spring Harb Perspect Biol. https://cshperspectives.cshlp.org/ content/8/6/a005918.full.

[59] Small DM, Veldhuizen MG, Green B. 2013. Sensory neuroscience: taste responses in primary olfactory cortex. Curr Biol. 23(4): PR157–R159.

[60] Stein BE, Burr D, Constantinidis C, Laurienti PJ, Meredith MA, Perrault TJ, Ramachandran R, Röder B, Rowland BA, Sathian K, et al. 2010. Semantic confusion regarding the development of multisensory integration: a practical solution. Eur J Neurosci. 31(10): 1713–1720.

[61] Andersen RA, Buneo CA. 2002. Intentional maps in posterior parietal cortex. Annu Rev Neurosci. 25: 189–220.

[62] Marozzi E, Jeffery KJ. 2012. Place, space and memory cells. Curr Biol. 22(22): R939–R942.

[63] Bailly F, Longo G, Montevil M. 2011. A 2-dimensional geometry for biological time. Prog Biophys Mol Bio. 106(3): 474–484.

[64] O'Neil D. 2012. Primate color vision. Palomar.edu; [accessed 2020 Mar 27. https://www2.palomar.edu/anthro/primate/color.htm.

65 Mills A. The most fascinating animal senses in the world. Animal Wised; [updated 2018 Sep 18; accessed 2020 Mar 18]. https://www.animalwised.com/the-most-fascinating-animal-senses-in-the-world-2635.html.

66 Neuroscience for kids: amazing animal senses. Washington.edu; [updated 2019 December 4; accessed 2020 Mar 18]. https://faculty.washington.edu/chudler/amaze.html.

67 Smith B. 2016. The incredible – and bizarre – spectrum of animal colour vision. Cosmos Magazine; [accessed 2020 Apr 20]. https://cosmosmagazine.com/science/biology/the-incredible-and-bizarre-spectrum-of-animal-colour-vision/.

68 Sensory systems/marine animals. Wikibooks; [updated 2018 January 12; accessed 2020 Apr 14]. https://en.wikibooks.org/wiki/Sensory_Systems/Marine_Animals.

69 Britannica. 2019. Photoreception. Encyclopaedia Britannica; [accessed 2020 Apr 27]. https://www.britannica.com/science/photoreception.

70 Photoreceptors. 2015. NC State: Agriculture and Life Science; [accessed 2020 Apr 20]. https://genent.cals.ncsu.edu/bug-bytes/senses/photoreceptors/.

71 Kerr S. 2018. Animal sensory systems. Organismal Biology; [accessed 2020 Mar 4]. http://bio1520.biology.gatech.edu/chemical-and-electrical-signals/sensory-systems-i/.

72 Cole B. 2016. The weirdest senses animals have that you don't. Wired; [accessed 2020 Mar 18]. https://www.wired.com/2016/06/weirdest-senses-animals-humans-dont/.

73 Shashar N, Cronin TW. 1996. Polarization contrast vision in octopus. London (UK): The Company of Biologists Limited.

74 Krapp HG. 2007. Polarization vision: how insects find their way by watching the sky. Curr Biol. 17(14): R557-R560.

75 Dacke M, Nilsson D, Scholtz CH, Byrne M, Warrant EJ. 2003. Insect orientation to polarized moonlight. Nature. 424(33).

76 Heinloth T, Uhlhorn J, Wernet MF. 2018. Insect responses to linearly polarized reflections: orphan behaviors without neural

circuits. Front Cell Neurosci. 12(50).

[77] Ferro S. 2015. 5 sounds you probably can't hear. Mental Floss; [accessed 2019 Jan 8]. https://www.mentalfloss.com/article/64572/5-sounds-you-probably-cant-hear.

[78] Harris T. 2001. How sharks work - shark senses. Howstuffworks; [accessed 2020 Mar 17]. https://animals.howstuffworks.com/fish/sharks/shark3.htm.

[79] Gabbatiss J. 2017. Plants can see, hear and smell – and respond. BBC; [accessed 2020 Mar 17]. http://www.bbc.com/earth/story/20170109-plants-can-see-hear-and-smell-and-respond.

[80] The Scientist Staff. 2016. Sensory biology around the animal kingdom. The Scientist; [accessed 2020 Mar 17]. https://www.the-scientist.com/features/sensory-biology-around-the-animal-kingdom-32941.

[81] Handwerk B. 2019. Evolution surprise: bacteria have "noses," can smell. National Geographic; [accessed 2020 Apr 5]. https://www.nationalgeographic.com/news/2010/8/100818-science-health-bacteria-noses-smell-evolution/.

[82] Top 11 animals with super sensors. 2020. BioExplorer; [accessed 2020 Mar 17]. https://www.bioexplorer.net/animals-with-best-sensors.html/.

[83] Chemoreceptors. 2015. NC State: Agriculture and Life Science; [accessed 2020 Apr 22]. https://genent.cals.ncsu.edu/bug-bytes/senses/chemoreceptors/.

[84] Salisbury D. 2014. Mosquito sperm have a sense of smell. Vanderbilt University; [accessed 2020 Apr 26]. https://news.vanderbilt.edu/2014/02/03/mosquito-sperm/.

[85] Bozza T. 2015. Sensory neurobiology: demystifying the sick sense. Curr Biol. 25(4): R153-R155.

[86] Invertebrate sensory receptors. 2015. Biology Boom; [accessed 2020 Mar 17]. https://biologyboom.com/write-notes-on-invertebrate-sensory-receptors/.

[87] Ortega A, Krell T, Zhulin I. 2017. Sensory repertoire of bacterial chemoreceptors. Microbio and Mol Bio Rev. 81(4): e00033-17.

[88] Bren A, Eisenback M. 2000. How signals are heard during bacterial chemotaxis: protein-protein interactions in sensory signal propagation. J Bacteriol. 182(24): 6865–6873.

[89] Jones G. 2011. Sensory biology: bats feel the air flow. Curr Bio. 21(17): R666-R667.

[90] Mechanoreceptors. 2015. NC State: Agriculture and Life Science; [accessed 2020 Mar 18]. https://genent.cals.ncsu.edu/bug-bytes/senses/mechanoreceptors/.

[91] Mishra RC, Ghosh R, Bae H. 2016. Plant acoustics: in the search of a sound mechanism for sound signaling in plants. J Exp Bot. 67(15): 4483–4494.

[92] Gagliano M, Grimonprez M, Depczynski M, Renton M. 2017. Tuned in: plant roots use sound to locate water. Oecologia. 184: 151-160. https://link.springer.com/article/10.1007/s00442-017-3862-z.

[93] The senses of the horse. 2008. Horsehints; [updated 2020 Jan 21; accessed 2020 Apr 5]. horsehints.org/Senses.htm.

[94] Tuthill JC, Azim E. 2018. Proprioception. Curr Biol. 28(5): R194–R203.

[95] Hill PSM. 2009. How do animals use substrate-borne vibrations as an information source? Naturwissenschaften. 96: 1355–1371.

[96] University of Geneva. 2019. How our body 'listens' to vibrations. Medicalxpress; [accessed 2020 Apr 21]. https://medicalxpress.com/news/2019-03-body-vibrations.html.

[97] Bullock TH, Bodznick DA, Northcutt RG. 1983. The phylogenetic distribution of electroreception: evidence for convergent evolution of a primitive vertebrate sense modality. Brain Res Rev. 6(1): 25-46.

[98] Welsh J. 2011. Dolphins' 'sixth sense' helps them feel electric fields. LiveScience; [accessed 2020 Mar 22]. https://www.livescience.com/15240-dolphins-sense-electric-fields.html2011.

[99] Lordzb. 2013. 10 unusual animal senses. Listverse; accessed [2020 Mar 17]. https://listverse.com/2013/04/13/10-unusual-animal-senses/.

[100] Raine NE. 2013. Bee positive: the importance of electroreception in pollinator cognitive ecology. Europe PMC; [accessed 2020 Mar 7].

http://europepmc.org/article/PMC/3713399.

[101] Abhishlasha R. 2019. Photoreceptors of photosynthetic pigments. Biology Discussion; [accessed 2020 Mar 23]. http://www.biologydiscussion.com/photosynthesis/photoreceptors-of-photosynthetic-pigments/39805.

[102] Biology for majors II: plant responses to light. 2020. Lumen; [accessed 2020 Mar 27]. https://courses.lumenlearning.com/wm-biology2/chapter/plant-responses-to-light/.

[103] Biology for AP® courses: 23.6 plant sensory systems and responses. Openstax; [updated 2020; accessed 2020 Mar 17]. https://openstax.org/books/biology-ap-courses/pages/23-6-plant-sensory-systems-and-responses.

[104] Rosen H. 2017. Octopus vision, it's in the eye (or skin) of the beholder. The Dish on Science; [accessed 2020 Mar 22]. http://thedishonscience.stanford.edu/posts/octopus-vision-is-in-the-skin-of-the-beholder/.

[105] Naisbett-Jones LC, Putman NF, Scanlan MM, Noakes DLG, Lohmann KJ. 2020. Magnetoreception in fishes: the effect of magnetic pulses on orientation of juvenile pacific salmon. J Exp Biol. 223: jeb222091.

[106] List of sensors. Wikipedia; [updated 2020 Sep 22; accessed 2020 Mar 27]. https://en.wikipedia.org/wiki/List_of_sensors.

[107] Modell H, Cliff W, Michael J, McFarland J, Wenderoth MP, Wright A. 2015. A physiologist's view of homeostasis. Adv Physiol Educ. 39(4): 259-266.

[108] Kleckner IR, Zhang J, Touroutoglou A, Chanes L, Xia C, Simmons WK, Quigley KS, Dickerson BC, Barrett LF. 2017. Evidence for a large-scale brain system supporting allostasis and interoception in humans. Nat Hum Behav. 1(0069).

[109] Schulkin J. 2004. Introduction. In: Schulkin J, editor. Allostasis, homeostasis, and the costs of physiological adaptation. Cambridge (UK): Cambridge University Presss. p. 1–16.

[110] Sterling P. 2004. Principles of allostasis: optimal design, predictive regulation, pathophysiology, and rational therapeutics.

major prebiotic transitions as stages of protocell development: three challenges for origins-of-life research. Beilstein J Org Chem. 13: 1388–1395.

[135] Chen IA, Walde P. 2010. From self-assembled vesicles to protocells. Cold Spring Harb Perspect Biol. 2(7): a002170.

[136] Egbert MD, Barandiaran XE, Di Paolo EA. 2012. Behavioral metabolution: the adaptive and evolutionary potential of metabolism-based chemotaxis. Artificial Life. 18: 1-25.

[137] Grandy WT. 2004. Time evolution in macroscopic systems. Found Phys. 34: 1–20.

[138] Styer DF. 2008. Entropy and evolution. Am J Phys. 76(11): 1031-1033.

[139] Wolfe J. 2015. Cellular thermodynamics: the molecular and macroscopic views. Chichester (UK): John Wiley & Sons, Ltd.

[140] Schrödinger E. 1944. What is life? The physical aspect of the living cell. Cambridge (UK): Cambridge University.

[141] Tiezzi EBP, Pulselli RM, Marchettini N, Tiezzi E. 2008. Dissipative structures in nature and human systems. WIT Trans Ecol Envir. 114: 293-299.

[142] Prigogine I. 1996. The end of certainty: time, chaos, and the new laws of nature. New York (NY): Free Press.

[143] Nicolis G, Prigogine I. 1977. Self-organization in nonequilibrium systems: from dissipative structures to order through fluctuation. New York (NY): John Wiley & Sons.

[144] Prigogine I, Stengers I. 1984. Order out of chaos: man's dialogue with nature. New York (NY): Bantam Books.

[145] Jantsch E. 1980. The self-organizing universe: scientific and human implications of the emerging paradigm of evolution. Oxford (UK): Pergamon.

[146] Prigogine I. 1977. Nobel lecture: time, structure and fluctuations. Nobel Prize; https://www.nobelprize.org/prizes/chemistry/1977/prigogine/lecture/ [accessed 2020 Feb 22].

[147] Goldbeter A. 2018. Dissipative structures in biological systems: bistability, oscillations, spatial patterns and waves. Philos Trans

Royal Soc A. 376(2124).

[148] Morrow SM, Colomer I, Fletcher SP. 2019. A chemically fuelled self-replicator. Nat Comm. 10(1011).

[149] Schreiber A, Gimbel S. 2010. Evolution and the second law of thermodynamics: effectively communicating to non-technicians. Evo Educ Outreach. 3: 99–106.

[150] Goldbeter A, Berridger MJ. 1997. Biochemical oscillations and cellular rhythms: the molecular bases of periodic and chaotic behaviour. Cambridge (UK): Cambridge University Press.

[151] Károlyi G, Péntek Á, Scheuring I, Tél T, Toroczkai Z. 2000. Chaotic flow: the physics of species coexistence. PNAS. 97(25): 13661–13665.

[152] Ozery G. 2019. Kinetics vs thermodynamics. LibreTexts Chemistry; [updated 2020 Aug 21; accessed 2019 Oct 23].

[153] Pascal R, Pross A. 2014. The nature and mathematical basis for material stability in the chemical and biological worlds. J Syst Chem. 5(3).

[154] Pross A. 2014. Life's restlessness. Aeon; [accessed 2017 Oct 25]. https://aeon.co/essays/paradoxes-of-stability-how-life-began-and -why-it-can-t-rest..

[155] Pascal R, Pross A, Sutherland JD. 2013. Towards an evolutionary theory of the origin of life based on kinetics and thermodynamics. Open Biol. 3(11).

[156] Pross A. 2005. On the emergence of biological complexity. Origins Life Evol B. 35: 151–166.

[157] Pross A, Pascal R. 2013. The origin of life – what we know, what we can know, and what we will never know. Open Biol. 3(3): 120190.

[158] Noncovalent bonding. 2011. Biology Pages; [accessed 2019 Oct 26]. https://biology-pages.info/N/Noncovalent.html.

[159] Pizzarello S, Shock E. 2010. The organic composition of carbonaceous meteorites. Cold Spring Harb Perspect Biol. 2(3): a002105.

[160] Macromolecules and their monomeric subunits. [date unknown]. Bioinfo.org; [accessed 2017 Oct 21]. http://www.bioinfo.

org.cn/book/biochemistry/chapt03/bio3.htm#head3_15.

[161] 24.1 Overview of metabolic reactions. [date unknown]. BC Campus; [accessed 2019 Dec 20]. https://pressbooks.bccampus.ca/dcbiol12031209/chapter/24-1-overview-of-metabolic-reactions/.

[162] Gabora L. 2006. Self-other organization: why early life did not evolve through natural selection. J Theor Biol. 241(3): 443-450.

[163] Dörr M, Löffler PMG, Monnard P. 2012. Non-enzymatic polymerization of nucleic acids from monomers: monomer self-condensation and template-directed reacti. Curr Org Synth. 9(6).

[164] Whitesides GM, Boncheva M. 2002. Beyond molecules: Self-assembly of mesoscopic and macroscopic components. PNAS. 99(8): 4769–4774.

[165] Lopez-Fontal E, Grochmal A, Foran T, Milanesi L, Tomas S. 2018. Ship in a bottle: confinement-promoted self-assembly. Chem Sci. 9: 1760-1768.

[166] Chan JM, Carlsson G, Rabadan R. 2013. Topology of viral evolution. PNAS. 110(46): 18566–18571.

[167] Crisp A, Boschetti C, Perry M, Tunnacliffe A, Micklem G. 2015. Expression of multiple horizontally acquired genes is a hallmark of both vertebrate and invertebrate genomes. Genome Biol. 16(50).

[168] The terms symbiogenesis, endosymbiosys, and endosym-biogenesis. 2011. Latintos; [accessed 2019 Dec 21]. https://golatintos.blogspot.com/2011/04/terms-symbiogenesis-endosymbiosis-and.html.

[169] Lindmark DG, Muller M. 1973. Hydrogenosome, a cytoplasmic organelle of the anaerobic flagellate tritrichomonas foetus, and its role in pvruvate metabolism. J Biol Chem. 248(22): 7724-7728.

[170] Biagini GA, Finlay BJ, Lloyd D. 1997. Evolution of the hydrogenosome. FEMS Microbiol Lett. 155(2): 133-140.

[171] BD Editors. Mitochondria. Biology Dictionary; [updated 2020 May 8; [accessed 2019 Dec 2]. https://biologydictionary.net/mitochondria/.

[172] Imachi H, Nobu MK, Nakahara N, Morono Y, Ogawara M, Takaki Y, Takano Y, Uematsu K, Ikuta T, Ito M, et al. 2020. Isolation

of an archaeon at the prokaryote-eukaryote interface. Nature. 577: 519–525.

[173] Gabaldon T, Huynen MA. 2007. From endosymbiont to host-controlled organelle: the hijacking of mitochondrial protein synthesis and metabolism. PLOS Comput Biol. 3(11): e219.

[174] Arora S. [date unknown]. Hypothesis and the origin of eukaryotic cell. Biology Discussion; [accessed 2019 Oct 16]. http://www.biologydiscussion.com/eukaryotic-cell/hypothesis-and-the-origin-of-eukaryotic-cell-biology/38563.

[175] Martin WF. 2017. Symbiogenesis, gradualism, and mitochondrial energy in eukaryote evolution. Period Biol. 119(3): 141–158.

[176] Aanen DK, Eggleton P. 2017. Symbiogenesis: beyond the endosymbiosis theory? J Theoret Biol. 434: 99–103.

[177] Fishkis M. 2010. Emergence of self-reproduction in cooperative chemical evolution of prebiological molecules. Orig Life Evol Biosph. 41: 261–275.

[178] Fellerman H, Sole RV. 2017. Minimal model of self-replicating nanocells. Philos Trans R Soc B. 362(1486): 1803–1811.

[179] Joyce NP, Gerald F. 2002. A self-replicating ligase ribozyme. PNAS. 99(20): 12733–12740.

[180] Von Neumann J. The general and logical theory of automata. In: Newman JR, editor. 1956. The world of mathematics. 4th vol. New York (NY): Simon and Schuster. p. 2070–2098.

[181] Bernhardt HS, Tate WP. 2015. A ribosome without RNA. Front Ecol Evol. 3(129).

[182] Johnston WK, Unrau PJ, Lawrence MS, Glasner ME, Bartel DP. 2001. RNA-catalyzed RNA polymerization: accurate and general RNA-templated primer extension. Science. 292(5520): 1319-1325.

[183] De Farias ST, Dos Santos AP, Rêgo TG, José MV. 2017. Origin and evolution of RNA-dependent RNA polymerase. Front Genet. 8: 125.

[184] Protein. [date unknown]. NCBI; [accessed 2020 July 14]. https://www.ncbi.nlm.nih.gov/protein.

[185] Diener TO. 1989. Circular RNAs: relics of precellular evolution? Proc Natl Acad Sci. 86(23): 9370-9374.

[186] Joyce GF, Schwartz AW, Miller SL, Orgel LE. 1987. The case for an ancestral genetic system involving simple analogues of the nucleotides. Proc Natl Acad Sci. 84(13): 4398-4402.

[187] Forterre P. 2010. Defining life: the virus viewpoint. Orig Life Evol Biosph. 40(2): 151-160.

[188] Briones C, Stich M, Manrubia SC. 2009. The dawn of the RNA world: toward functional complexity through ligation of random RNA oligomers. RNA. 15(5): 743–749.

[189] Belousoff MJ, Davidovich C, Zimmerman E, Caspi Y, Wekselman I, Rozenszajn L, Shapira T, Sade-Falk O, Taha L, Bashan A, et al. 2010. Ancient machinery embedded in the contemporary ribosome. Biochem Soc Trans. 38(2): 422–427.

[190] Kun Á, Szilágyi A, Könnyú B, Boza G, Zachar I, Szathmáry E. 2015. The dynamics of the RNA world: insights and challenges: The dynamics of the RNA world. Ann N Y Acad Sci. 1341: 75–95.

[191] Szostak JW. 2012. The eightfold path to non-enzymatic RNA replication. J Syst Chem. 3(2).

[192] Robertson MP, Joyce GF. 2012. The origins of the RNA world. Cold Spring Harb Perspect Biol. 4(5): a003608.

[193] Caetano-Anollés G, Sun F. 2014. The natural history of transfer RNA and its interactions with the ribosome. Front Genet. 5: 127.

[194] Deamer D, Dworkin JP, Sandford SA, Bernstein MP, Allamandola LJ. 2002. The first cell membranes. Astrobiol. 2(4): 371-381.

[195] Manrubia SC, Briones C. 2007. Modular evolution and increase of functional complexity in replicating RNA molecules. RNA. 13(1): 97–107.

[196] Jeffares DC, Poole AM, Penny D. 1998. Relics from the RNA world. J Mol Evol. 46(1): 18-36.

[197] Sankaran N. 2012. How the discovery of ribozymes cast RNA in the roles of both chicken and egg in origin-of-life theories. Stud Hist Philos Biol Biomed Sci. 43(4): 741–750.

[198] Yaris M. 2002. Primordial genetics: phenotype of the ribocyte. Annu Rev Genet. 36: 125-51.

[199] Le Vay K, Salibi E, Song EY, Mutschler H. 2020. Nucleic acid

catalysis under potential prebiotic conditions. Chem Asian J. 15: 214 – 230.

[200] Monnard P. 2016. Taming prebiotic chemistry: the role of heterogeneous and interfacial catalysis in the emergence of a prebiotic catalytic/information polymer system. Life. 6(4): 40.

[201] Saladino R, Botta G, Pino S, Costanzo G, Di Mauro E. 2012. From the one-carbon amide formamide to RNA all the steps are prebiotically possible. Biochimie. 94(7): 1451-1456.

[202] Ralser M. 2014. The RNA world and the origin of metabolic enzymes. Biochem Soc Trans. 42(4): 985–988.

[203] Rout SK, Friedmann MP, Riek R, Greenwald J. 2018. A prebiotic template-directed peptide synthesis based on amyloids. Nat Commun. 9(234).

[204] Tsogoeva SB. 2010. Organoautocatalysis: challenges for experiment and theory. J Syst Chem. 1(8).

[205] Kim KM, Caetano-Anollés G. 2012. The evolutionary history of protein fold families and proteomes confirms that the archaeal ancestor is more ancient than the ancestors of other superkingdoms. BMC Evol Biol. 12: 13.

[206] Danger G, Boiteau L, Rossi JC, Pascal R. 2014. Systems chemistry of □-amino acids and peptides. BIO Web Conf. 2.

[207] Vasasa V, Szathmáry E, Santos M. 2010. Lack of evolvability in self-sustaining autocatalytic networks constraints metabolism-first scenarios for the origin of life. PNAS. 107(4): 1470–1475.

[208] Liu Y, Sumpter D. 2018. Spontaneous emergence of self-replication in chemical reaction systems. Metabolism. 293(49).

[209] Alberti S. 1999. Evolution of the genetic code, protein synthesis and nucleic acid replication. Cell Mol Life Sci. 56(1-2): 85–93.

[210] Alberti S. 1997. The origin of the genetic code and protein synthesis. J Mol Evol. 45(4): 352–358.

[211] Saladino R, Crestini C, Pino S, Costanzo G, Di Mauro E. 2012. Formamide and the origin of life. Phys Life Rev. 9(1): 84–104.

[212] Islam S, Powner MW. 2017. Prebiotic systems chemistry: complexity overcoming clutter. Chem. 2(4): 470–501.

[213] Gordon KH. 1995. Were RNA replication and translation directly coupled in the RNA (+protein?) World? J Theor Biol. 173(2): 179-193.

[214] Yarus M. 2013. A ribonucleotide origin for life – fluctuation and near-ideal reactions. Orig Life Evol Biosph. 43: 19-30.

[215] Fishkis M. 2007. Steps towards the formation of a protocell: the possible role of short peptides. Orig Life Evol Biosph. 37(6): 537-553.

[216] Rouch DA. 2014. Evolution of the first genetic cells and the universal genetic code: a hypothesis based on macromolecular coevolution of rna and proteins. J Theor Biol. 357: 220-244.

[217] Goldford JE, Segrè D. 2018. Modern views of ancient metabolic networks. Curr Op Syst Biol. 8: 117-124.

[218] Schrum JP, Zhu TF, Szostak, JW. 2010. The origins of cellular life. Cold Spring Harb Perspect Biol. 2(9): a002212.

[219] Froese T, Ikegami T, Virgo N. 2012. The behavior-based hypercycle: from parasitic reaction to symbiotic behavior. Artificial Life. 13: 457-464.

[220] Koonin EV, Senkevich TG, Dolja VV. 2006. The ancient virus world and evolution of cells. Biol Direct. 1(29).

[221] Shirt-Ediss B, Ruiz-Mirazo K, Mavelli F, Solé RV. 2014. Modelling lipid competition dynamics in heterogeneous protocell populations. Sci Rep. 4: 5675.

[222] Munteanu A, Attolini CS, Rasmussen S, Ziock H, Solé RV. 2007. Generic Darwinian selection in catalytic protocell assemblies. Phil Trans R Soc B. 362: 1847-1855.

[223] Hunding A, Kepes F, Lancet D, Minsky A, Norris V, Raine D, Sriram K, Root-Bernstein R. 2006. Compositional complementarity and prebiotic ecology in the origin of life. Bioessays. 28(4): 399-412.

[224] Shenhav B, Oz A, Lancet D. 2007. Coevolution of compositional protocells and their environment. Philos Trans Royal Soc B. 362(1486): 1813-1819.

[225] Monnard P, Deamer DW. 2001. Nutrient uptake by protocells: a liposome model system. Orig Life Evol Biosph. 31: 147-155.

[226] Piedrafita G, Monnard P, Mavelli F, Ruiz-Mirazo K. 2017. Permeability-driven selection in a semi-empirical protocell model:

the roots of prebiotic systems evolution. Sci Rep. 7(3141).

[227] Segré D, Ben-Eli D, Deamer DW, Lancet D. 2001. The lipid world. Orig Life Evol Biosph. 31(1-2): 119–145.

[228] Liu K, Ren X, Sun J, Zou Q, Yan X. 2018. Primitive photosynthetic architectures based on self-organization and chemical evolution of amino acids and metal ions. Adv Sci. 5(6): 1701001.

[229] Olasagasti F, Moreno A, Peretó J, Morán F. 2007. Energetically plausible model of a self-maintaining protocellular system. Bull Math Biol. 69(4): 1423–1445.

[230] Follmann H, Brownson C. 2009. Darwin's warm little pond revisited: from molecules to the origin of life. Naturwissenschaften. 96(11): 1265–1292.

[231] Weiss MC, Sousa FL, Mrnjavac N, Neukirchen S, Roettger M, Nelson-Sathi S, Martin WF. 2016. The physiology and habitat of the last universal common ancestor. Nat Microbiol. 1(16116).

[232] Marshall M. 2009. Timeline: the evolution of life. NewScientist; [accessed 2019 Dec 18]. https://www.newscientist.com/article/dn17453-timeline-the-evolution-of-life/.

[233] Timeline of the evolutionary history of life. Wikipedia; [updated 2020 Jan 15; accessed 2020 Jan 20]. https://en.wikipedia.org/wiki/Timeline_of_the_evolutionary_history_of_life.

[234] Kitadai N, Maruyama S. 2018. Origins of building blocks of life: a review. Geosci Front. 9(4): 1117-1153.

[235] Pigliucci M, Finkelman L. 2014. The extended (evolutionary) synthesis debate: where science meets philosophy. BioScience. 64(6): 511-516.

[236] Müller GB. 2017. Why an extended evolutionary synthesis is necessary. Interface Focus. 7(5).

[237] Noble D. 2015. Evolution beyond neo-darwinism: a new conceptual framework. J Exp Biol. 218: 7-13.

[238] Pigliucci M, Müller GB. 2010. Evolution–the extended synthesis. Cambridge (MA): MIT Press.

[239] Pigliucci M, Finkelman L. 2014. The extended (evolutionary) synthesis debate: where science meets philosophy. BioScience.

64(6): 511-516.

[240] Units and levels of selection. 2005. In: Stanford encyclopedia of philosophy. Stanford (CA): The Metaphysics Research Lab, Center for the Study of Language and Information ; [updated 2017 Apr 14; accessed 2020 June 20]. https://plato.stanford.edu/entries/selection-units/.

[241] Dawkins R. 1995. River out of eden: a Darwinian view of life. New York (NY): Basic Books.

[242] Dawkins R. 1989. The selfish gene. Oxford (UK): Oxford University Press.

[243] Guerrero R, Margulis L, Berlanga M. 2013. Symbiogenesis: the holobiont as a unit of evolution. Int Microbiol. 16(3): 133-143.

[244] Frost LS, Leplae R, Summers AO, Toussaint A. 2005. Mobile genetic elements: the agents of open source evolution. Nature. 3: 722-732.

[245] Jönsson ME, Garza R, Johansson PA, Jakobsson J. 2020. Transposable elements: a common feature of neurodevelopmental and neurodegenerative disorders. Trends Genet. 36(8): 610–623.

[246] Rankin DJ, Rocha EPC, Brown SP. 2010. What traits are carried on mobile genetic elements, and why? Heredity. 106: 1–10.

[247] Sokurenko EV, Hasty DL, Dykhuizen DE. 1999. Pathoadaptive mutations: gene loss and variation in bacterial pathogens. Trends in Microbiol. 7(5): 191-195.

[248] Aziz RK. 2009. The case for biocentric microbiology. Gut Pathog. 1(1): 16.

[249] Eisen JA. 2007. Environmental shotgun sequencing: its potential and challenges for studying the hidden world of microbes. PLoS Biol. 5(3): e82.

[250] Handelsman J, Rondon MR, Brady SF, Clardy J, Goodman RM. 1998. Molecular biological access to the chemistry of unknown soil microbes: a new frontier for natural products. Chem Biol. 5(10): R245–R249.

[251] Thomas T, Gilbert J, Meyer F. 2012. Metagenomics - a guide from sampling to data analysis. Microb Inform Exp. 2: 3.

[252] Paez-Espino D, Eloe-Fadrosh EA, Pavlopoulos GA, Thoma AD, Huntemann M, Mikhailova N, Rubin E, Ivanova NN, Kyrpides NC. 2016. Uncovering earth's virome. Nature. 536: 425–430.

[253] Whitman WB, Coleman DC, Wiebe WJ. 1998. Prokaryotes: the unseen majority. Proc Natl Acad Sci. 95(12): 6578–6583.

[254] Mukherjee S, Stamatis D, Bertsch J, Ovchinnikova G, Sundaramurthi JC, Lee J, Kandimalla M, Chen IA, Kyrpides NC, Reddy TBK. 2020. Genomes OnLine Database (GOLD) v.8: overview and updates. Nucleic Acids Res. 49(D1): D723–D733.

[255] Robbins RJ, Krishtalka L, Wooley JC. 2016. Advances in biodiversity: metagenomics and the unveiling of biological dark matter. Stand Genomic Sci. 11(1): 69.

[256] Norman A, Hansen LH, Sørensen SJ. 2009. Conjugative plasmids: vessels of the communal gene pool. Phil Trans R Soc Lond B Biol Sci. 364(1527): 2275–2289.

[257] Cleland CE. 2013. Pluralism or unity in biology: could microbes hold the secret to life? Biol Philos. 28: 189–204.

[258] Locey KJ, Lennon JT. 2016. Scaling laws predict global microbial diversity. PNAS. 113(21): 5970–5975.

[259] Bashford JD, Jarvis PD. 2008. Spectroscopy of the genetic code. In: Abbott D, Davies PCW, Pati AK, editors. Quantum aspects of life. London (UK): Imperial College Press. p. 147-186.

[260] Bach M. 2020. 139 optical illusions & visual phenomena. Michael Bach; [accessed 2020 June 7]. https://michaelbach.de/ot/index.html.

[261] Purves D, Morgenstern Y, Wojtach WT. 2015. Perception and reality: why a wholly empirical paradigm is needed to understand vision. Front Syst Neurosci. 9: 156.

[262] Purves D, Wojtach WT, Lotto RB. 2011. Understanding vision in wholly empirical terms. PNAS. 108: 15588–15595.

[263] Purves D, Monson BB, Sundararajan J, Wojtach WT. 2014. How biological vision succeeds in the physical world. PNAS. 111(13): 4750–4755.

[264] Merikle PM, Smilek D, Eastwood JD. 2001. Perception without

awareness: perspectives from cognitive psychology. Cognition. 79(1-2): 115-134.

265 Lee A. 2013. 25 weirdest superstitions and rituals in sports. Bleacher Report; [accessed 2020 May 9]. https://bleacherreport.com/articles/1478386-25-weirdest-superstitions-and-rituals-in-sports.

266 What ancient civilizations teach us about reality [video]. 2020, 16:44 minutes. TEDx Talks. YouTube. [accessed 2020 Dec 12]. https://www.youtube.com/watch?v=1geJGnzJ87Q.

267 Raypole C. 2019. How to hack your hormones for a better mood. Healthline; [accessed 2021 Jan 25]. https://www.healthline.com/health/happy-hormone.

268 Brookshire B. 2013. Dopamine is _. Slate; [accessed 2020 June 25]. https://slate.com/technology/2013/07/what-is-dopamine-love-lust-sex-addiction-gambling-motivation-reward.html.

269 Ferguson S. 2020. Does masturbation have positive or negative effects on the brain? Healthline; [accessed 2020 June 25]. https://www.healthline.com/health/healthy-sex/masturbation-effects-on-brain.

270 Wu K. 2017 Feb 14. Love, actually: the science behind lust, attraction, and companionship [blog]. Science in the News. [accessed 2020 June 25]. sitn.hms.harvard.edu/flash/2017/love-actually-science-behind-lust-attraction-companionship/.

271 The 4 major stress hormones. 2017. Its Psychology; [accessed 2020 May 20]. https://itspsychology.com/stress-hormones/.

272 Jade. P vs. NP - the biggest unsolved problem in computer science [video]. 2020 Jan 21, 15:32 minutes. Up and Atom. YouTube. [accessed 2020 Sep 3]. https://www.youtube.com/watch?v=EHp4FPyajKQ.

273 NP-completeness. 2020. Wikipedia; [accessed 2020 Sep 3]. https://en.wikipedia.org/wiki/NP-completeness.

274 Thakchoe S. 2011. The theory of two truths in India. In: Stanford encyclopedia of philosophy. Stanford (CA): The Metaphysics Research Lab, Center for the Study of Language and Information ; [updated 2016 Oct 20; accessed 2017 Oct 22]. https://plato.stanford.edu/entries/twotruths-india/.

275 Buddharakkhita A, translator. 1985. The Dhammapada: the Buddha's path of wisdom. Kandy (LK): Buddhist Publication Society; [accessed 2017 Oct 24]. www.buddhanet.net/pdf_file/scrndhamma.pdf.

276 Smith J, editor. 1998. Breathe sweeps mind (tricycle book). New York (NY): Riverhead Books.

277 Aurelius M. 167 ACE. The meditations. The Internet Classics Archive; [accessed 2019 July 2]. http://classics.mit.edu//Antoninus/ meditations.html.

278 Ogunjimi A. [date unknown]. What is main purpose of protein in living things. Sciencing; [updated 2018 Nov 28; accessed 2020 Mar 4]. https://sciencing.com/what-is-main-purpose-of-protein-in-living-things-7317884.html.

279 Lipid. [date unknown]. Wikipedia; [updated 2021 Jan 2; accessed 2021 Jan 25]. https://en.wikipedia.org/wiki/Lipid.

280 Overview of metabolic reactions. [date unknown]. Github; [accessed 2019 Jan 12]. https://oerpub.github.io/epubjs-demo-book/content/m$^{46489}$.xhtml.

281 The significant difference between micelles and liposomes. [date unknown]. BiologyWise; [accessed 2019 Nov 22]. https:// biologywise.com/difference-between-micelles-liposomes.

282 What are the five functions of lipids? [date unknown]. Reference; [updated 2020 Mar 25; accessed 2019 Oct 17]. https://www. reference.com/science/five-functions-lipids-bbbc5fcd62af62c0.

283 Kee T, Monnard P. 2016. On the emergence of a proto-metabolism and the assembly of early protocells. Elements. 12(6): 419-424.

284 Biology for AP® courses: 22.3 prokaryotic metabolism. Openstax; [updated 2020; accessed 2020 June 20]. https://openstax.org/ books/biology-ap-courses/pages/22-3-prokaryotic-metabolism.

285 Grosberg RK, Strathmann RR. 2007. The evolution of multicellularity: a minor major transition? Annu Rev Ecol Evol Syst. 38: 621-54.

286 Bonner JT. 1999. The origins of multicellularity. Integr Biol. 1(1): 27-36.

287 Gilbert SF, Sapp J, Tauber A. 2012. A symbiotic view of life: we have never been individuals. Q Rev Biol. 87(4): 325-341.

288 Superorganism. 2020. Wikipedia; [accessed 2020 Feb 14]. https://en.wikipedia.org/wiki/Superorganism.

289 Fan L, Reynolds D, Liu M, Stark M, Kjelleberg S, Webster NS, Thomas T. 2012. Functional equivalence and evolutionary convergence in complex communities of microbial sponge symbionts. PNAS. 109(27): E1878–E1887.

290 Boxma B, de Graaf RM, van der Staay GWM, van Alen TA, Ricard G, Gabaldón T, van Hoek AHAM, Moon-van der Staay SY, Koopman WJH, van Hellemond JJ, et al. 2005. An anaerobic mitochondrion that produces hydrogen. Nature. 434(7029):74-79.

291Metabolism without oxygen. 2013. Lumen; [accessed 2020 Apr 17]. https://courses.lumenlearning.com/boundless-biology/chapter/metabolism-without-oxygen/.

292 Bębenek A, Ziuzia-Graczyk I. 2018. Fidelity of DNA replication—a matter of proofreading. Curr Genet. 64: 985–996.

293 Gerstein MB, Bruce C, Rozowsky JS, Zheng D, Du J, Korbel JO, Emanuelsson O, Zhang ZD, Weissman S, Snyder M. 2007. What is a gene, post-ENCODE? history and updated definition. Cold Spring Harb Labor Press. 17: 669–681.

294 Deveson IW, Hardwick SA, Mercer TR, Mattick JS. 2017. The dimensions, dynamics, and relevance of the mammalian noncoding transcriptome. Trends Genet. 33(7): 464-478.

295[295] Finegold DN. 2019. Factors affecting gene expression. Merck Manual Professional Version; [accessed 2020 Aug 3]. https://www.merckmanuals.com/professional/special-subjects/general-principles-of-medical-genetics/factors-affecting-gene-expression.

296 Aryal S. 2018. Gene expression. Microbe Notes; [accessed 2020 July 15]. https://microbenotes.com/gene-expression/.

297 Cell signalling. 2020. OpenLearn; [accessed 2019 Nov 12]. https://www.open.edu/openlearn/science-maths-technology/cell-signalling/content-section-1.5.

[298] Rosenbaum DM, Rasmussen SGF, Kobilka BK. 2009. The structure and function of G-protein-coupled receptors. Nature. 459(7245): 356–363.

[299] Cell surface receptors: types & downstream mechanisms. 2020. Lecturi; [accessed 2020 Apr 29]. https://www.lecturio.com/magazine/cell-surface-receptors-types-downstream-mechanisms/.

[300] Pause BM. 2012. Processing of body odor signals by the human brain. Chemosens Percept. 5(1): 55–63.

[301] Proprioception. 2020. Physiopedia; [accessed 2020 Mar 4]. https://www.physio-pedia.com/Proprioception.

[302] Ritchie JB, Carruthers P. 2015. The bodily senses.; [accessed 2020 Apr 1]. http://faculty.philosophy.umd.edu/pcarruthers/The%20Bodily%20Senses.pdf.

[303] Taube JS. 2007. The head direction signal: origins and sensory-motor integration. Annu Rev Neurosci. 30: 181–207.

[304] Efeyan A, Comb WC, Sabatini DM. 2015. Nutrient sensing mechanisms and pathways. Nature. 517(7534): 302–310.

[305] Segelken R. 2002. Structure of key protein that enables quorum-sensing bacteria to communicate and spread infection is solved by research team. Cornell Chronicle; [accessed 2020 Jan 6]. https://news.cornell.edu/stories/2002/06/structure-key-protein-enables-quorum-sensing-bacteria-communicate-and-spread.

[306] Lin Y, Guo YR, Miyagi A, Levring J, MacKinnon R, Scheuring S. 2019. Force-induced conformational changes in PIEZO1. Nature. 573: 230–234.

[307] Pesheva E. 2018. Ending 40-year quest, scientists reveal 'hearing' protein. The Harvard Gazette (Cambridge, MA). [accessed 2020 April 12]. https://news.harvard.edu/gazette/story/2018/08/hearing-protein/.

[308] Zaru R. 2020. Pattern recognition receptors (PRRs) ligands. British Society for Immunology; [accessed 2020 Apr 12]. https://www.immunology.org/public-information/bitesized-immunology/receptors-and-molecules/pattern-recognition-receptor-prrs.

[309] Zedalis J, Eggebrecht J. 2018. Biology for AP® Courses: 27.3 taste and smell. OpenStax; [accessed 2020 Apr 17]. https://openstax.org/books/biology-ap-courses/pages/27-3-taste-and-smell.

CPSIA information can be obtained
at www.ICGtesting.com
Printed in the USA
BVHW091137030621
608729BV00005B/1789